The

Story

Book

David Baboulene

Extracts from *The Inimitable Jeeves* by kind permission of The Estate of P.G. Wodehouse.

Extract from *Minority Report* by Philip K. Dick by kind permission of The Estate of Philip K. Dick.

Extracts from *Back to the Future* by kind permission of Universal.

Published in 2010 by:

DreamEngine Media Ltd.

Email: publishing@dreamengine.co.uk

www.dreamengine.co.uk

Printed and bound by JF Print Ltd., Sparkford, Somerset.

ISBN: 978-0955708923

Writing, like driving a car and making love, is one of those activities which every Englishman thinks he can do well without instruction. The results are of course usually abominable.

Tom Margerison (1923 –)

To Katy, from the world's best driver...

Contents

Acknowledgments

This book has been drawn from my own experience as an author, scriptwriter, and story consultant, and my academic study of stories down the ages. However, from the outset, I was determined that this would be a book that was useful to aspiring writers living and breathing in the real world, so a healthy dose of reality was required. I set about discussing story theory with individuals who have found success through stories, and as you can see from the list of luminaries below, I got very lucky.

So I would like to thank as warmly as an acknowledgements page allows, the following people for their contributions:

From Film: Bob Gale – the Hollywood legend behind *Back to the Future* and the writer, director or producer of more than a dozen other movies.

From Theatre: Willy Russell – *Educating Rita, Blood Brothers, Shirley Valentine* – is there a more influential name from the theatre in the last 100 years?

From Novels: Lee Child – around 16 million Jack Reacher novels sold in 29 languages and 43 countries – need I say more?!

From Television: John Sullivan – *Only Fools and Horses*, Just Good Friends, Citizen Smith – a television comedy legend.

From Acting: Mark Williams – *The Fast Show*, *Harry Potter* movies, *Shakespeare in Love, 101 Dalmatians* – insights from the actors' viewpoint from this fascinating man.

From Publishing: Stewart Ferris – Author of around 40 books and ex-head of Summersdale Publishers – a leading independent UK publishing house. Stewart tells us how to put on the salesman's hat, package our work and approach the media industries.

My thanks go to these fine gentlemen for providing me with some fascinating days and wonderful insights.

Introduction – What lies between a writer and success?

Writing is like mining for gold hidden in the hillsides of your mind. The young writer, realising he has brilliant story ideas within him, goes to the publisher and points at the hillsides, shouting, 'There's gold in them thar hills! Give me money and I will return you pots of gold!'

The publisher wants gold, but he's heard it all before from thousands of prospectors. They never have the gold they claim. They rarely have any gold at all. He doesn't even lift his eyes.

But this writer is determined to prove himself. He buys some tools, goes to the hills and spends two years away from his family. He toils and he sweats and he makes his fingers bleed digging out nuggets. Over time, he becomes swift in locating them; perceptive in sorting them; discerning in choosing them. He begins to discard those of low quality and keep only the best. He collects them carefully in a bucket until he has an impressive and weighty haul.

The writer returns to the publisher and with wild hair and torn clothes he proclaims, 'You have to acknowledge me now! I have spent years digging nuggets out of the hills for you. Look at this gold, gold, GOLD, I tell you!'

The publisher unblinkingly indicates to either side of the writer, who realises he is in a line of a thousand other weather-beaten obsessives, who have similar weighty buckets and are shouting the same imploring mantra at the man who must decide.

Put yourself in the position of the publisher. He knows that the hit rate is low; checking every mud-filled bucket is simply not an option, but he must deal with these prospectors every day, and it is his business to find what little gold there might be. So answer this question: which writer should he choose from this line of thousands? They all have talent. They have all made sacrifices, gained skills, shown commitment and worked hard. But which bucket-full of supposedly precious stones really holds a fortune? How can he know? What would you do? Think about it, and we'll come to the answer in a minute.

Let me get to the point. There are four clear steps to getting success:

- Create a story of unrivalled excellence and tell it brilliantly.

- Package the story to the industry's preferred form.

- Market your story to the agents or directly to the publishers/ producers.

- Enjoy public adulation and respect from all sides (although you don't have time for all that because you're too busy counting money).

Unfortunately, most writers, in their rush to get feedback and to announce their talent to those who they feel need to know, rather tend to skip over step 1. Instead of 'creating a story of unrivalled excellence and telling it brilliantly', they do half that job at best, and then go on to number 2, hawking their work around the market looking for interest and collecting rejections. The questions I'm most commonly asked when I deliver my seminars are all to do with steps 2 and 3: 'Can you help me find a producer? How do I get a publishing deal? Tell me the secret of success!'

And I answer: 'Great news! Getting a deal is easy! A piece of cake! All you need is a story of unrivalled excellence and to tell it brilliantly. Go away and do that and I'll give you a publishing deal myself.'

What people *don't* ask me is this: 'How do I turn my creative ideas into fully fledged stories of unrivalled excellence? What can I do to improve my completed stories? How can I know if I am telling my stories to their finest effect? What should I do to identify and fix story problems? What steps must I take to master the craft of creating great stories?' These are the questions we should be asking, and these are the questions this book attempts to help you to answer in the context of You.

The majority of this book is dedicated to making the very most of the story ideas you have. From there, the good news is this: if you have a great story, and tell your story well, you *will* get a publisher, agent, production deal or all three. Have no doubt about it, publishers, film companies and the agents that pitch to them are desperate for good, original, well told stories.

According to the Motion Picture Association of America, Hollywood churns out around 600 movies a year (610 in 2008), at an average overall cost of more than $100 million dollars a throw. But despite this staggering investment in each and every one of the 600+ stories that get released into cinemas, how many are actually any good? One or two percent are worth watching (let's be generous – say, ten movies a year) and of *those* how many are genuinely excellent? One? Two? And these few nuggets are drawn from approximately one-hundred-thousand scripts submitted formally to the industry in America every year. And that's just America. And that's just those that get copyrighted.

A couple of genuinely excellent movies a year, drawn from all that investment, all those written scripts, and a worldwide box office of just under $29 billion (2009). On the book side, approximately 300 books are published *every day* in the UK (1000 every day in the US). How many of them are any good? How many authors make any money from a consumer book market valued at around £3 billion in 2009 in the UK and $24.3 billion in the USA? [1]

People think these numbers work against them, but make no mistake, if you can write something that is better than most, you will get a deal. Become a master of this particular craft, and you will get a privileged view of just how few writers there are out there who really know what they are doing.

Going back to our original question, then: Who, from the thousands of writers proffering gold-filled buckets in the line and stridently proclaiming their value, will the publisher select? Look along the line. The writer he will deal with is easy to spot, because he's not holding a bucket full of hard-won nuggets. He is holding up a cut and polished, solid gold necklace.

And he's not shouting at all.

---

[1] Figures from The UK Publisher's Association and the Association of American Publishers.

THE ROOTS OF STORY

Stories are the architects of the human mind

1   Why do stories exist?

Once upon a time...

...around 100,000 years ago, a simple and apparently mundane evolutionary change took place in a hominid somewhere: The position of his hyoid bone in the upper front of the throat changed relative to a descending larynx. And the planet was changed forever.

Whereas the neanderthal and early hominids made a range of sounds comparable to those of a chimp, this tiny change in throat architecture enabled suitably endowed hominids to produce complex sounds. Complex sounds allowed the hominid to develop language, and this, in its turn, led to levels of co-operation that had previously been impossible. Sophisticated co-operation meant that ten hominids working together were suddenly the most powerful creature on Earth, and the roots of civil society were put down. If you think about civilisation, it is simply co-operation taken to its logical extreme, and language was fundamental to our progress.

Story-telling

Although nobody has been able to put a precise date on the first story-telling, it is believed that stories came along with the hominids just as soon as the language was sophisticated enough to facilitate it. Cave paintings had shown an innate desire to express events in what we would now recognise as a story structure, but it was all very static and unsatisfactory. Language was a multi-media leap for the hominid story-teller, which was of far more significance to humankind than the electronic communications revolution we have experienced in the last fifty years.

It is reasonable to assume that hominids made this leap, but it raises an awkward question for the academics: why would a hominid *want* to tell stories? Times were hard 100,000 years ago. It was a struggle simply to survive the day, and if a hominid had any spare energy, you could be pretty sure he'd be using it to survive tomorrow or prepare for the winter. Why would he give time and precious energy to indulge in story telling?

The answer is this: in the same way that language had a massive part to play in the ability to build a sophisticated society, so stories have a practical purpose in maintaining and advancing that society. Sophisticated co-operation requires learning, so stories were told because they helped others to understand how to co-operate and therefore to maintain the society that was so important to the success of the human race. Stories were told precisely because they helped hominids to get through the day and to prepare for the winter. As civilisation became more complex, so the stories that teach people how to behave in society-appropriate ways became comparably complex. In this respect, stories are as valuable today as they were to our ancestors.

People need to learn – but why stories? Why not other forms of teaching?

Stories and learning
Human beings learn principally in one of two ways.

Firstly, we learn through experience. When we take an action we get real-time, real world understanding of what the world gives us in return. This is the most powerful learning, but often the most painful, because we are learning 'emotionally', and learning in a cold sweat as we go along. If our hominid decides to kill a sabre-toothed tiger for dinner, he will learn rapid and stern lessons about how best to go about it. If he survives, he will get better and better at tackling sabre-toothed tigers each time he takes one on. We learn from experience.

Secondly, we learn 'analytically'. We sit in retrospect, perhaps in a classroom or laboratory, strip out the emotion and understand events through clinical analysis of the facts over an appropriate time period. A hominid might study the physical properties of the sabre-tooth he has killed and thereby gain insight in how he might better despatch the next one.

Learning through emotion and learning through analysis are mutually exclusive. If we learn emotionally, our instincts are in charge and there is no analysis going on in real time. If we learn analytically, the emotion, by definition, has been stripped out. We cannot learn both emotionally and analytically at the same time.

Except we can. There is one situation in which we get the raw power of emotional learning combined with the holistic understanding of analysis: When we absorb a story. Story locks us on to the emotional journey of a protagonist. We 'go there' with him, and learn his lessons as if we are experiencing the events emotionally for ourselves. That is why a story can frighten us or reduce us to tears. But at the same time we are safe behind a book or in a cinema, and our brains have the freedom to simultaneously undertake analysis of events. We fly back through what has gone before to understand cause and effect, and we project with our imagination out along the road forming up ahead to guess what might happen from here. The lessons we learn when we absorb a story are more thoroughly learned than through any other teaching method. That is why there is no more powerful learning tool in human life than stories. That is why stories are so pervasive and critical. That is why, since our hominid predecessors first recounted an experience, human beings have used stories to teach ensuing generations how to lead their lives in order to propagate an ongoing and successful civilisation.

And that is why stories are the architects of the human mind.

1.1 Model 1 – Freud

OK. So I know things are a little academic at the moment, but stick with me. We will get on to real world, your stories and meaty practical stuff shortly. However, I am sure you will find this material valuable in your writing too, so hang in there.

Given that stories are powerful and essential, how do they work? What happens that makes a story so elemental in the way it resonates with our minds?

Our psychological make-up is most easily understood using Freud's *Structural Apparatus of the Psyche*, which proposes that the mind is made up of three components know as the Id, the Super-ego and the Ego. Below is a representation of Freud's Structural Apparatus, simplified for our purposes.

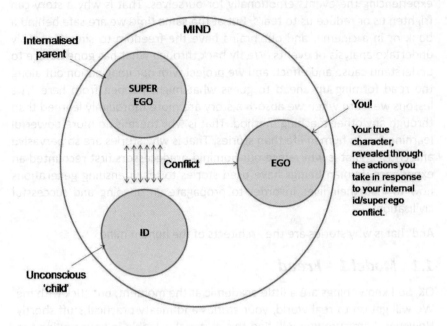

The Id is the animal in all of us; the part of us that is driven entirely by our instincts. It functions at the unconscious level, doesn't understand the word 'no', refuses to negotiate and demands instant gratification. It makes instinctive decisions based solely on seeking pleasure and avoiding pain. The id is concerned with the self-centred basics: eating, drinking, sex, safety and security, warmth, breathing and so on. The new-born child has no knowledge, awareness or moral code – it is 'id-ridden'. It has its instincts and that is all. And this is where we all start.

Super-ego. The super-ego develops in direct opposition to the id as we are forced into a world of co-operation. We gain social awareness and build a moral code. It is the rule book we develop as we learn to be civilised. It is our conscience – the part of us that applies rules as we learn to co-operate over and above the selfish demands of the animal id. The super-ego is known as the 'Internalised Parent' and is often in conflict with the instinctive demands of the id. The id says, 'I see chocolate! I want it and I want it now,' and instructs us to take it.

However, the super-ego says, 'No! You haven't paid for it! That would be stealing!'

The super-ego understands that taking things is against the better interests of civilised society and presents the case against the id's instinctively self-centred response.

Although characterised as 'the parent', the rules and social conscience we internalise in developing a super-ego come from other sources too, most notably life experiences, civil authorities, cultural guides (school, church, teams, clubs and groups), friends, teachers and relatives. (These non-parental factors are also known as the 'cultural super-ego'.)

Note that your cat doesn't have a super-ego to worry about. Its mind looks like this:

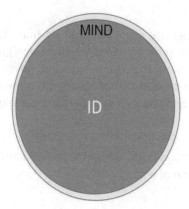

Your cat is 'id-ridden'. Like every other animal, every decision it ever makes is purely instinctive. It has no super-ego to temper its id, so it behaves as dictated by nature. It sees a blackbird and it wants to kill it. You cannot reason with the cat. You can't convince it of a higher moral position: 'Don't kill the blackbird! You aren't even hungry! I feed you twice a day! You're approach to this situation is morally abhorrent!'

Even if you thrash the cat every time it chases a bird, it will go out and do the same thing again as soon as it sees another one. The cat is at one with nature and lives and dies by the id-driven decisions it makes without a second thought.

Human beings are uniquely encumbered by the need to subdue the id and develop a dominating super-ego. The resultant conflict between the id and the super-ego is at the basis of our being. On the positive side, the presence of a ruling super-ego means we have a civilised society to live in. On the down side, we have stress, quandary and conflict at our basis, because our instinct drives us one way, and the learned behaviours required by society drive us another. We are eternally in conflict, because every decision is initially made instinctively by the id and then tempered, adjusted or changed completely by the super-ego.

The Ego is the individual that results from this conflict between the id and the super-ego. 'Ego' is Latin for 'I' and that is exactly what it is: the individual that is you; and you are defined by the decisions you make having balanced the conflicting demands of your id and your super-ego. Faced by chocolate in a shop, the id-ridden might choose to steal the chocolate; The id-affected might only steal it if they think they can get away with it; the super-ego dominated might pay for the chocolate even if there's no shopkeeper present and put the change into the charity box. Your ego is you, you are defined by the decisions you make, and your decisions are a result of the conflict between your id and super-ego.

The id and the super-ego are more generalised than the ego – all human beings start off with very similar instinctive drives and grow towards similar social codes that populate the super-ego and govern civilised society. However, the ego – the character that results from the conflict – is unique to you as an individual, and changes with personal development over time.

So what?

The key point to note at this point is that the earlier illustration could just as easily be a representation of a story:

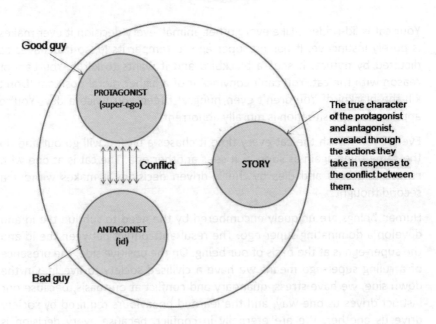

A story results from the conflict between the 'forces of good' doing positive things towards a civilised society (Our Hero represents the super-ego); and the 'forces of antagonism' – traditionally the 'bad guy' – who is self-absorbed and doing self-centred things to benefit only himself (the id). The paths of protagonism and antagonism are in opposition. They go into conflict and the journey through that conflict is the story: The actions and true characters that are revealed through the protagonist's response to the conflict, leading to a resolution of that conflict and life lessons being learned.

As we shall see in the body of this book, conflict is the lifeblood of story, and we, as human beings, are uniquely encumbered by specific types of conflict peculiar to our species, and inextricably paralleled with our id/super-ego battle.

Stories resonate with us when, either directly or through metaphor, they deal with a common conflict we all face – a conflict between id and super-ego. A good story embodies this conflict and shines a light on the route forwards for us in the real world.

All good stories do this. We are given a protagonist with whom we empathise. We lock on and take a journey with that protagonist through the conflicts represented. The behaviour of the protagonist leads us through the story, and we learn a lesson for how we should behave when faced with related conflicts in our own lives. Of course, this is not a conscious, stated lesson. When we were two years old, we enjoyed the story of the race between the hare and the tortoise. At no point does it pointedly state: 'slow and steady wins the day', but that is the lesson that will benefit a person in their progress in society. At the same time, when we were two and we approached a task with impatience, we found we failed. We went into conflict with the task, and found that the more we rushed at it, the less successful we became until we smashed it on the floor and burst into tears. The conflicts and lessons of *The Hare and the Tortoise* story resonated with the truth we found in life, so we 'got something' from the story. We liked it. It rang true, and our ego grew a little more society-appropriate.

Many other stories, with similar underlying messages, affirm similar learning, until we just know that 'slow and steady wins the day'. We don't know how we know it, we just do. Stories taught us good life behaviour in meaningful ways, and far more effectively than if some old bloke had stood up in front of us wagging his finger and saying, 'slow and steady wins the day.'

So, if all good stories shine a light on the route ahead for us on our journey from id-driven to super-ego appropriateness, what does this journey look like in words we all understand and can use as writers?

1.2   Model 2 – Maslow

Abraham Maslow shows us that same journey, from id-ridden baby to mature social adult. In his 1954 book *Motivation and Personality*, he proposed a Hierarchy of Human Needs, which set out our priorities for different stages of personal growth and identified the path we take – quite naturally – in our quest for what he called 'self actualisation' (personal fulfilment).

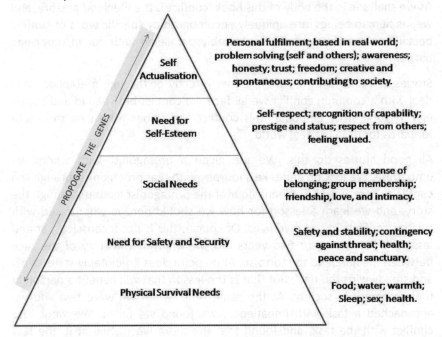

We can see that the lower levels relate very strongly to the demands of the id. The basics of life must be satisfied – water, food, sleep, warmth, health, security, sanctuary and the avoidance of threat. Each successive level in the hierarchy must be satisfied to a minimum before the individual can turn his mind to higher things. If a person cannot get enough to eat, he will compromise on his social agenda, or even his safety and security, to find food. However, once a person feels safe and secure, his or her focus will naturally move on to, for example, relationships, love, his place in a group and a sense of belonging.

Building further, the individual wishes to be respected and recognised, to build knowledge, self-esteem and status. The progression leads, ultimately, to 'self-actualisation'. Here, a person has predominantly reconciled his id and his super-ego. He feels fulfilled (whatever that might mean for him), is self-aware, grounded in the real world, creative and spontaneous, and has a personal system of morality that is fully internalised and independent of external coercion (e.g., he doesn't need a 'parent' to tell him not to steal or commit rape). Note that a 'self-actualised' person satisfies his demands at each level. He doesn't *remove* his id or its animal demands, but he controls and works with his demands for power, sex, safety and so forth to ensure they are society-appropriate.

Running as a powerful theme throughout all these levels are the needs dictated by our genes to propagate the next generation. I think it is interesting to note that in a society that is obsessed with sex, it is a factor that exists on every level of the hierarchy: it is a basic need; it makes us feel safe and secure to be in the arms of another; it gives us a sense of belonging, intimacy and a sense of success in relationships – possibly even group membership(!); we gain status and pride amongst our peers; and we feel a sense of satisfaction and fulfilment that is perhaps all too brief in our troubled lives. Intimacy works at all levels and at any time in our growth. That is why we always like it.

I ask again: so what?

All right, all right. Here is the key for a writer. As we discovered, your cat doesn't need an instruction book for development of an appropriate self, because she is id-driven for her whole life. In this respect, unlike us, she is, like all other animals, at peace with herself. She knows exactly how to handle every situation. She is at one with nature. There are no dilemmas; no difficult choices to make. Every decision is easy for the id-driven.

However, the journey we humans make from instinctive, id-ridden animal at birth to self-actualised, society-appropriate individual is a long and tortuous one, and, critically, one which has no map from Mother Nature. There are no instructions apart from those we humans invent for ourselves for handling the quandary, dilemma, conflict, stresses and strains of becoming 'civilised'. And for this journey, our id is not useful; indeed, it must be overcome. There is only one way to learn how to behave appropriately in society, and that is from each other.

If the civilised world we humans have created beyond the id is to flourish and progress, then every individual's development towards personal fulfilment needs guidance. Over the centuries of human civilisation, the visionaries developed philosophies to show people how we should lead our lives; to help us to climb the hierarchy towards self-actualisation, to contribute to the perpetuation of the society that supports human life, and to be fine parents (i.e., teachers) to the next generation. Philosophy is, by definition, the study of the world beyond the id; philosophy attempts to define that rule book for how people should lead their lives over and above their instinctive drives.

For example, which are the most influential philosophies that guide humanity? Religions. And how are they encapsulated? In story. At their base, religions are all stories, conveyed to us by writers. And all stories – religious or otherwise – are, beneath it all, a symbolic or analogous representation of a good guy learning the right things to do to climb the hierarchy personally (and progress the needs of the civilised world), and/or a bad guy being 'ego-centric' and failing in his self-serving, anti-social agenda. As the heroes and villains face their challenges and succeed and fail respectively, we recognise in ourselves the conflicts they face and we learn the behaviours that will succeed or fail for us. It's as simple as that. Biblical stories are all concerned with guiding our thoughts and actions. Stories are – almost exclusively – providing signposts for where to go next to climb the hierarchy towards the betterment of society, and towards personal fulfilment in that society.

Time and time again the stories to which we are exposed reaffirm the same messages, and therefore shape our minds. Once we have grown beyond the messages a story is trying to deliver, that is when we are able to *consciously* identify the moral message. From this elevated position of enlightenment, we decide that stories reflect society. They do, but only for those of us who have already learned the lesson; only then are we able to see a reflection. For all people before they have learned the moral message or faced the inner conflicts, the story will be a guiding light for future behaviour. *Society reflects stories*.

1.3   Get real, please...

When you try to relate this chapter to the stories you know, I feel sure you will feel somewhat sceptical. Do stories really have a key role in driving our social and psychological development? In a moment I will present an example using a story choice a sceptic would be proud of, but the real proof of how important stories are to the soul of civilisation comes from the stories that *don't* exist.

For all the outrageous stories you have ever experienced, for all the ground-breaking authors and for all the Machiavellian directors who strut about basking in how controversial they are, what you have never seen is a story that breaks the furthest bounds of acceptable civilised behaviour. You don't often see a good guy lose out at all, but when you do, it will usually be a tragedy in personal terms but a win for the greater good. 'Jesus died to save us all'. What it will not do, for example, is show genuine evil winning: a paedophile gaining control of a class of two-year-olds, for example, and having the kind of story resolution such a character might want. This is because ultimately we, as humanity, demand that stories guide a fine society. We don't mind a fictional story in which a traditional bad guy wins out occasionally – it simply serves to highlight the good that 'lost' and the path that 'good' should have taken in order to prevail. But true evil never gets to win, because such a story would be morally abhorrent and nobody would want to read or see it. It doesn't even have to be that extreme. *The Simpsons* was banned in certain countries in the world, because the programme was deemed to glamorise behaviour that is negative to civil society. Deep down in our psyche, this is unacceptable. We need our stories to lead our society in the right direction. [2]

Returning to stories that do exist, let's try an example. In this book I focus on *Back to the Future*, written by Bob Gale and Robert Zemeckis, as my case study for a 'standard', classically structured story. My claim is that all good stories will depict a character growing and advancing through conflict towards self-actualisation, so the question can be asked of *Back to the Future*: how does a light-hearted, science-fiction, adventure story about teenage time travel possibly relate to the principled advancement of my soul through life's journey? [3]

Back to the Future – initial values

Clearly, the surface story shows a protagonist dealing with events that bear no obvious relationship to the psycho-social issues discussed here. But we don't have to dig too far beneath the surface to find the underlying messages. Across the full arc of the story, what measurable changes take place in the protagonist's life? Well, Marty McFly (played by Michael J. Fox) begins in a family comprising a mother who drinks Vodka at the dining table, a weak and subservient father being bullied by his peers, an overweight sister who can't get a boyfriend, and a brother working in a fast-food joint. They live in run-down conditions and are going nowhere in life.

In terms of Maslow's hierarchy, look at the values in the frame: At the basic levels, we see drinking and obesity – threats to health. The family is bullied by Biff Tannen (Thomas F. Wilson), so economic security and 'freedom from threat' are under the cosh. The sister 'can't get a boyfriend' – the chances of high quality genes propagating to the next generation are under threat and she is unfulfilled at the level of 'love', 'acceptance' and 'group membership'. The mother, Lorraine McFly (Lea Thomson) looks on the father rather sadly – clearly no great love and affection here despite their marriage. The father George McFly (Crispin Glover) symbolises all of them at the 'self esteem'

---

[2] Most cultures recognise that, far from glamorising socially unacceptable behaviour, audiences learn appropriate behaviour from their understanding of how wrong the featured behaviours are.

[3] Incidentally, it would be really useful to watch *Back to the Future* if you can. Most of my examples are drawn from this story, which features just about all the principles that lie beneath a good story.

level. He is weak and riddled with self-doubt; he lacks prestige or status. Even Marty lacks self esteem: he doubts his musical ability, an area where he is desperate to win acceptance and to gain status. Even the time travel itself – the main adventure plot line – is presented as a threat, not simply because of its inherent dangers, but because it puts the future of the McFly gene pool in jeopardy. Marty and his siblings are being wiped out by his interference in past events and, worse still, the gene pool of Biff Tannen – the representative of the ego-centric dark side of life – is going to profit his own gene pool from Marty's time travel (indeed, these issues are central to the sequel).

Back to the Future – final values

By the end of the story look what has changed. Marty's journey, his experience and the actions he has taken mean that the family as a whole has climbed up a level of Maslow's hierarchy in all areas. All aspects of the home exude prestige and fulfilment. All the family members are healthy and slim. The parents are back from the country club where they've been playing golf and radiate love, affection, togetherness and contentment. The cars on the drive and the fixtures of the house ooze status and achievement. Biff has been subdued and is now, himself, forced into subservience by a strong and assertive, self-actualised father (his first book is published – a clear symbol of fulfilment if ever there was one!). The sister is fighting off multiple boyfriends. The brother is smartly and proudly heading off to his office profession. Marty gets the car he wanted (presented from the start of the story as the prestige symbol) and he gets the girl (Jennifer, played by Claudia Wells), thereby securing the next generation (indeed, we meet their kids in the sequel). The dragon is slain by the brave knight who ends the story in a luxurious kingdom and in the arms of his adoring princess.

It should be possible to analyse all good stories in these terms, and it is through these mechanisms that a story touches a chord in all of us. A set of values can be measured at the start, and will be seen to have symbolically or actually changed across the course of the story, depicting a clear move up the hierarchy. I suggest that in answering the subjective question of what factors are present in every 'good' story, a measurable character progression up the hierarchy towards fulfilment would be a common factor. This is, incidentally, why few movies manage to deliver a successful sequel. All the characters have made their great journey, and once they have achieved a higher self, particularly if they achieve self-actualisation, there is no further personal journey they can satisfactorily take, so any subsequent story can only fail to resonate. *Back to the Future* handled this by moving on to the next generation, 30 years into the future, where Marty and Jennifer's children are struggling on the lower levels of the journey towards their own self-actualisation and can be helped back onto and along the correct path through the adventures portrayed.

This said, the transition doesn't have to be as obvious and broad as *Back to the Future*. A good novel may take 500 pages and shift its protagonist from a position of delusion to one of belief. Indeed, an ironic story may take its protagonist back to where he started. It doesn't matter; it's the highlighting of a positive journey that gives the story its irony, so the principle remains the same.

Stories, like our personalities, are born out of conflict. I think it is hardly a coincidence that the journey through life is the story of our character development as an individual (ego) developing towards self-actualisation, and the journey through a story is that of a 'character's' development as an individual (protagonist's ego) towards self-actualisation.

1.4 Some quotes

The point is, a developing human is naturally wired up to interpret the world and learn his way using story structures. Stories are a reflection of how our brains want to understand and organise things. Don't just take my word for it. Here are some quotes from university types:

> **Bruner (1990).** "Psychologists have learned that 'fictional' story forms provide the structural lines in terms of which real lives are organized."

> **Pinker (1997).** " 'Intelligence' is the ability to attain goals in the face of obstacles by means of decisions and actions based on rational rules. The quality 'intelligence' is awarded to those who follow story structure."

> **Polkinghorne (1998).** "Narrative [story telling] is a scheme by means of which human beings give meaning to their experiences."

> **Boyce (1996).** "...stories are the most basic form used to filter, internalize, make sense of, and evaluate new experiences and information."

> **Kendall Haven (2006).** "The brain is predisposed to think in story terms. This predisposition is continuously reinforced and strengthened as the brain develops up through age 12. Adults arrive dependent on interpreting events and other human's behaviour through a specific story architecture."

Are you getting the point yet?! As writers, we must ensure that our stories – in fact or in metaphor – resonate with conflict and with human truth if they are to grip and engage an audience. If they do, then they will be appreciated, because:

Stories are the architects of the human mind.

2 A story definition

The dictionary tells us that a story is:

'A narration of an incident or a series of events designed to interest, amuse or instruct.'

Fair enough, I suppose, from the viewpoint of a consumer of story. However, as writers we need to dig a little deeper to understand how these events are 'designed'.

A good story delivers three elements, via three basic mechanisms for delivery:

Deliverable story element...	...Delivery mechanism is...
A structured narrative (the 'telling' of the story)	The choice of events selected for narration, the order of those events and the words used to describe them.
Character development	Action through conflict leading to at least one participant in the story changing, growing, and/or learning a 'life lesson'.
The underlying story (subtext)	Knowledge gaps. Information gaps in story events leaving space for audience projection and interpretation.

We will of course be going into detail in all three areas. For the moment, an introduction.

2.1 The structured narrative

This refers to the telling of your story; the presented, top level story as told. The actual words that are written on the page, their literal, face-value meaning, and the story events they portray. The term 'structured' narrative is carefully chosen, because the structure of your story is also generated by the events you choose to narrate and the order in which you place them.

Structured narrative – delivery mechanism

For a story to be well told, it must comprise 'meaningful' events. In general, events can only be meaningful if they are relevant to the story you wish to tell, and carry power in themselves because they affect change in the protagonist's emotional position. We will look in detail at this shortly.

Most fine stories fall into a very small number of common structures on which we shall focus, but they do not have to.

2.2 Character development

For a story to resonate effectively with an audience, at least one character in the story is likely to be challenged to change and grow across the arc of the story. As a result of their success or failure, at least one participant in the story will learn lessons about life and how it should be lived.

In *Back to the Future*, we have already described how the family progressed up Maslow's hierarchy towards self-actualisation across the telling of the story. This is a fine example of 'growth', but which character personified that growth?

George McFly is the one who changed and grew, from a weak and down-trodden boy to a strong and confident man. He didn't *consciously* learn any life lesson, because to him his actions were all that ever happened, but we watched him change and grow. It was us, the audience, who learned the life lesson from his story: fate is in our hands. The actions we take will define the path of our lives.

Character development – delivery mechanism

Characters must be forced to make difficult decisions through conflict. Characters placed under pressure of dilemma, a choice of evils or conflict triangulation will reveal their genuine character through the actions they take, and the audience will understand the life lessons from the decisions they get right... and wrong...

Most fine stories demonstrate a clear character development through one of the participants learning a life lesson, but not always.

2.3 The underlying story (subtext)

If a story is to distinguish itself from an instruction manual or a straightforward factual diary, there must be more going on than the surface-level narration. It must deliver an underlying story, known as the subtext. The underlying story is the one the audience perceives through their own interpretation of the narration. The truth they understand beyond the simple literal meaning of the words that comprise the narrative.

The underlying story – delivery mechanism

The means of delivery of the underlying story is through 'knowledge gaps'. A knowledge gap is the difference in knowledge held by different participants in a story. The participants are the protagonist, antagonist, other characters, the audience and the author. If, for example, one character knows more than another, we have a knowledge gap. If the audience knows more than the protagonist, then we have a knowledge gap, and so on. In *Back to the Future*, Marty is a time traveller from 1985, living in 1955. We, the audience, know that, but the 1955 characters, including his future parents, do not. This gap in the knowledge held between the participants gives all the events implicit story power. This is an example of one type of knowledge gap.

> **Note:** most writers think they must write <u>subtext</u> in order to deliver an underlying story. This is wrong. We write <u>knowledge gaps</u> in order to deliver a subtext. The underlying story *is* the subtext, and the subtext is a consequence of bedding in knowledge gaps.

There are no less than ten types of knowledge gap, created through questions, dialogue, action, promise, subplot, subterfuge, implication and suggestion, misinterpretation, subconscious aims and through metaphor. We shall look at this whole area in great detail later.

**If the story is *created* using knowledge gaps, then the real story
is *received* in subtext.**

Not all these three elements are always present in all stories, it would be fair to say that, in principle, most good stories have all three elements; and of course, although any given story might major on the factual narrative, another on the subtext and another on the character and life lessons, there are inevitable overlaps between the elements that make some presence of each almost unavoidable. However, **deep and pervasive subtext is always present in all good stories**.

As the designers of story, it is critical that we writers understand these elements, so this book focuses strongly on the mechanisms for delivery – story events, knowledge gaps and character action through conflict.

2.4 The roots of story – summary

Great stories resonate with the human mind because they reflect the conflicts our minds have to deal with as we learn and grow in life.

Stories are the most effective method of teaching and learning, because they combine the power of learning emotionally through direct experience with the objectivity and accuracy of unemotional analytical learning.

Stories are made up of a narrative (the telling), an underlying story (or subtext) and character development through learning life lessons. The substances of story that delivers these elements are:

A narrative structure (the events that are chosen and the order in which they are placed).

Character growth and learning through conflict.

Knowledge gaps (differences in knowledge held by the different participants in a story).

NARRATIVE AND STRUCTURE

A writer who denies the need for structure in his work is like a squash
player who claims his brilliance removes the need for a wall.

Me. (1960 –)

Introduction

Narrative – the story as told – is the tip of the iceberg. As we write our
words, we build a world, we create characters, we select and describe
events, we inspire images, we bed-in knowledge gaps, we capture conflicts
and reactions and, imperceptibly beneath the surface, nine-tenths of the
story is generated in an underlying structure.

However, as we create our story, we don't work on structure. Structure is a
consequence of our words, not a template for our words. And this is the
message I will go to some pains to get across: structure is not a part of the
creative process. Structure is an outcome of the creative process.

Many 'rule books' for writers begin with a classic three-act structure and
give orders for you to populate that structure with brilliance. 'Describe your
mood and timeframe on page 1.' 'Introduce your protagonist by page 3.'
'Put a turning point in the life of the protagonist on page 25.' And so on.
Cobblers. All utter, utter cobblers. Don't be tempted. It's ridiculous.
Structure is a consequence of the events you choose to narrate and the
order in which you narrate them. As soon as you take structure as a starting
point, you are frustrating your creativity and murdering your story. It is
dead in the water. Pack up and go home.

If you are going to build your perfect house, you start with a vision: your
preferred layout for the kitchen, you plan the en suite bathroom, and think

about colours and decoration and living space and landscaping and interior design and dream of what it will be like to live there. Of course, once you know what you want, you have to think about the viability of your dreams in terms of an underlying structure that can support them and bring them to life. You need to make sure that it has solid foundations, walls, a roof, plumbing for water, pipes bringing gas and so on, but that's not your starting point as the visionary. It never could be. Your vision *drives* the eventual structure. If you begin with an existing structure, your vision and dream will have to be bent to fit. Stories are the same. Begin with your imagination and creativity, and think about structure later. If the story emerges perfectly from your creative outpouring, who cares what the structure is?

This said, knowledge of structure is extremely valuable when it comes to retrospective analysis of a story event and fixing story problems. When you know there is something wrong with your story, and you cannot put your finger on the problem, turning the story upside-down and analysing the structure can generally reveal why it isn't working as you intended. This is the main value of structure: fault finding and optimisation <u>after</u> the creative outpouring is complete and we are in rewrite mode.

In this section, we shall understand how structure works. This essentially means identifying the creative components of the narrative that drive in structural pillars. We will be looking at:

What is structure? A definition and explanation.

A classic three act structure. The importance and derivation of the most common form.

Protagonist aims. The incidents that define your story and the structure.

Turning points and conflict.

Steps away from classical form. We all like to be different – the benefits and dangers of a 'different' structure.

And we shall repeat as a mantra, and never forget, that structure must be our slave and not our master:

Structure is not a starting point for creative development. Start with a creative outpouring of free expression The value of understanding structure comes in retrospective analysis and fixing story problems <u>after</u> the initial creative phase.

3   What is structure?

Story structure is an unavoidable consequence of the events you choose to narrate and the order in which you choose to arrange them. When you arrange your story events you generate a story structure.

3.1.1   What is an event?

A **story event** is the generic term for any structural element – a scene, chapter, sequence, act, or even an entire story. When I talk about 'the events you choose to narrate', the important consideration is that all events must be relevant to the story you want to tell, and for them to be **'meaningful story events'**, it means they affect change in the protagonist's emotional position.

If the protagonist has 8 hours sleep, Coco Pops for breakfast, uses the loo and drives to work, we have no emotional charge (unless something awful happens on the loo) and so we have no interest. These are events we choose not to narrate.

3.1.2   A classic three act structure

Structure begins from the simplest of birthplaces: All stories have a beginning, a middle and an end, and although it might sound a little trite, these are, effectively, the three acts of classical form that you have heard so much about. Because all stories have no choice but to have some sort of beginning, middle and end, there are structural imperatives that go with these unavoidable factors, and that is why the three act structure has become the *de facto* standard. Let's look at a standard story structure example.

Beginning

The beginning, or Act I, is the setup for the story. We gain an understanding of the world in which the story is set, the nature and presence of the protagonist, the nature and presence of forces of antagonism, and all the information we need in order that the **inciting incident**, when it hits, has us, the audience, asking the correct **key question**.

Middle

The inciting incident throws the established world out of balance. It is the trigger for a story-wide confrontation between the protagonist and the forces of antagonism. The conflict between them is fought from both sides, complicated by further events, and generally deepened by attempts at resolution. Matters approach a head. The ultimate battle at which the protagonist and forces of antagonism will go head to head with a winner-takes-all confrontation that will resolve the conflict one way or the other.

End

The climactic confrontation takes place between the protagonist and forces of antagonism. One wins out, the other loses with a degree of finality that means there can be no further battles in this story. The key question that was raised at the point of inciting incident is addressed satisfactorily. (This doesn't necessarily mean it was 'answered', but it usually does.)

Act I (Beginning)	Act II (Middle)	Act III (End)
Set up to an **inciting incident** which raises a **key question**.	**Progressive complications** as protagonist engages with antagonistic forces.	**Climax and resolution**, addressing key question raised.

These are the boundaries of a classic three act structure. Act I is the setup – the beginning – and that lasts up to the inciting incident. Once we have our key question, we are into Act II (the middle) which lasts up until we enter the climax, which is the beginning of Act III, more commonly known as 'the end', at which the key question raised is addressed satisfactorily, and the story is finished.

All stories have a beginning, a middle and an end. It's unavoidable, and that is fundamentally why a classic three act structure exists in every story. Whenever you hear about other structural forms – five acts, seven acts, no structure – in reality, what results will usually be easily interpreted in a three act form. It is, pretty much, the only game in town, and has been since the time of Aristotle, 2,300 years ago. Yes, there are other structures that have worked, but I recommend you embrace this classic form, at least until you feel your apprenticeship is over, and you are ready to push the boundaries knowledgeably.

OK. So let's take a look at these principal creative components – the inciting incident, key question and the resolution – that define the top-level structure of your story.

3.1.3   The inciting incident

The reason the inciting incident is so important is because it raises a key question in the mind of the audience that gives your story its fundamental direction; it orientates your audience to the aims of the protagonist, grips them and sets them up for the long haul across the arc of the entire story as they interpret the narrative in terms of what each event must mean in answering the key question.

The inciting incident raises a key question in the mind of the audience that is held open across the course of the story and addressed satisfactorily at resolution.

The key question

Questions are, obviously, a fundamental type of knowledge gap, and opening a 'grand' key question that arcs across the full telling of the story is a fine way of ensuring a pervasive, ever-present knowledge gap and therefore ensuring the story-wide engagement of the audience. It is not essential to have a key question that is raised early on, and answered at resolution – indeed, many of the finest stories do not, as we shall see – but the vast majority do.

Back to the Future provides a fine example. Marty accidentally propels himself back in time from 1985 to 1955. We know that he doesn't want to be there – he has a life and ambitions in 1985 – and he sets about trying to make the journey back to his own time. The fundamental question is raised: 'Will Marty make it back to 1985?' And that question will keep us in our seats until the end of the story, when we expect that the question will be answered by the action of the climax and resolution.

Your audience members know they are in good hands once they have been handed a good solid key question. It gives the story direction, and gives the audience a reference point for interpreting all the events that happen. They commit to the story and become intrigued and engaged as they anticipate an equally well-crafted journey and a resolution that will satisfactorily address that key question.

Studios and publishers have also learned to spot a key question. They can see when a key question has been raised and even the accountant can check if it is nicely paid off at resolution (sadly, the bean-counters are often the ultimate gatekeeper to a story's progress, and are often overly obsessed with these identifiable structural elements). When they see these elements it makes them feel confident that the writer knows what he is doing and that his work contains some of the basic substance they find in stories that make money. Indeed, so common is it, that some studios make it a basic requirement of their story department that a clear key question is raised (usually through an inciting incident that they also like to be able to identify) and that the story ending answers the key question. Sad, but true.

Example

Imagine that you are a friend and fellow parent, and you've dropped into my house for a cuppa after the morning school run. I am quick to tell you:

"My son fell into a hole this morning."

What is your reaction? "Oh, my God! Is he OK? How did that happen? What sort of hole? How big was it? How did you get him out? Is he in hospital?"

Immediately, there is a clear set of obvious questions that most people would naturally ask. That's because the report of my son falling into a hole is an inciting incident. The story of my son falling into a hole will not be complete until these obvious questions are answered satisfactorily.

Note carefully however, that I didn't give you just the one line. I sneakily set up the situation with the preamble about my house, our friendship and a school run. This provided a context in which you and I are friends having a cup of tea together somewhere in the western world. This gives you preconceptions of a real world drama with real world rules, and therefore real world questions.

A different type of setup could have raised different questions. If the context had been a man on stage in a spangled suit, leaning on a microphone and saying through a big smile, 'my son fell into a hole this morning', you might have started to smile, got an amusing image in your head of a child disappearing haplessly into a hole, and the question raised in your mind might be: 'so what's the punch line?' (A possibly inappropriate response to an anxious parent.) If the context had been that we were on holiday in India tracking with hunters on elephants when my son fell into a hole, you could sensibly have asked the key question: 'was there a tiger in the hole?' (Again, somewhat inappropriate to an anxious parent in Sussex.)

This is important, because this setup ensures that my inciting incident raised the *correct* key question in your mind.

In terms of the story as a whole, this gives us the whole point of Act I and the inciting incident in a nutshell:

1. The inciting incident raises the key question that will grip to the end of the story.

2. Act I is the build up to the inciting incident. Act I provides the setup required to ensure that the inciting incident raises the *correct* key question.

3. The story's act III climax and resolution answers the key question.

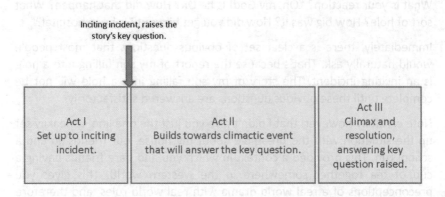

Inciting incident, raises the story's key question.

Act I	Act II	Act III
Set up to inciting incident.	Builds towards climactic event that will answer the key question.	Climax and resolution, answering key question raised.

Take a simple example: *Tom and Jerry*. A mouse flies round the corner of the house, followed hotfoot by a cat. This is the inciting incident. The key question is raised: 'Will the cat catch the mouse?' And we are away. All the information we need is there and we are gripped to the end to get the answer to the key question.

This is the simplest trick in story-telling. You set your audience up so that the inciting incident will raise the questions you want raised. The story then spends Act II grappling with the question from all sides as it builds towards the climax. The ending (Act III) is where the key question is answered and the story resolved. This is exactly story structure.

Let's do another one.

"Sammy puts lingerie on under a big fur coat and goes into town to surprise Bobby at work."

We're intrigued of course, but look at the difference. There is no setup here. We don't have a context for this event. This inciting incident has no Act I to set it up, so we don't know the right question to ask. Yes, we can ask, 'what happens next?' but that should always be the case. If we want to be sure to engage our audience we need a more specific key question. With Sammy dressing in lingerie, we don't know what to ask or why she is doing it or if it's a murder mystery or a relationship drama or a porn film or a sci-fi novel or a comedy.

The Act I setup of a plotline provides the rules that will govern what key question is raised. Depending on the setup, Sammy could be an assassin, adulteress, an alien or even a man! And there is a wholly unsatisfactory level of detail about the lingerie, but maybe that's just me.

Perhaps it should be a picture book. Anyway, the 'rule books' will tell you that the inciting incident must come at around a quarter of the way through your story, or 25 minutes for a film. I am saying this is cobblers. It should come at the appropriate time for your story. This is the earliest time after you have set the audience up to form the right key question from the inciting incident. But it must come as soon as possible in order to get the audience gripped. Once we have them asking the correct key question, we can start to have some fun, but until then, we are in danger of losing our audience because they don't yet know what question(s) the story is trying to ask and answer.

Some stories, like our *Tom and Jerry* example, begin with the inciting incident – an excellent way to start, provided it raises the correct key question. Some stories begin after the inciting incident, if that makes sense. I recently enjoyed a stage production of *Death and the Maiden*, by Ariel Dorfman. The premise is this: a rapist unwittingly reappears in the life of one of his victims, fifteen years after the brutal event. She recognises his voice immediately.

It becomes evident to us, as the story unfolds, that the rape of Paulina fifteen years previously was the inciting incident in the current story and we get hold of the key question: 'Will Paulina exact a brutal revenge on her rapist?'

If there is too much set up without an inciting incident, the audience will become confused as the story meanders without aim before the key question ever gets asked. If the inciting incident is too early, then the wrong key question may be raised in the mind of the audience and the story will lack the correct direction.

3.2   Lots of examples from all types of story

Let's take a look at a range of inciting incidents from all the different story media, beginning with a film. Can you identify the inciting incident in *Back to the Future*? The event that invoked that key question in your mind ('Will Marty make it back to 1985')? No peeking ahead...

3.2.1   *Back to the Future* – inciting incident

I said no peeking.

Marty McFly and Emmett 'Doc' Brown (Christopher Lloyd), the inventor of a time machine built into a DeLorean, are in a car park planning carefully for Doc Brown's first time travel experiment. They are attacked by terrorists who want revenge for the Doc having stolen their plutonium. Marty leaps into the DeLorean and drives off to escape the attack. The terrorists sure mean business – Marty sees them shoot Doc Brown in cold blood – then they come after him. In fleeing from the terrorists Marty takes the DeLorean up to 88m.p.h. – the trigger speed for time travel to take place – and he is propelled back in time to the year 1955.

Out of interest, how long do you think Marty is in his contemporary 1985 world of Act I before this inciting incident sends him back in time? I'll tell you. There are almost thirty minutes of Act I – one third of the whole story – all in 1985, setting us up to ask all the right questions and interpret events as the writers intended. We have locked on to Marty as our protagonist, so we understand what he wants from life and we are now immediately asking ourselves: 'Will Marty ever get back home?' The key question is in place, and there's no way we will leave our seats until we know the answer.

3.2.2   *The Giggler Treatment*

For the novelists amongst you, the inciting incident in Roddy Doyle's children's book, *The Giggler Treatment* comes at the end of Chapter 1, when we are told that the protagonist, Mr Mack, is four paces away from treading in a large dog poo on the pavement; a dog poo that has been placed there deliberately for him by mysterious powers. The key question is raised – will he tread in the poo? Who put it there? Why? And the rest of the entire book covers these four paces and the events causing, surrounding and leading up to the climax when this key question is answered. Wonderful.

This is a fine example of what we are after. It doesn't matter what the story is about, but if you are sure you have an inciting incident, and manage to raise a clear key question in the mind of your reader or viewer, you definitively have the essence of a story. And no, I'm not going to tell you if he treads in the poo.

3.2.3   *Hamlet*

The inciting incident in Shakespeare's *Hamlet* is when his dead father comes to him as a ghost and tells him that he was murdered by his own brother who has now taken Hamlet Senior's crown and wife as well as his life. The ghost demands that *Hamlet* avenge his death. The key question is raised: will Hamlet believe the voices in his head and take revenge? Will he murder his own uncle on the orders of a ghost? Is he mad, or has a crime been committed?

The inciting incident of most crime stories is when the crime takes place and Inspector Cop-With-Personal-Problems-and-Self-Destructive-Tendencies is put on the case to solve it. Will the cop solve the crime and bring the perpetrators to book? A clear key question is easily raised in crime stories, and a clear society-appropriate life-lesson can be taught about how crime doesn't pay, which is why crime stories are so common.

3.2.4   Adrift

The film story, *Adrift*, by Adam Kreutner, is an interesting story setup. A group of young friends takes a large yacht out a long way from land. After a few beers and some fun and games, the inciting incident occurs when someone shouts, 'last one in's a sissy!' (or some such) and they all jump over the side to muck about in the sea. All great fun... until they realise nobody put the ladder down. They can't reach to get back on board, they are many miles from land, and there's nobody on board... except the baby. The yacht drifts slowly on as the group begins to argue amongst themselves, raising the key question: will they find a way back on board, or will they die trying? (Unfortunately, this film is a fine example of a good inciting incident not necessarily leading to a good story...)

3.2.5   Idomeneo

In the opera by Mozart of the Greek Tragedy *Idomeneo*, the inciting incident is in two parts. Idomeneo is at sea in a storm and fears he will never see his home and family again. He prays to King Neptune and promises that if Neptune saves him, he will sacrifice to him the first living soul he encounters back on dry land. The storm instantly abates and Idomeneo survives. Upon hearing the news of his father's safe return, Idomeneo's son, Idamante, hurries to the beach and he is the first to arrive and meet Idomeneo. The father must sacrifice his own son to Neptune... or risk the wrath of the Gods... What question immediately springs to mind?

3.2.6   Toy Story

In *Toy Story*, the inciting incident is the moment that the new toy on the block, Buzz Lightyear, is discovered on the bed of the young boy who owns the toys (Andy). This occurs at around 13 minutes. The toys are surprised, because Buzz is in the place on the bed usually belonging to their current leader, Woody, who has always been Andy's favourite toy, until now... The toys start chattering that Woody might have been replaced. They are then doubly surprised – and mightily impressed – to find that Buzz is apparently not a toy. He is a real live space ranger. He is packed with modern gadgetry and titanium wings. He is digital and capable. Woody feels inadequate with his string pull voice and no gadgetry... and Andy loves his new toy. The question is raised: is Woody finished as the leader of the toys? Is Buzz going to replace Woody as Andy's favourite toy?

It is interesting to note that the complete delivery of the inciting incident and the raising of the key question takes around 12 minutes in *Toy Story* (this is explained in detail later). In general, these elements tend to all come at once as part of the same story event, but, as I say, this is not a rule book. *Toy Story* requires this inciting incident along with the Act I turning point 12 minutes later to put the full and correct key question is in place. The story of *Death and the Maiden* also took the inciting incident (the rape fifteen years earlier) and the Act I turning point (when Pauline reveals to us that the dinner guest was her rapist) to raise the key question.

It is often quite tricky to isolate the precise inciting incident; there may be several events that successfully cause a key question to be raised without a single, obvious inciting incident. This is done to be absolutely sure the correct key question is very clearly in place – particularly important in a children's story, so you can be sure the audience 'gets it'. You have to do what is right for your story. In principle, if yours is a good story and is to be well told, it will have an inciting incident which will raise a clear key question.

We could go on all night, identifying the inciting incident and key question for every story we can think of. Try it on a few for yourself, and I would wager that you will find a correlation between clear inciting incidents/key questions and the success of the story concerned.

3.3   When is a key question not a key question?

Once you have written a few stories with inciting incidents that raise clear questions that lead to satisfying resolutions then you will be well qualified to experiment with more subtle inciting incidents, less clear key questions, and resolutions that raise as many questions as they answer. We shall take a closer look at the options for stepping away from classical form in '**3.10 – Structure and non-classical form**', but let me just say a few words on this now.

There are many successful stories – perhaps the *most* successful stories – that do not have a glaring key question presented to the audience on a plate in neon capitals one-third of the way through the story. This doesn't mean that there is no key question – what there will be instead is a focus on subtext, or on character growth and learning. Perhaps there will be a more subtle gap in knowledge that needs *understanding* rather than a question that needs answering. The protagonist may not even be aware that he is trying to fill this knowledge gap; he is certainly not aware of any key question, so he cannot knowingly set about answering it.

So, for example, the protagonist may be labouring under misapprehension, or be misguided in their approach to life, and the story may be about their growth into understanding and embracing change. For example...

3.3.1   *A Christmas Carol*, by Charles Dickens

Never out of print since 1843, this classic novel is a perfect example of a great story, but it has no blatant key question. It has an inciting incident, when the ghost of Ebenezer Scrooge's ex-business partner, Jacob Marley, visits him, but no key question is raised beyond 'what will happen next?' However, we are primed by the ghost to expect three spirits to visit Scrooge, and we are riveted by the gap in knowledge – what will happen when the ghosts descend upon this cold hearted, money grabbing man? The foreshadowing of these future scenarios will keep us gripped, and in the end it is the personal growth of the protagonist that will satisfy us at resolution. Scrooge journeys from id-dominated at the beginning – greedy, bullying, selfish, money-grabbing – to super-ego dominated by the end – generous, society-appropriate, warm-hearted and fulfilled by generosity. He learns the kind of lessons we want all people to learn, and we love the story for that. The key to holding our attention without a key question is that we can project forwards to the three encounters with ghosts and we want to know what these individual story events will entail. In essence, the story is actually about Scrooge's personal journey and his learning of life lessons. Indeed, the resolution to the story doesn't involve ghosties at all; that's all done with by that point – the climax and resolution are all about Scrooge's personal growth.

This is the common method of story delivery in the more complex and sophisticated novels and films, and some of the most successful are like this (*Goodfellas* and *The Godfather* being two top ten films of all time that do not have a clear key question); but for a less deep example, look at *Groundhog Day*. A magical, hugely successful film... with no key question.

3.3.2   *Groundhog Day*

The knowledge gap in *Groundhog Day* is huge and fascinating – weatherman, Phil (Bill Murray) is having the worst day of his life – and is reliving that same day over and over again. We, the audience, know that he is stuck in some sort of time loop and that the same day keeps repeating, but the people he meets every day – behaving exactly the same way every day – do not. There is a gap in knowledge between what we, the audience, know (along with Phil) and what the other characters in the story know. This is a fine example of a deep, persistent, continuous knowledge gap, but there is no 'question' arising from it. Again, we can project forwards to future sequences – we know he is going to relive the same day again and again, and we are interested to know how he is going to handle the same day multiple times, but with increasing experience of it. This keeps us gripped whilst the personal journey of growth and learning builds us a satisfying resolution. How does Phil change and grow through the telling of the story?

Once Phil realises he is going to be reliving the same day time and time again he sees selfish opportunities to take advantage of the predictability of the people around him. He uses his fore-knowledge of daily events to steal money, gain gratuitous sex, even commit murder; and yet despite these opportunities he becomes less and less happy with his lot. His character, and the story, progresses when he changes his approach to society. He gives up the hollow dissatisfaction he gets from self-centredness, and experiences personal growth and learning when he changes to altruistic, society-benefiting behaviours. He becomes a finer person, devoting his day and using his prescience of the day's events to save lives, learn piano, indulge romance, help the elderly and so on. Once he becomes a genuinely good person, the spell is broken, society gives him his rewards and he is free to move on with a happy life. Or, to put it another way, his super-ego (altruistic good guy) wins out over his id (selfish bad guy), and society rewards him with a princess (Rita, played by Andie MacDowell). Clear and evident progress up Maslow's hierarchy helps make this a great story based not on a key question, but on character development.

We will look in greater depth at knowledge gaps shortly, but we can safely say that a story which not only has a key question but also deep and pervasive knowledge gaps and clear and evident character growth across its course has the best of all worlds and is all the stronger for it.

3.3.3   The Truman Show

I would suggest that *The Truman Show* is an example of a story that exhibits all aspects of excellent story foundation – a strong inciting incident/key question; a massive basis in subtext; excellent character growth; and learning for us, the audience.

Written by Andrew Niccol, the story stars Jim Carrey as Truman Burbank, a man whose life has been filmed since he was in the womb. He is the star of a reality show, and has no idea that the entire world around him is a film set created for his part and that everyone in his world is an actor working on his personal soap opera. The TV show that is Truman's life becomes a global phenomenon; a reality show watched by billions around the globe 24/7. **The inciting incident** raises a clear key question: will Truman ever find out that his life is one enormous fabrication? What will happen when he does?

The subtext is deep and persistent: everyone knows – I mean everyone on earth, including the film audience and all the actors participating in Truman's life – that his life is a reality TV show, except Truman himself. There are also many other levels of knowledge gap, but this single excellent, pervasive, deep and persistent knowledge gap keeps us gripped and intrigued throughout.

In terms of **character growth**, the story is magnificent, firstly because Truman changes and grows out of his prison over the course of the film (all other characters remain static), and secondly, because we, the audience can learn lessons about life. At what point does reality TV shift from innocent entertainment to unjustifiable, dangerous, intrusive and unacceptable? For those who wish to get right into it, Truman's experiences can be seen to reflect the normal psychological development we all experience in the transition from the restricted world of a child under the eye of benign but controlling parents, escaping and growing into the freedom of adulthood. We can also move into the metaphorical – *The Truman Show* has sparked religious analogy (for example, does the Programme Director, Christoff, played by Brian Delate, represent God... or the devil?) and prophesy with regard to 'Big Brother' watching us, and the obsessive human drive for fifteen minutes of fame. (More on these aspects of subtext later.)

Andrew Niccol's story idea found instant success from a single page treatment, and I strongly believe that it is the clear presence of all the basic story elements that brought him this success.

3.4   Resolution

The area we focus on as soon as we can in the writing process is the ending. Given that we have our inciting incident and key question, it is important to know how things are going to turn out in the end. The ending 'resolves' the key question raised by the inciting incident, so these two events – the inciting incident raised early in the story and the resolution at the end – are the king-pins of the story. If we don't know the ending, we don't know where the goal is. We have no direction with which to write the Act II events that lead up to the resolution with any degree of confidence. It is interesting to note that all the experts I spoke to agreed: we need to know the ending before we can truly write our story.

However, sometimes we do not know at this early stage of development *exactly* what our ending is going to be. Even if we think we do, as we become ever more familiar with the world we are creating, new possibilities may emerge that will cause the ending to change.

The key, then, is to work at both ends of the process at the same time: on the one hand we need to get our mitts on the ending, because once we have that, we can write the whole story. On the other hand, we must keep our story fluid and flexible to easily embrace new and interesting ideas. We achieve this by resisting detail and by working with a Step Outline (more on which in Chapter **10 – The step outline**).

Many writers simply write 'page 1' at the top, begin at the beginning, and write their entire story from front to back, discovering their ending when they get there. Although this is a common 'method', it is not a wise approach. It might work sometimes if you are lucky, and is certainly a reasonable approach with a short story. However, if the ending, when it finally shows its face, is something of a revelation to you, it will cause more problems than it solves, because, firstly, the story will have become screwed into place here and there, and secondly, changing the ending will require extensive changes through the body of the story. The whole thing rapidly becomes unmanageable, and – more often than not – the full potential we set out with will never be realised.

This said, do not worry if you don't have your ending yet; simply provide a general answer to your key question. *Back to the Future*'s key question is: "Will Marty make it back to 1985?" Initially, Bob Gale and Robert Zemeckis knew only this about the ending: "Yes, he will make it back to 1985, and it will be a better 1985 than the one he left behind."

Suffice to say, if you can provide anything from a single sentence to a complete ending at this stage, we are heading in the right direction.

Don't forget, although we have focussed on the whole story as our story event example in this section, the same is true for all story events. Be they entire stories, acts, sequences, or scenes, they all have a beginning, a middle and an end, and, in theory, will need an inciting incident raising a key question that is answered at resolution in order to be meaningful. Of course, this is not the case in practice. Not all events need to carry massive power, or possibly could, but if an event is to be meaningful, it will contain an inciting incident/key question, and/or knowledge gaps, and/or character development. If it doesn't it will need to have a damn good reason to be there in terms of the wider story events of which it is a passive component.

3.5   Turning points

When a writer wants to see the connection between his created narrative and the resultant structure, he looks for turning points.

A turning point has a rather unique position in a story because:

> **A turning point is a measurable element of the creative side.** Turning points are generated through the interactions and behaviours of your characters in a story event.

> **A turning point is a measurable element of structure.** Turning points can be clinically identified, pointed at and evaluated through analysing the structure of a story event.

When desirable *creative* elements come together appropriately, they deliver a turning point which is 'visible' from the *structural* viewpoint. This can be very useful when analysing a story because testing for a turning point will tell us if any critical creative component is missing from an event that is failing to please us.

Turning points define the presence of a change in the protagonist's emotional position, and that can only happen effectively through conflict. You can't have a story without conflict, and you can't have *effective* conflict without generating a turning point, so this next bit is worth understanding.

A turning point

occurs when the protagonist's emotional 'charge' switches across the course of an event (scene/act/sequence/story...)

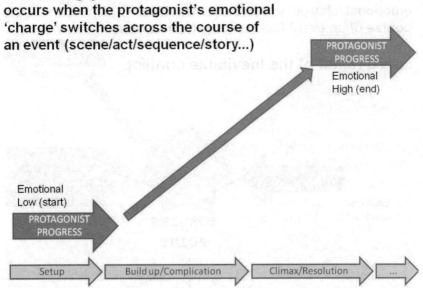

We should be able to take any given event and 'measure' the change in the values at stake for the protagonist across the course of that event, and therefore confirm firstly, that it has a turning point, and secondly, that it is probably a meaningful event.

What do we mean by 'meaningful? To be meaningful, the emotional transition has to take place **through conflict**. As we shall see, conflict is critical – the life blood of story – and the transition across an event is pointless unless it is achieved through conflict.

In order for the turning point to occur through conflict, the following elements need to be present:

- A protagonist with a protagonist aim for the event.

- An antagonist (or forces of antagonism), set in direct opposition to the aims of the protagonist.

- The two go head to head – an irresistible force against an immovable object.

- One wins and the other loses as a result of the conflict.

A turning point occurs when the protagonist's emotional 'charge' switches across the course of an event (scene/act/sequence/story...)

...as a result of the inevitable conflict.

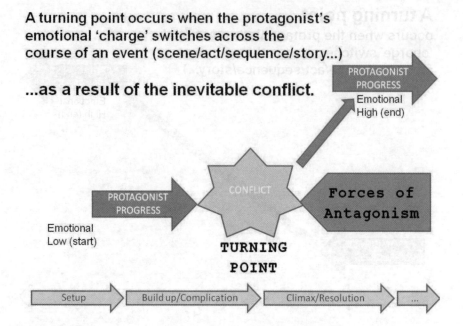

For example?

Hopefully, you have watched *Back to the Future* by now. In the pivotal scene in which George McFly finally stands up to the bully, Biff, in order to save Lorraine, he has several emotional values under threat across several simultaneous events at the different story levels (scene, sequence, act and story). If you have yet to watch *Back to the Future*, the sequence under scrutiny involves George McFly, racked with self-doubt and lacking assertiveness, stumbling across the muscle-bound bully, Biff, sexually attacking Lorraine in a parked car – the girl George loves and desires but is too weak to win. The scene forces George into a choice of evils: stand and fight, and risk a severe beating from the bully, or walk away and leave the woman of his dreams to be abused; and any chance of a future with her gone forever. Despite the odds, he chooses to stand and fight, and – steeled by a build up of anger towards the bully and by his love for Lorraine – he makes a fist for the first time in his life... and punches Biff's lights out. His self-doubt gone, he takes the adoring Lorraine by the hand and leads her off into the school dance.

This event is pivotal to the story, changing the fortunes of George, Lorraine, their future son Marty and the bully Biff. On the basis that we all agree this scene works, I would wager that I can find turning points – changes in emotional values for the protagonists – in the story at the scene, sequence, act and story event levels through this single action, so let's try to identify the structural elements we would expect to find if the event has a turning point.

The elements we are looking for at each level are: a protagonist (with an emotional value under threat); an antagonist with aims in direct opposition to those of the protagonist; inevitable conflict between them; and a switch in the protagonist's emotional value between the start and the end as a result of the conflict.

Scene level

At the scene level, the protagonist is George. The antagonism in the scene comes from Biff. George's scene aim is **to defeat the bully**. They both want the girl, so the conflict is inevitable and only one can win out. George's chances of defeating the bully are apparently zero at the scene's inciting incident (the moment George inadvertently challenges Biff to a fight), however, he succeeds, so his emotional position transitions to the positive by the end when he has overcome the bully. This measurable transition in the protagonist's fortunes, achieved through conflict, indicates that the scene has a turning point.

Sequence level

In the context of the wider story event of which that scene is a component, George's aim, as protagonist, is **to win Lorraine's hand**. The antagonism comes from his own 'self-doubt', which inhibits the dynamism required to get the girl (who, expressly desires a 'strong man'). At the sequence inciting incident, when George opens the car door and finds Biff in front of him, he goes into conflict with his own self-doubts. We know from what has gone before that his chances of a future with Lorraine look to be at an all time low. A few precious seconds (and a left hook) later, and he has gone from weak and unattractive to confident and attractive. The emotional value of 'self-doubt' has, for George, gone from negative to positive.

Act level

At the still-wider act level, of which this sequence is a component, the protagonist is Marty – George's son. Marty's emotional position in terms of 'death' begins at the negative – he looks unlikely to exist in the future because he inadvertently stopped his parents from meeting. The forces of antagonism are represented by the difficulties of getting history back on track in order for him to be born; specifically, his stated protagonist aim is: **to get his future parents to kiss on the dance floor at the Enchantment Under the Sea Dance**. That will put history right back on track.

At the beginning of the act, his mother is not remotely attracted to his father and his father is so riddled by self-doubt that it seems impossible that

Marty might fix up history. By the end of the act his parents kiss on the dance floor and his future existence is assured. His personal safety has gone from negative to positive.

Story level

Marty's emotional value of 'happiness' is still under threat at the wider story level, where the key question raised at the inciting incident was, 'Will he make it back to 1985?' At this level, his upcoming attempt to return to 1985 relies upon his coinciding with a bolt of lightning that will be used to power time travel. However, the sequence event, above, must complete first if history is to be put back on track, so the force of antagonism principally in play during this scene is the clock is ticking down. Can Marty resolve the subplot in time to make it to the bolt of lightning and return to 1985? As George's scene with Biff commences it seems Marty has no chance of getting his parents to fall in love and still make it to the bolt of lightning on time. He takes on the clock, and when he succeeds, his chances of future happiness move from negative positive.

Turning point?

Within each event, the turning point should be clearly identifiable as the very moment when the protagonist's fortunes shift from negative to positive, or vice versa in each of the events. The exact moment of the turning point can be identified as when George connects his left hook with Biff's chin. It is precisely in this single story beat, lasting but a couple of seconds, that all those emotional values at stake switch, directly or indirectly, and at every level of the story in motion, from negative to positive. Now **that** is a turning point.

3.5.1   Note on turning points

The examples above are all a switch from negative to positive, but things can equally move in the other direction, of course. Indeed, the shift only has to be 'relative'. A turning point can represent a shift in a protagonist values from positive to negative; the shift can be from positive to dramatically more positive; or from negative to extremely negative. There simply has to be a relative and appreciable shift.

Note on the protagonist and antagonist

Note that the term 'protagonist' doesn't mean 'the good guy'. It means **the entity whose story is being told**. Yes, this is usually the main actor or actress, and usually the good guy, but might be a criminal, a team, the devil, an animal, a family, an alien, an army or a lump of putty, just as long as it is their story that is being told. Equally, the protagonist may succeed or fail in his aims, but even in a tragedy, the outcome of a good story will shine a light on appropriate behaviours for handling human conflicts. Note also that the protagonist for a given story event doesn't have to be the same throughout the story. As you saw above, the protagonist in *Back to the Future* changed, for the different story events, between George and Marty. In general, if the protagonist in any given event is not the protagonist for the top level story, the event will still impact the emotional position of the story-wide protagonist. In other words, although Marty is the protagonist for the wider story, George's protagonist role in his confrontation with Biff had a clear and evident impact on Marty's story.

Similarly, the antagonist is simply the term for the forces ranged in opposition to the aims of the protagonist. Again, this will most usually be 'the bad guy' in conflict with the good guy protagonist, but you may have a criminal as your protagonist (Robin Hood; Butch and Sundance; Jack Sparrow; Delboy Trotter; Norman Stanley Fletcher...), and the antagonistic forces might therefore be the victims or the police. Forces of antagonism can include the weather, the dog, the protagonist's insecurity or delusions, acts of God and many others. We shall address this in much greater detail later, for the moment:

The protagonist is the entity whose story is being told. Forces of antagonism are any forces which are in conflict with the aims of the protagonist.

3.6 The major turning points

We also need to talk about the mid-act turning point, and the differences between an inciting incident and a turning point. We shall then use *Back to the Future* to show how the whole package shapes up in a real example.

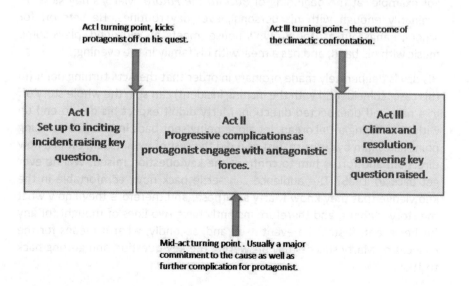

Act I turning point, kicks protagonist off on his quest.

Act III turning point – the outcome of the climactic confrontation.

Act I
Set up to inciting incident raising key question.

Act II
Progressive complications as protagonist engages with antagonistic forces.

Act III
Climax and resolution, answering key question raised.

Mid-act turning point . Usually a major commitment to the cause as well as further complication for protagonist.

In these terms, *Back to the Future* conveniently represents the common form. There are usually three main turning points in the plot of a classically structured film story, as shown above. The first one is, more often than not, also the inciting incident (but certainly doesn't have to be). The key feature that distinguishes an Act I turning point from the others is that it should set the protagonist off on his quest for the ultimate goal, and we should understand from this his story-wide purpose and see his direction change as he sets about fulfilling it.

This change in direction is often part of the mechanism for raising the key question, as it gives a good indication to the audience of the overall goal of the protagonist, and therefore helps to raise that all-important key question. Whereas most turning points represent a change in some value for the protagonist – from positive to negative or vice versa – the act I turning point, being so early and therefore having no relative values against which it can relate – sets the story direction and provides a 'baseline' measurement against which future emotional transitions can be related. In other words, George's single punch in *Back to the Future* was a beat in a scene about two boys fighting over a girl in a school car park. But we interpreted it for its importance in a different boy's story-wide aims to exist in the future and to get back to 1985.

In the common case, the Act I turning point is a 'call to action' for our hero, which identifies clearly what is required of him. It is likely that it will propel the protagonist in a wholly unexpected direction, and define his goal (perhaps more clearly than the inciting incident alone) and might refine or help to clarify the key question raised.

For example, at the beginning of *Back to the Future*, Marty's day kicks off ordinarily enough with his personal, everyday routines. He sets off for school, hangs out at Doc Brown's house, meets his girlfriend, plays some music with his band, and has a meal with his family in the evening.

His day is deliberately made ordinary in order that the Act I turning point (in this case, coincidental with the inciting incident) can spin the whole story off in a new and unexpected direction. Marty didn't expect his day to end up with him driving a DeLorean, let alone being sent back in time. The turning point takes him by surprise, just as it did the rest of us, sets him off in a new direction, and forces him to confront the key question raised. Will he ever get back to 1985? The audience can settle back now, comfortable in the knowledge that they know Marty's purpose, and therefore they know what the story is about, and therefore instantly have two lines of thought for any further event: firstly, the event itself and, secondly, what it means for the chances of Marty successfully answering the key question and getting back to 1985.

In *Toy Story*, the inciting incident is when Buzz Lightyear is discovered in Woody's place on Andy's bed. The key question is raised: will Buzz replace Woody as leader of the toys and Andy's favourite toy? But this is not yet a turning point for the protagonist, Woody. The first major turning point comes some twelve minutes later, when Woody hatches a plan to 'lose' Buzz down behind the chest of drawers. This simple plan will solve everything. However, when he executes his plan, it goes wrong. He accidentally knocks Buzz out of the window. The other toys see Woody do it and lose trust in him. They think he's a murderer. His attempt at fixing his first problem has had the opposite effect, and multiplied his problems. He is now no longer Andy's favourite toy, he is no longer the respected leader of the toys, he has no friends and stands accused of murder. This turning point sets Woody off in a new direction, and with a defining quest – to find and save Buzz Lightyear in order to prove to his friends that he didn't murder Buzz and to regain the respect he needs to be their leader.

The Cohen Brothers' film, *No Country for Old Men* is different again, in that there are two time-separated events that comprise the entire Act I turning point and inciting incident, but in this case, the two things must be taken in combination in order to get all the information across. Llewelyn Moss (Josh Brolin) stumbles across the carnage of a drugs deal turned shoot-out in the remote desert of West Texas. Everyone is dead but for a dying Mexican, stuck in the driver's seat of a car, who begs Moss for water. Moss leaves him to die, finds two million dollars of drugs money and gets clean away with the cash, leaving no link to himself whatsoever. This is surely a turning point in his life – his fortunes have changed dramatically – but there is no key question raised yet. Although such a sum of money is surely 'life changing', his story has yet to be given its direction. As he lies in bed in the middle of the night, he feels guilty that he left the Mexican to die. He returns to the scene of the shoot-out to give the man water... and his car is discovered by police. This is the real turning point. His identity is now known and the chase is on from both the police and the psychopathic and relentless bad guy, Anton Chigurh (played by Javier Bardem), who will hunt him without mercy to get the drug lords their money back. Now Moss's fortunes have gone massively to the negative, his direction is changed and the key question is raised: can Moss outrun the police, and Chigurh, and get away with the money? Both events are needed before the full inciting incident/turning point job is done, and we, the audience, are orientated.

The mid-act turning point

A full-length story tends to meander during Act II if there isn't a new major turning point at some stage. Hence, a modern story tends to have a mid-act turning point, which divides Act II into two. If you think about it, a mid-act turning point is also a natural requirement if three acts are going to deliver a happy ending. The turning point at the climax of Act I will have sent fortunes downwards, and the dynamic for the major turning point at climax must go from an all time low at the entry to Act III to a high point for the story to end on a positive.

That's confusing... Hold on, I'll draw a picture... There.

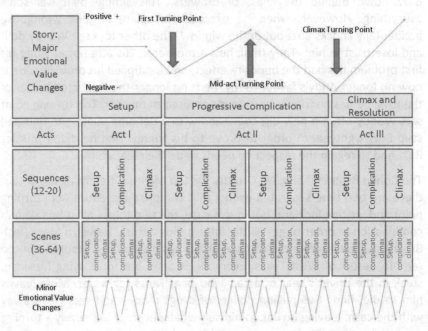

As you can see, Act II begins from an emotional low (as a result of the climax to Act I), and ends with a low (in order for Act III to end high and deliver a happy ending). In between, it is most common and logical therefore to arc fortunes high by the centre of Act II in order to be able to drop back to the second low at the end of Act II.

The diagram is the structure of *Back to the Future*, showing the major emotional swings for the protagonist. This is a classic structure with a happy ending.

Marty's emotional position begins flat in his normal school day, but takes a big negative hit when he gets sent back in time. It rises gradually as he finds Doc Brown and gets a plan together for how to return to 1985, but takes a massive hit at the mid-act turning point when he realises he has interfered with future events; his parents are not going to meet and, even if he can return to 1985, he will not exist when he gets there. Things continue to an all-time emotional low, until the climax turning point when his dad finally makes a fist, all the problems resolve and his emotional position swings to finish at an all time high.

Subplots

The turning point is equally a mechanism by which we trigger subplots. Every full-length story is likely to have more than one thread running through it – indeed, a full length novel might have many subplots – and every significant subplot is a story event, so it needs its own key question and resolution, so it also needs an inciting incident to set it off in the right direction and a turning point to ensure it is an effective, clear event with direction. A mid-act turning point is usually positioned at the end of a longer sequence or an act, and serves to payoff a 'mini storyline' in which our protagonist has addressed an element of the greater story and ends up being a step nearer – or more likely, considerably further away from – his ultimate aim, which is now complicated by a new plotline with its own demands that must be satisfied before the main plotline can be completed.

For example, the first sequence after the main plot inciting incident in *Back to the Future* (i.e., in the diagram above, the Act II setup sequence) has Marty discovering where – and when – he is: Hill Valley, 1955. He bumps into his 17-year-old future father, follows him and finds him up a tree peeking through a bedroom window at a girl undressing. His future father, George, then falls out of the tree, on to the road in front of a car. Marty, quite naturally, runs to save his father's life. In doing so, he gets hit himself and knocked unconscious by the car. The car that should have hit his father. His father runs off. The car driver takes the injured Marty into his house to look after him.

However, the girl George was ogling in the house was Marty's future mother. She is now tending Marty back to health instead of tending his future father... and this accident was how his parents originally met.

When Doc Brown realises that Marty has interfered with the sequence of events that were supposed to lead to his birth, he tells him he must reunite his parents in love or be erased from existence, and this is both the mid-act turning point and the inciting incident for the main subplot. Things have just taken a new and unexpected downturn. Marty cannot now go back to 1985 (the aim of the main plot line) as planned without first ensuring that his mother and father meet and fall in love (the aim of the dependent subplot), or else he's never going to exist. Marty must sort this out before he can leave 1955, so we now have a new direction and a new key question that must be answered for the protagonist and story. Structurally, we have our mid-act turning point and a subplot is bedded into the story.

The mid-act turning point does not have to trigger a subplot, of course. Indeed, it doesn't have to exist at all. If it does, it does because it represents a major reversal of fortune for the protagonist.

The climax turning point

Act III is defined by the final turning point which gives the protagonist his final change in fortune in the main plot storyline and leads irrevocably to the story ending. In simplistic terms, it is the final conflict between good and evil; the moment when the hero wins or loses against the forces of antagonism in the final battle that will result in the end of the road for the forces of good or the forces of evil; a change in fortune through conflict that has a finality that means that this particular story can go no further.

The climax turning point in *Back to the Future* is a clear and single event. Marty's battle against the forces of antagonism (the physics and viability of time travel) reach the turning point – the one shot Marty has at a return to 1985 – when the DeLorean hits 88 miles-per-hour at exactly the moment the lightning is fed into the flux capacitor. Marty travels through time, back to 1985. Marty's direction and fortunes have changed to the positive once more; indeed, significantly more positive than they were when he left 1985 in the first place. The key question has been answered with finality and the adventure is complete.

Turning points are critical to a writer's work. Apart from these story-level (major) turning points, every scene, sequence and act is probably defined by a turning point, each one being a major, moderate or minor reversal in the fortunes of the protagonist.

3.6.1   Acts and story length

You will have noticed that Act II is actually double the length of Act I and Act III, with a setup, progressive complications and act climax (at the mid-act turning point), followed by another setup, progressive complications and act climax. Why is it called a three act structure when there are patently four acts here? The division of Act II into two 'acts' does not create a classic 4 act structure, because the mid-act turning point does not have an imperative component associated with it that would mean it will always be there. As we have seen, the Act I and Act III boundaries are characterised by story imperatives (beginning, middle, end), which is why a three act structure is defined, with or without a tangible mid-act turning point.

If your story is long, or multiple inciting incidents demand it, your structure may need to extend to five or seven acts. Most novels will be at least this. Do this by extending to a second and third Act II. In other words, your story dynamic should go 'Act I –> (Act II.a and Act II.b) > (Act II.c and Act II.d) > (Act II.e and Act II.f) > Act III.

Does that make sense?! We know that in a standard three-act structure Act II, because of the need for a mid-act turning point, actually has the structure of two acts, hence the linkage of II.a and II.b.; II.c and II.d; and so forth.

Whatever length and complexity of a story, it will all be wrapped up in an Act I setup and an Act III climax and resolution.

3.6.2 Sequences

The variations in classical structure are only related to complexity and length of story. We have already discussed the elements that define the story dynamics at this top level which give us our act boundaries.

Acts consist of a set of linked events called 'sequences' that change the emotional state of the protagonist through moderate turning points, leading up to the major story turning points at the end of the act. Although there are no rules as to how many sequences make an act, a classically formed film story is likely to comprise three to five sequences before each major turning point, so perhaps 16 to 20 across the course of a story. As can be seen in the diagram below, each sequence in its turn is a recognisable component of the individual structure of the act, in this case let's assume that this is the second half of Act II from the story's mid-act turning point to the end of Act II.

> Note: You will have noticed that Act II is actually double the length of Act I and Act III, with a setup, progressive complications and act climax (at the mid-act turning point), followed by another setup, progressive complications and act climax. The division of Act II into two 'acts' does not create a classic 4 act structure, because the mid-act turning point does not have an imperative component associated with it that would mean it will always be there. As we have seen, the Act I and Act III boundaries are characterised by story imperatives (beginning, middle, end), which is why a three act structure is defined, with or without a tangible mid-act turning point.

For the purposes of clarity, I divide Act II into two – Act II.a. is before the mid-act turning point, and Act II.b after it. We shall look closely at Act II.b of *Back to the Future*.

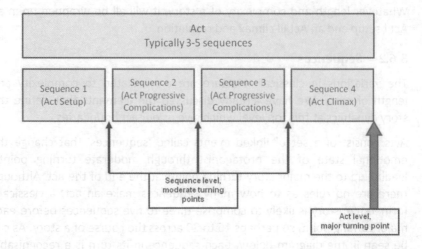

As we know from earlier, at the story level, Act II.b should be a complication in the protagonist's main story goal (Marty's aim is to get back to 1985), so let's see if it does that job.

Act II.b has the inciting incident whereby Marty interferes with his parents' meeting, meaning he will not exist in the future. The key question is raised: can Marty get his parents to kiss on the dance floor at the Enchantment Under the Sea Dance? This is the definitive event which will put history back on track. This is, indeed, a complication for his wider aim to return to the future, because he will not exist in the future if he doesn't fix his parents up first, so he has to achieve this through the course of Act II.b before he can attempt to return to 1985 in the climax and resolution of the main story.

Given that each act must have its own internal structure to maintain audience interest and pay off with a major turning point, there are five sequences that represent the internal development of Act II.b's own internal storyline:

Sequence 1 is the act setup

Sequence 2 is the act 'progressive complication'

Sequence 3 is the (optional) further act progressive complication

Sequence 4 is the act climax.

As you can see in the diagram above, this structure sets up Act II.b as a story in its own right – the story of how Marty got history back on track. A moderate reversal pays off each sequence, until the final sequence, which is also the act climax and a major turning point in the main story.

A sequence, like each of the other structural events of a story, should have a protagonist with his sequence aims, an antagonist (and/or antagonistic forces) with his sequence aims in opposition to those of the protagonist, an inciting incident and key question, a turning point and climax/resolution. The protagonist for a sequence does not have to be the same protagonist as that for the main story, although it usually will be. If it is not, it is most likely that the sequence storyline will have a major impact in the progress of the main story protagonist. For example, George is the protagonist for the scene in which he punches Biff's lights out, however, this is a pivotal event in the main plot storyline, for which Marty is the protagonist.

Let's take a closer look at Act ll.b., in other words, the sequences that define the second half of Act ll, from the mid-act turning point, when Marty realises that he has to reunite his parents in order to repair history, to the end of Act ll.

Act ll.b sequences:

Setup: A photograph of Marty from the future shows he is fading away. Doc Brown tells Marty that his interference in 1955 has led to his parents' failing to meet. The new path of history that Marty's interference has created means that Marty will not be born. He is being wiped from the future. He has to get his parents to meet and fall in love, or fade from existence.

> **Inciting incident** (at the Act level): Marty is disappearing from the photograph.

> **Key Question** (for the act): Can Marty get his parents to meet and fall in love (achieved if they kiss on the dance floor)?

Complication(s): Three attempts to get George to ask Lorraine out meet with problems: Firstly, George is too weak and unassertive for Lorraine. Secondly, she is infatuated with Marty, because he is brave and fights for her honour. Thirdly, she loves Marty (and why wouldn't she? She doesn't know it yet, but she's his mother after all!).

Complication: Biff enters the picture. He too wants a piece of Lorraine and, true to his character, he will get his way by force. Lorraine isn't strong enough to stop him by herself. Marty is brave, but isn't strong enough to stop him either, and George – well, his lack of assertiveness is a problem that everything seems to hinge on.

Complication: Marty and George concoct a role-play. They will stage a fight that will allow George to apparently rescue Lorraine from Marty's inappropriate advances and simultaneously show Lorraine how strong and macho he is by apparently beating Marty up.

Climax: George enters the car park to act his part in the role-play, but instead of Marty play-acting his inappropriate advances towards Lorraine, George finds Biff making serious inappropriate advances towards Lorraine.

Biff threatens George to back off, and when he doesn't back away, Biff attacks him physically. But George's anger is such that he overcomes his own inadequacy and takes Biff out with one punch.

At Resolution, George takes Lorraine into the dance where they kiss on the dance floor. History is back on track.

So these sequences give Act II.b an effective structure all of its own, with an inciting incident raising a key question for the act which is answered at climax. Although the story is moving fast through Act II, and the interaction with events at other levels causes the sequences to be split up and intertwined with others, each of these sequences must have its own structure which defines it.

3.7   Scenes

So to recap, each act of a story is a mini-story in itself, with a setup, complications and its own climax and resolution which provide both a major turning point at the main story level and a launch point for the next act. The component parts of the act are called sequences.

And guess what. Sequences, too, are standalone story events, comprising their own setup, complications, climax and resolution. These component parts of a sequence are called 'scenes', and each one should carry a minor turning point all of its own, building towards the more significant sequence and act level turning points.

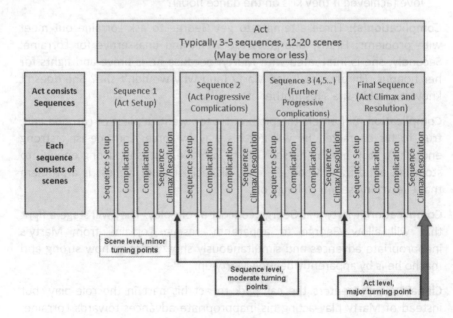

Scenes are the manageable, 'bite size' events of story that can be worked in their own right. I try very hard in my writing to ensure scenes carry their own impact and power, firstly, because they do a critical job in maintaining interest second by second, beat by beat. Secondly, I originally got belief in myself that I could actually write by writing short pieces. We all do – that's where we start. Scenes are the fun bit, where we can let loose and *write*!

What we don't realise is that stepping up from a 1000 word article, short story, or a ten minute play, to a 100,000 word novel or a 100 minute film story involves an entirely different approach to writing. By breaking a story down into scenes, the job at hand becomes a short story job again: to write that scene. As long as we know exactly what the purpose of the scene is in terms of the bigger picture, we are back where we feel comfortable, structuring up a 'story' of a page or two only.

So a sequence consists of a number of scenes (generally 3-5 in *Back to the Future*, but this is not a rule book and yours may be very different!) and carries an entire plot event through its own setup, complications, climax and resolution. Because we know the objective of the sequence, we therefore know the objective for each scene it comprises, so each scene can be carefully constructed to ensure that it carries all the necessary elements, firstly to deliver its part in the sequence, and secondly, to carry power and depth all of its own.

Let's take a look at a single sequence which is a component part of the Act II.b deconstruction above: sequence 5 is the sequence climax:

3.7.1   Sequence breakdown

Scene 1 – Sequence setup – George arrives in the car park to act out his part in the role-play, rescuing Lorraine from the inappropriate advances Marty is making towards her in the car. George doesn't know that it is Biff in the car making genuinely inappropriate advances, not Marty play-acting.

> **Inciting incident**: George tears the door open and, expecting Marty, says his rehearsed line: 'Hey you! Get your hands off her!' But it's not Marty making inappropriate advances. It's Biff, and Lorraine is in serious trouble...

> **Key Question:** Will George rescue Lorraine?

Scene 2 – Sequence Progressive Complication. Biff threatens George and orders him to leave. George looks like he will go. Lorraine begs him for help. George gulps back his fear – it's a choice of evils – but he stands his ground.

Scene 3 – Sequence Climax. Biff gets out of the car and attacks George, but is distracted by Lorraine attacking him too. Biff laughs at Lorraine and pushes her back into the car. George is so driven by love for Lorraine and anger towards the bully that he clenches his fist, shakes with rage... and lays Biff out with one punch.

Scene 4 – Sequence Resolution. George takes Lorraine on his arm proudly into the dance.

The sequence key question is answered: Yes, George will rescue Lorraine.

Notice that the protagonist in this scene is George, not Marty. Every scene (sequence, act, story...) must have a protagonist, but it doesn't always have to be the same one. As a general rule, any events that centre around a different protagonist from the story-wide protagonist must still climax with results that are significant to the main plot protagonist.

3.8 Beats

Beats are the moment by moment actions and reactions that build into scenes. Ideally, every 'action' will raise a question in the mind of the audience, and the reaction will pay it off in an interesting or unexpected way, simultaneously raising a new question. The progress of the protagonist towards the scene aim is thus continuously moving from positive to negative and back again, and the audience is constantly exercised as to what will happen next and which way the overarching events will go.

Take the scene above, for example. George appears in the car park feeling positive – he and Marty have hatched a plan to make him look strong that will win him the girl. Does the plan work? No. He opens the door and Biff is inside. The plan is in tatters before it's barely begun, and George's prospects swing to the negative. Biff threatens George. Does George run? No he doesn't. He stands his ground (positive). But Biff throws Lorraine to one side and gets out of the car to give George hell (negative). George throws a punch at Biff (positive). Biff catches his arm and twists it up his back (negative). What's going to happen next? Unexpectedly, Lorraine leaps out of the car. Does she run away now she has a chance to escape? No. She leaps on top of Biff and tries to wrestle him off George (positive). Biff is distracted by Lorraine, but she is no match for him. He shoves her back hard into the car and laughs at her humiliation (negative). What next? The humiliation steels George. He clenches his fist, sets his jaw to destiny and whilst Biff laughs at Lorraine – he lays him out with a single left hook (positive).

Clearly, these beats continuously jerk the protagonist from positive to negative and back. They also keep the audience guessing as to what will happen and continuously deliver the unexpected. (For the finest imaginable example of continuously delivering the unexpected, watch the 2004 horror film *Saw*, by Leigh Whannell and James Wan. Yes, it's slasher horror and gore, but it's a terrific story, delivered brilliantly.)

When a story progresses like this, the audience is exercised at all times. Not only are they trying to monitor events beat by beat in the scene, they are trying to keep up with the all-important subtext, firstly for what the beats really mean, and secondly for their implications for what will happen towards the key questions already in mind at the scene, sequence, act and story levels. As we have seen, when George punches Biff, he not only overcomes the bad guy in the presented action by winning the immediate conflict (their fight impacts the sequence level key question), he also rescues the girl (answers the scene level key question), with the implications for Marty's future existence (impacts the act level key question), removes the main obstacle to returning to 1985 (impacts the story level key question), and gives himself the confidence to lead a completely different life with Lorraine from that moment onwards.

This punch – a single beat of a single scene, leaves us trying to absorb all these implications at all these levels as the story moves us into climax and on back to 1985 where George's life of personal strength and confidence has created a completely different 1985 from the one we left at the end of Act I, with prestige and status, and with Biff subservient to the successful and fulfilled author, George McFly. All from the one punch in one scene in one sequence in one act of the story.

A story that exercises its audience on so many levels simultaneously and continuously stays one jump ahead of our searching minds is a winner. This must be your aim, to build unexpected beats into great scenes that deliver powerful sequences that build into act level turning points that leave us breathless as we absorb the entire story.

3.9   Some structural myths

If you read any theory on creative writing, or attend classes, or even just pick up on themes under discussion on the internet, you are sure to stumble across one or two of the following arguments put forward.

Herewith the definitive truth on these areas, in terms of which I am right, and everyone else is wrong:

"There are only seven stories."

We've all heard this one – sometimes it's five stories, or three, or even one – and, it can be a fascinating and convincing argument. The fact is that the perpetrators are really talking about structure, so in that respect, they are right; as discussed earlier, there are very few sensible *structures* that can work for your story. However, the fact that there are only a very few sensible structures doesn't change the fact that there are an infinite number of different stories that can be built on top of those very few sensible structures. Most artistic endeavour is limited by structure; a painter is limited by the size of his canvas and the number of colours, a musician limits himself with his instruments and the rules of harmony. All creative people build their millions of unique works on limited underlying structures. Indeed, every single one of the seven billion people on this planet is built on the same basic skeletal structure. We are all identical, and yet absolutely unique. Don't fight it – embrace it – a good foundation sets your creativity free, it doesn't constrain it.

"Formal learning of writing theory can damage your creative capability."

I have some sympathy for this contention, but only because too much teaching material, particularly in screenwriting, provides a rule base for how to write based on structure as a starting point. Yes, that is damaging to your writing. What they are doing is taking the classic structure as a starting point, and then trying to tell you how to populate that structure with your brilliance. This *is* limiting and damaging to your creativity.

The answer is to ensure that you always begin with the free and unfettered pouring of story from your imagination. Care not a jot (at first) for how many sets your play might be limited to, how many commercial breaks your sitcom must accommodate, what budget the production company has set for your film story; just let the story flow, without any thought for practical issues. Later on, if there are problems with your story, or imposed practical issues to deal with, use your knowledge of structure to root out those problems or satisfy those practical demands. The value of structural understanding is in story optimisation and problem resolution, not as a creative starting point. Ideally, your ideas will pour out and there will be no problems with the story you have written; in which case who cares what the structure is? Creativity first, always and forever. Structure secondarily, and only as a tool for analysis and repair.

"There is no need for structure in your stories. The best stories do not obey the rules of structure."

This is difficult to understand, and I won't name the story consultant, currently at large in the Los Angeles area, who makes this claim. Structure is, by definition, a consequence of, firstly, the events you choose to narrate from your protagonist's life and, secondly, the order in which you choose to place them. Structure is therefore going to happen to your story *whether you like it or not*, so isn't it better to understand structure and work with it? I agree that structure should not drive your creative process, however, there is no such thing as a story without structure.

3.10 Structure and non-classical form

So far we have stayed strictly in the mainstream of straight-down-the-middle classic structure. I would define classical form as having: three acts and a single, positive, proactive protagonist battling against external forces of antagonism towards a clear goal. The story is a series of logically linked events, played out in chronological order to an ending that answers the key question raised at the point of inciting incident. The story is based in a human reality and resolves to a happy ending.

There are many valid stories that are not in the mainstream. Indeed, it would be true to say that the most acclaimed and sophisticated stories are most definitely off to one side of the mainstream, if not actually up the bank and off into the Jungles of Poo-story that flank the river.

In this section, I intend to list the common steps away from orthodox form that can be reasonably taken towards the wilds of non-classical form. The list is constructed in order of risk taken. In other words, the further down the list you tick a box for your story, and the more boxes you tick, the further you are likely to be getting from a mainstream audience and a commercial deal. This said, the first three listed steps away are often associated with the very best stories, and, if these departures from classical form are well managed, are the stuff of Oscars and Booker prizes.

Don't forget, we are still primarily in the realm of narrative and structure; we haven't begun to address the other main strands of a fine story – character development and subtext.

Ironic Ending – the story carries two main plot threads in the one main story line (known as the conscious and the unconscious plot lines) and they end in opposites – one positive, one negative. This can work well and be satisfying. For example, in *Gerry McQuire*, Tom Cruise's character turns down the opportunity to accept the millions and business success he stated as his goal at the outset, but instead finds his soul and the true love he never even realised he was seeking. The most successful stories are often structured along these lines, but they have to be managed well and care must be taken. To work best, the goal that is foregone will be something we all relate to (in this case, making millions) but requires self-centred behaviour to achieve (perhaps through evident 'greed'), and is therefore, at least symbolically, a component of 'the dark side', and the unexpected success will come in the form of something 'finer' from the forces of good (generosity, achievement, status, acceptance, love, and so on) that renders the protagonist a 'better' person than he would have been if he'd simply got rich. The story events pay off negatively (he is forced, or volunteers, to give up the riches), but the character development pays off positively (his character learns and grows; his soul is enriched).

In the film *I am Legend* (from the 1954 novel of the same name by Richard Matheson), Doctor Robert Neville (played by Will Smith), is the last man alive in a future New York. He must find a cure for a disease that is wiping out humanity (he is immune) before the zombies that now rule the streets catch and devour him. The ending to the story has him die in the process of saving humanity. This is a fine, tragic twist on an ironic ending; the light of future civilisation survives at the expense of one brave 'legend' who gives his life for the greater good.

Interestingly, the original 1954 novel ends with a new form of humanity taking over, with Neville as the last of the old 'species', now mistrusted and hated, just as the infected were when the human race was dominant. A finality of tragic and total bleakness is unacceptable to Hollywood, which is why, I assume, they tried to force a more palatable ironic ending. Two other endings are portrayed in two other film versions of this same story – *The Last Man on Earth* (1964), and *The Omega Man* (1971). Only the novel succeeds in satisfying at the ending, with a pure human tragedy, but tempered by the ironic potential for the new master race to create an even better society than ours. The others all have good potential endings that are not well executed. This is how careful one has to be when trying to weave together a personal tragedy that is intended to show a wider benefit to humanity.

Down-Ending and Tragedy. Other stories major on the tragic, ending at the negative in both threads. In *Atonement* (2007), the unwise, naive and incorrect rape allegation of Briony Tallis (played by Saoirse Ronan) at age 13 sends her sister Cecilia (Keira Knightly) and Cecilia's one true love, Robbie (James McAvoy) on a downward spiral from which their relationship is unlikely ever to recover. However, they apparently recover at least to the extent that they share a single tender time together in love before their ultimate deaths. As adults, Briony apologises to her sister and they regain communication. However, we learn at resolution that this was not really what happened. Cecilia and Robbie never recovered from the downward spiral; Briony, (Vanessa Redgrave), now seventy years old and dying herself, wrote the story we have just seen as an act of atonement, in which Cecilia and Robbie's love is given life and time in that one precious union. Her novel becomes a best-seller, providing a horribly, wonderfully hollow irony to the real truth: Briony was never brave enough to apologise and re-establish contact with her sister; and as we watch Robbie and Cecilia walk together to a cosy seaside cottage to consummate their love, we realise that it never happened. The family never reunited and their love was never given its time. Briony's 'atonement' ends in her making lots of money and fame from the story's success, which simply serves to cut the wounds of guilt all the more deeply. The story events turn out to be tragic, as does the character development in the subtextual strand. This story was drawn from the novel of the same name, written by Ian McEwan.

As we've seen, a simple down ending is often balanced ironically by wins in other plot-lines. An audience is likely to feel a story is a little grim if a protagonist sets off on a quest and simply fails – unless there is food for thought provided through irony or other considerations. The most successful stories, in terms of critical acclaim and awards won, are indeed, tragedies. From the Greeks – who turned tragedy into an art form – through *Hamlet*, *Macbeth* and *Romeo and Juliet*, to the Oscar wins in 2007 for *Atonement* and *No Country for Old Men*, and many, many other fine works in between, we are most moved by a tragic ending. The reason is clear. Although we feel less disturbed by a happy ending, and often wish to escape from reality in our recreational hours, the fact is that tragedies best reflect real life.

Life IS a tragedy. We will all die in the end, and a story that reflects this truth, however much we don't want to face it, is more likely to ring true. Aristotle himself, who first documented the genre, said that tragedy provides an 'emotional cleansing' (catharsis) through experiencing emotions in response to the suffering of the characters in the drama. In short, we are fascinated by emotions we do not wish to experience in our own lives – a version of the reason we slow down to gawp at the misfortune of others in a car crash as we go past.

It is interesting to note that research has shown that people who have suffered genuinely in life are more satisfied by tragic stories than other people, and embrace them more readily than people who have not experienced suffering in the real world, who look to hide from tragic stories and wrap themselves in the comfort of happy or escapist stories.

Hidden or disguised inciting incident/unclear key question/unanswered key question. Many, many stories raise an unclear or poorly defined key question, and although a story with no clear key question can definitely work, it is more often associated with a weak story. It predominantly works well when the audience or reader is still gripped, even if only by the simple and pervasive question: 'what's going to happen?', or when sequence level key questions are able to keep the audience engaged, and can even be used as a highly powerful mechanism when the inciting incident and key question are revealed later, causing the viewer to rush back through the story so far, filling in the detail with the new information concerning the questions they should have been asking all along. I would place 'Atonement' in this category. It is extremely unclear, during first viewing of the film, where it is going, and even becomes irritating as it meanders off to war with one of the secondary characters for long stretches of Act II. For most of us, I suspect, it is only with discussion and hindsight (or through knowing the book version) that the full story behind *Atonement* is revealed, and a second viewing is demanded, this time fully armed with the correct key question.

As we discussed earlier, some stories, such as *Groundhog Day* and *A Christmas Carol*, manage to deliver such strong character arcs and knowledge gaps, that the lack of a clear key question is not a hindrance. However, you must be very careful to find another method of giving good direction to your story if it lacks a clear key question.

WARNING! If you have a most powerful twist in the tail of your story, study it to ensure it isn't really the inciting incident. If it is, you are likely to be about to produce a loser. Try to shift the inciting incident to the earliest you can to raise the key question, and let the power of the story come through in ways other than a twist which is utterly amazing when you get there, but which has kept the key question hidden for so long that the audience are in the pub or the book is on the fire long before you deliver your killer revelation. I know it's a powerful ending, but nobody will be left in the theatre to watch it. Think about what Willy Russell says about his own stories: "I actually tell my audience early on exactly what is going to happen in the end. It adds immense power and tension to the telling when everyone knows – even subconsciously – where it's all going to end up."

Multiple Protagonists. It is important to note that multi-protagonist stories carry a health warning that makes them somewhat harder to write. It is easier to have an audience latch on to an individual and empathise with their plight, but with a group it is much harder. It can be done, of course – think of all the buddy movies (Buzz and Woody, *Romeo and Juliet, Butch and Sundance*), through *Three Amigos, Four Musketeers, the Famous Five, Can't Think of a Six, the Magnificent Seven* and beyond through *Ocean's 11, Cheaper by the Dozen*; families (*Honey, I Shrunk The Kids; The Incredibles*), teams (*DodgeBall; Space Jam*), groups and gangs (*The Full Monty; Calendar Girls; West Side Story*), institutions, communities and populations (Prison films; War films; intergalactic films). There are endless examples where multiple protagonists have driven successful stories. Irritatingly, I don't know of a story with six protagonists except for the first half of the film *Twelve Angry Men*, which, as a suggestion, isn't even funny.

If you cannot avoid a multi-protagonist, the key to success is two-fold:

The group should behave and succeed or fail as a single entity. The story is about the group, so it must live and die in and of itself, like a single protagonist. Individual members can have different fortunes, but it is important never to lose sight of the overarching story, which tracks the fortunes of the group.

One member of the group should represent the group symbolically. This is the one whose character and fortunes best represents the group's journey. This is why you can only remember the name of one of the *Three Musketeers* (D'Artagnan – who wasn't even a musketeer!), one of *the Magnificent Seven* (actually, we tend to remember the actor who played the lead – Yul Brynner – rather than his character, Chris, despite the presence of bigger name actors, such as Charles Bronson and Steve McQueen), only Norman Stanley Fletcher in *Porridge*, and so on.

Open Ending. Some stories end with no clear answer to the key question raised. This is often the case with 'art house' movies, although I tend to think that most art house movies end up being defined that way because of what they are like, rather than anyone deliberately setting out to make the thing that way from the beginning. Often, the whole point is to leave you to discuss the story with others and work your own ending out for yourself. As with the other alternatives, it is perfectly possible to create an absolute classic with an open ending. Woody Allen's *Manhattan* springs to mind, whereby the whole point is brilliantly made that for most of the time, nothing changes despite the vain and fatuous activity of desperate people trying to find their identity and gain social standing. How can anyone manage to write a story showing how 'nothing changes' without having a story in which nothing changes, and keep that story from being a bore? More often than not, in the hands of the inexperienced writer, an open ending is unsatisfying and wishy washy, unless it is balanced by character arcs that provide story progression.

Non-Linear Time – requires great skill to deliver. As with most unorthodox forms, it is amazing when it works (*Memento*, by Christopher Nolan, as an example straight from the top drawer), but it rarely works beyond the comfortable context of flashbacks and really obvious time shifts, such as dream sequences, flagged clearly to the viewer or reader and within an otherwise linear time delivery. Interestingly, *Back to the Future* represents linear time, because, through the eyes of the protagonist, Marty McFly, events were in that order despite the different time periods he visited.

Coincidence. It is fatal to a story to allow coincidence to resolve a plot line; specifically dangerous to have coincidence resolve the main plot line. At any point, this is very unlikely to satisfy outside the context of madcap humour, such as in Monty Python's *The Meaning of Life* (I think it was), in which the timely and totally coincidental passing of an alien spacecraft accidentally saves the protagonist from a fatal fall. Coincidence can legitimately be used elsewhere in a story, for example as part of the inciting incident, but not at the resolution of a plot line. Coincidence features highly in the events that allow the protagonist to win out in *Slumdog Millionaire*, written by Simon Beaufoy. The protagonist, Jamal Malik (played by Dev Patel), despite his childhood in the slums and rubbish heaps of Mumbai, just happens to have experienced a miraculous series of events in his life to gain precisely the knowledge required to answer most of the set of *Who Wants to be a Millionaire?* questions required to make a million, and indeed, the story twice makes the blunt assertion 'It Is Fated', providing one of the main (and I think unnecessary) overarching themes for the story. Don't get me wrong, this is not a bad thing. Most stories need something exceptional to happen for the story to be exceptional, and you should not shy away from the possibilities a little coincidence can open up. Just do not use coincidence to **resolve** a plot line.

Breaking Genre Rules – effectively creating a new genre. When a writer tells me he has a totally different story that has never been done before, I tend to worry... Most good genres have been invented already, so if your story doesn't fit an existing genre, you need to be very sure of yourself. Being unique and different can mean being special in a good way. Or you can be unique and different by throwing yourself off Beachy Head. In story terms, as in life, this kind of uniqueness isn't necessarily a good thing.

Stepping away from classical structure along these lines, can lead to works of genius... or works of unspeakable disaster. The only way to know what you are doing is to work your apprenticeship in the mainstream and move out – knowledgeably – from there. Spielberg may be famous for wonderfully unconventional and 'important' stories, such as *Schindler's List* and *Saving Private Ryan*, but a three act structure often shines through these, and don't forget the classically structured works that characterised his earlier career, such as *Jaws, E.T.,* and of course, *Back to the Future*.

3.10.1 Narrative and structure – summary

Write from the heart. Let it all flow and say balls to structure. Rewrite and fix problems using your head and theoretical knowledge to be sure to get the structure right.

If your story has problems, check the problem event for a turning point (protagonist with event goal; forces of antagonism in opposition; they go into conflict; only one wins out). If you are sure that the event does have a turning point, ask yourself if the whole event is germane to the story. If it is a scene, is it a logically linked event contributing to the sequence? If it is a sequence, is it a logically linked event contributing to the act? Don't forget that structure is a consequence of selecting the right events from the protagonist's experience. We don't want to know about some hilarious or dramatic event that isn't really part of the story. This is another common problem – a writer has an iconic scene, or hilarious event he has thought up, and is going to crowbar it in at all costs. This is a mistake, of course. It may be hilarious or iconic, but if it's in the wrong story, it must go. Take it out and save it for when it truly fits.

Of course, what I have presented in this section cannot be seen as a panacea. A fast-paced action adventure story might have seven acts, a four minute first act, 200 scenes and be three hours long. Any novel is likely to be much longer than a film story and have many more sequences and subplots. Overall, however the structure above, and the underlying principles, will be broadly identifiable in all good stories.

And lastly, remember that structure is a consequence of the events you choose to narrate and the order in which you place these events. It happens anyway. There *are* alternative structures to the orthodox one used for demonstration purposes here, so do not be scared to read more and break out a little, particularly if you story is based on strong character growth and/or significant subtext. Structure is important, but it is just structure. Ultimately, you need to do what works for you, but have no doubt: a human being without a skeleton is not going to work like a human being. A story without a workable structure is not going to work like a story.

3.11 Practical exercise – the story baseline

Structurally, there is a set of 'baseline' criteria that can help you prove to yourself that your story is well defined at the highest level, so let's make a list and revisit it whenever we have more information with which to flesh it out. The concept of our story must be easily encapsulated and the basic foundation stones must be easily identifiable. So, let's write a paragraph that answers the following questions and gives the story its 'baseline':

What is the title, genre, theme and setting of the story? (we'll address this later.)

Who is the protagonist?

What is his problem?

What is his goal?

What is the inciting incident?

What is the key question raised?

What opposes him in achieving this goal?

Who is the antagonist?

What is his goal?

What happens in the end?

At this stage, you may not have all these elements clear in your mind, but addressing these questions is still a valuable exercise, and you must keep returning to them until your answers are complete and accurate before you begin to write the first full draft. The list above – or something like it – will often be used, particularly in the film industry, as the first test of a story's worth. If a junior story editor cannot identify these things, it will be unlikely to get a reading from anyone senior. (They also tick boxes for many other things, but let's not depress ourselves with such clinical deconstruction.)

By presenting the story in the form of these questions, it should be clear if it has (or lacks) a good, solid spine. If the story is fundamentally right, then these questions look almost ridiculous. *Back to the Future* is a complex, multi-layered story, with many subplots, but answering the basic questions gives us this:

The protagonist is: Marty McFly.

His problem is: He is accidentally propelled back in time to 1955.

His goal is: To return to 1985.

He is opposed by: The technical difficulties of time travel in the 1950s.

The inciting incident is: the time machine takes him back to 1955.

The key question raised is: Will he make it back to 1985?

The antagonist is: Biff Tannen.

The antagonist's aim is: to change the course of history to his advantage through physical bullying.

The resolution is: Marty defeats Biff and makes it back safely to 1985.

Clearly, this story has a well defined spine. This is a great sign that the story will grip the audience from early on and make them feel satisfied by the resolution. It is no coincidence that *Back to the Future'*, despite its complexity, has at its root a simple, clear premise.

In analysing problem stories, listing out this baseline information, including the inciting incident, key question and resolution, is highly revealing about where problems might lie. I recommend that you keep updating your baseline information as you grow your story. If you have problems answering the baseline questions it is a good indicator that you are not yet ready to begin writing the first draft.

3.11.1 Baseline your story

So let's make a start on a story baseline. Write a paragraph filling in the <bits between the chevrons> for your story:

My story is called <story title>. It is a <genre, location in time and space, setting, mood and theme(s)>. (Skip this at the moment. We will look at genre, setting and mood later. Come back and fill it in after that.)

My protagonist is <name of protagonist>. His problem is <identify problem(s)>.   His   goal   is   <identify   protagonist's desire/goal/quest/mission>.

The inciting incident occurs when <identify inciting incident> and raises the key question <identify overarching question that must be resolved by the story events>.

He is opposed in his quest by <insert problems and forces of antagonism here>.

He is directly opposed by the antagonist: <enter identity of the bad guy>. The antagonist's goal is <identify antagonist's goal(s)>.

At resolution <identify what happens in the end>.

This summary will become very useful as part of the package of material we will use to take your story to market after it is written, so it is well worth working on this form. However, as I mentioned before, don't be too concerned if you are not able to identify all these elements accurately straight away, particularly as we haven't gone into details on certain areas, such as genre, theme and the difference between the antagonist himself and the more general antagonistic forces. And of course, we haven't even begun to properly consider character growth or subtext. Don't worry about it. Keep going, because it is making us think along the right lines, and bear in mind that you should return to this process and fill in the blanks as you gain understanding of your own story.

4 Knowledge gaps

OK. Pay attention, chaps. This is probably the most important chapter in the book, so we need to remain vigilant. We're a third of the way through, and we're all getting tired, but this really is the time to dig deep, up the caffeine, put the matchsticks in your eyes and read everything twice.

If I am ever to have an impact on your ability as a story-teller to the extent that you will one day search me out and fall on my neck, thanking me for making your story into a work of acclaimed wonder and telling me how gorgeous I am, it sits in this chapter. Am I getting through, here? This next bit's important.

I'll tell you what, just to prove how important this chapter is, I'm going to make it a whole new section. I'm just wild like that. Brace, brace, brace...

KNOWLEDGE GAPS AND SUBTEXT

...what lies beneath...

Introduction

As we have discovered, the presence of a physically functioning skeleton and a fine set of vital organs is structurally essential, and defines the presence of a human being... but it does not mean that the body is alive. A story is similarly incomplete if it only has structure and conflict. In this section, we come to the real differentiator: Knowledge Gaps. Knowledge gaps deliver the spirit of your story. Knowledge gaps are the only way that your story can live and breathe. Without it, your story will have no soul. Remember, all stories are delivered in subtext, because the real story is the underlying story. Knowledge gaps are the mechanism by which writers deliver a story in subtext.

Without subtext there is no story.

So, let's get a bit more background on the way the brain works and where the power of story lies. After that, we will define what knowledge gaps really are.

4.1 The brain and questions

My cat is, right now, sitting on the arm of my sofa, watching the bumble bees in the bush that is outside the living room window. When a bee comes close to her, she leaps to get it, concertinas herself, nose-first, up against the window, lands in a heap on the floor then checks to see if the dog saw anything. She goes back to her vantage point on the sofa arm where she regains her dignity and starts washing herself as if nothing happened. Two minutes later, when another bee comes close, her instincts kick in, and she does it again. Round and round the same painful loop, time and time again. She's three years old now. I don't know how long it will take her to overcome her instincts, but I fear that the window will give out first.

Now, the dog also sees the bee, but after only two years of banging his head on the window, he now has the foresight to run in the other direction, round to the kitchen and out into the garden (battling through the flap in the door put there for the cat), round to the bush where he successfully catches and eats a bee (it could be argued that this is not good evolutionary progress), whilst the cat looks on, utterly mystified by events. Until she sees another bee come close, and her instincts kick in and she haplessly starfishes herself up against the window again.

The key is imagination. The dog is able to project a series of actions that will take him from the existing state (separated from the bee) to a new, imagined future state that will solve his problem (to catch the bee). He takes these actions and reaps the rewards (he gets stung in the mouth).

We human beings project future scenarios all the time. From simple matters, like how to get from one location to another, to bigger problems to solve, like how to start and run a successful business or how to go and walk on the moon. We continuously take an existing state of our world, imagine a future, desired state, map out the necessary activities that must take place to make the future scenario a reality, and set about taking those steps. It's a basic human mode of operation and one that is fundamental to our success as individuals and as a race. Pretty much everything you do, from getting a meal on the table to bringing up a child, involves sitting in a current state, imagining a future desired state, and mapping out a plan for how to get from the current state to a desired future state.

To reprise the words of Steven Pinker in his 1997 book, *How the Mind Works*:

> " 'Intelligence' is the ability to attain goals in the face of obstacles by means of decisions and actions based on rational rules. The quality 'intelligence' is awarded to those who follow story structure."

Projecting a desired future state and mapping a route to getting there is a basic capability associated with intellect. Indeed, there are entire theories on the nature of thought that claim the intelligence afforded to the human mind is purely the ability to think in metaphor. We understand the solid labels we give to people and things (nouns) and the concepts that are empirical to worldly existence (time, location, movement, causality), and it is our ability to make abstracted concepts from these fundamentals that are the essence of intelligent thought. Above the basics, we only think in metaphors, and theories along these lines are largely accepted as valid.

If we accept that stories are simply metaphors for life, and metaphors are the basis of intellect, clearly, stories are therefore a means of training, honing and exercising our most fundamental and critical mental capabilities. In the same way that cats practice their hunting skills on each other, on balls of wool and on window panes, we humans can learn and develop real skills for life through absorbing stories. When we have a gap in knowledge we set about understanding and filling it, and until we have the correct information to fill the gap, we try out different possibilities to see which ones might fit. We project different answers into the gap, and when we find one that seems right, we use it and build on it to project further. And this is how we create an underlying story, a subtextual story in our own minds, all by ourselves. The author gives us a current state and a sum of information, and we fill in all the gaps he leaves for us all by ourselves.

A well crafted story continually invites us to project from the current given state in the story to some future desired state that we would like to see brought to fruition. The writer relentlessly adds to the sum of knowledge so we have to reassess our understanding of the current state (which may or may not be accurate) and reconfigure our projected path to our desired outcome state. Our brains instinctively do this; our brains love to do this; our brains automatically and relentlessly do this, so the writer uses this to his advantage. He grips the audience and maintains interest by constantly cracking open gaps in the knowledge held by different participants and, crucially, that available to the audience. Sometimes the audience has more knowledge than the protagonist, sometimes less. Sometimes the audience has the same knowledge as the protagonist, but less or more than another player. The author always knows more than everybody else, usually until the final outcome of the story.

In a good story there is always, always a difference in the knowledge possessed by at least one participant when compared to the audience.

It is in this knowledge gap that the brain gets busy; flying backwards through the delivered information trying to attain the knowledge that will fill this gap and flying forwards in the story to try and project a justifiable sequence of events that will take us to the desired story outcome (i.e., satisfactorily answering the key question; or to put it another way, to fill the main, overarching knowledge gaps). Each knowledge gap is fascinating to us every time. Each knowledge gap is critical to the successful delivery of story. Each instance of imagined material that the audience uses to fill the knowledge gaps is the underlying story.

Knowledge gaps and the audience
Although there are 12 major types of knowledge gap, all can be categorised in terms of their position relative to the audience as either 'revelation gaps'

or 'privilege gaps'. The former is concerned with the situation where we the audience know less than the protagonist, and the latter is where the audience knows more.

4.1.1 Revelation gaps

Say we are absorbing a crime story. We have seen everything the detective has seen, we know all the suspects, we've seen all the clues, we can project forwards from the current state to several possible arrest scenarios, and we've decided we're getting close to the truth. Then suddenly, the detective makes his move. He arrests the blonde, and we think: 'Wha- What?! Why did he do that?! Surely, she's a victim, not a suspect! What's going on?!' and we go into a tailspin trying to rebuild an accurate current state from the information available, and reconfigure the story from this new known state to some sensible projected state that accommodates this new turn of events.

As you can see in the illustration below, the author has built in a knowledge gap between the detective and the audience that keeps the audience behind the curve. The detective is making his moves on the basis of knowledge that the audience hasn't picked up on. This is an example of a revelation gap. At some point we get to find out the motivation for the detective making the move he has made, and the revelation closes this knowledge gap.

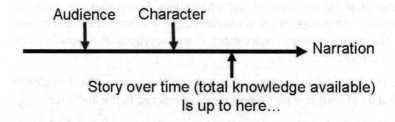

Throughout any mystery story, the antagonist has made several more moves ahead of the known information, giving the detective (and the audience) more puzzles to solve, and layering in the knowledge gaps to lead to future revelation.

4.1.2 Privilege gaps

Also known as 'dramatic irony', this is the situation whereby the audience knows more than a character such that a 'privilege' gap is created. Let's say that our detective is climbing the creaky staircase towards the spooky attic space of an old mansion. He carries a candle to light his way as a portentous chill blows around him and he shivers with unhappy expectation. As well he should, because we already know that there is a large, mad, axe-wielding murderer lying in wait for him behind the door at the top of the stairs. As the detective creeps ever nearer to an axe in the head, and the cold wind blows his candle out, we find ourselves on the edge of our seats, and we realise, finally and forever, that a privilege gap characterises 'suspense'.

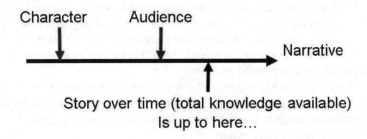

It should be possible, in any decent story, and at pretty much any time during that story, to find measurable gaps in the knowledge possessed by the audience when compared to some or all the other players.

Let's look at a story example to help us work our way deeper into this definition. The following extract is from my favourite author – two chapters from the P.G. Wodehouse book, *'The Inimitable Jeeves'*. The two chapters together act as a standalone short story which I hope you will enjoy in itself.

The story concerns the young master, Bertie Wooster, who is the narrator telling his story, and his butler, Jeeves, whose enormous intellect is forever required to dig the young master out of the holes into which he puts himself. I have removed one or two sentences that pertain to previous chapters. Enjoy the read, notice how the narrative – the words on the surface – tells a different story from the one you create for yourself. You know lots more than the narrator himself, who is also the protagonist! Afterwards, we will analyse for knowledge gaps.

4.1.3   Extract from The Inimitable Jeeves By P.G. Wodehouse

Chapter 5 – The Pride of the Woosters is Wounded

If there's one thing I like, it's a quiet life. I'm not one of those fellows who get all restless and depressed if things aren't happening to them all the time. You can't make it too placid for me. Give me regular meals, a good show with decent music every now and then, and one or two pals to totter round with, and I ask no more.

That is why the jar, when it came, was such a particularly nasty jar. I mean, I'd returned from Roville with a sort of feeling that from now on nothing could occur to upset me. I little thought that... Well, look here, what happened was this, and I ask you if it wasn't enough to rattle anybody.

Once a year Jeeves takes a couple of weeks' vacation and biffs off to the sea or somewhere to restore his tissues. Pretty rotten for me, of course, while he's away. But it has to be stuck so I stick it; and I must admit that he usually manages to get hold of a fairly decent fellow to look after me in his absence.

Well, the time had come round again, and Jeeves was in the kitchen giving the understudy a few tips about his duties. I happened to want a stamp or something, and I toddled down the passage to ask him for it. The silly ass had left the kitchen door open, and I hadn't gone two steps when his voice caught me squarely in the eardrum.

'You will find Mr Wooster,' he was saying to the substitute chappie, 'an exceedingly pleasant and amiable young gentleman, but not intelligent. By no means intelligent. Mentally he is negligible – quite negligible.'

Well, I mean to say, what!

I suppose, strictly speaking, I ought to have charged in and ticked the blighter off properly in no uncertain voice. But I doubt whether it is humanly possible to tick Jeeves off. Personally, I didn't even have a dash at it. I merely called for my hat and stick in a marked manner and legged it. But the memory rankled, if you know what I mean. We Woosters do not lightly forget. At least, we do – some things – appointments, and people's birthdays, and letters to post, and all that – but not an absolute bally insult like the above. I brooded like the dickens.

I was still brooding when I dropped in at the oyster-bar at Buck's for a quick bracer. I needed a bracer rather particularly at the moment, because I was on my way to lunch with Aunt Agatha. A pretty frightful ordeal, believe me or believe me not, even though I took it that after what had happened at Roville she would be in a fairly subdued and amiable mood. I had just had one quick and another rather slower, and was feeling about as cheerio as was possible under the circs, when a muffled voice hailed me from the north-east, and, turning round, I saw young Bingo Little propped up in a corner, wrapping himself round a sizable chunk of bread and cheese.

'Hallo-allo-allo!' I said. 'Haven't seen you for ages. You've not been in here lately, have you?'

'No. I've been living out in the country.'

'Eh?' I said, for Bingo's loathing for the country was well known. 'Whereabouts?'

'Down in Hampshire, at a place called Ditteredge.'

'No, really? I know some people who've got a house there. The Glossops. Have you met them?'

'Why, that's where I'm staying!' said young Bingo. 'I'm tutoring the Glossop kid!'

'What for?' I said. I couldn't seem to see young Bingo as a tutor. Tough, of course, he did get a degree of sorts at Oxford, and I suppose you can always fool some of the people some of the time.

'What for? For money, of course! An absolute sitter came unstitched in the second race at Haydock Park,' said young Bingo, with some bitterness, 'and I dropped my entire month's allowance. I hadn't the nerve to touch my uncle for any more, so it was a case of buzzing round to the agents and getting a job. I've been down there three weeks.'

'I haven't met the Glossop kid.'

'Don't!' advised Bingo, briefly.

'The only one of the family I really know is the girl.' I had hardly spoken these words when the most extraordinary change came over young Bingo's face. His eyes bulged, his cheeks flushed, and his Adam's apple hopped about like one of those India-rubber balls on the top of the fountain in a shooting-gallery.

'Oh, Bertie!' he said, in a strangled sort of voice.

I looked at the poor fish anxiously. I knew that he was always falling in love with someone, but it didn't seem possible that even he could have fallen in love with Honoria Glossop. To me the girl was simply nothing more nor less than a pot of poison. One of those dashed large, brainy, strenuous, dynamic girls you see so many of these days. She had been at Girton, where, in addition to enlarging her brain to the most frightful extent, she had gone in for every kind of sport and developed the physique of a middle weight catch-as-catch-can wrestler. I'm not sure she didn't box for the 'Varsity while she was up. The effect she had on me whenever she appeared was to make me want to slide into a cellar and lie low till they blew the all clear.

Yet here was young Bingo obviously all for her. There was no mistaking it. The love-light was in the blighter's eyes.

'I worship her, Bertie! I worship the very ground she treads on!' continued the patient, in a loud, penetrating voice. Fred Thompson and one or two fellows had come in, and McGarry, the chappie behind the bar, was listening with his ears flapping. But there's no reticence about Bingo. He always reminds me of the hero of a musical comedy who takes the centre of the stage, gathers the boys around him in a circle, and tells them all about his love at the top of his voice.

'Have you told her?'

'No. I haven't had the nerve. But we walk together in the garden most evenings, and it sometimes seems to me that there is a look in her eyes.'

I know that look. Like a sergeant-major.'

'Nothing of the kind! Like a tender goddess.'

'Half a second, old thing,' I said. 'Are you sure we're talking about the same girl? The one I mean is Honoria. Perhaps there's a younger sister or something I've not heard of?'

'Her name is Honoria,' bawled Bingo reverently.

'And she strikes you as a tender goddess?'

'She does.'

'God bless you!' I said.

'She walks in beauty like the night of cloudless climes and starry skies; and all that's best of dark and bright meet in her aspect and her eyes. Another bit of bread and cheese,' he said to the lad behind the bar.

'You're keeping your strength up,' I said.

'This is my lunch. I've got to meet Oswald at Waterloo at one-fifteen, to catch the train back. I brought him up to town to see the dentist.'

'Oswald? Is that the kid?'

'Yes. Pestilential to a degree.'

'Pestilential! That reminds me, I'm lunching with my Aunt Agatha. I'll have to pop off now, or I'll be late.'

I hadn't seen Aunt Agatha since that little affair of the pearls; and, while I didn't anticipate any great pleasure from gnawing a bone in her society, I must say that there was one topic of conversation I felt pretty confident she wouldn't touch on, and that was the subject of my matrimonial future. I mean, when a woman's made a bloomer like the one Aunt Agatha made at Roville, you'd naturally think that a decent shame would keep her off it for at any rate a month or two.

But women beat me. I mean to say, as regards nerve. You'll hardly credit it, but she actually started in on me with the fish. Absolutely with the fish, I give you my solemn word. We'd hardly exchanged a word about the weather when she let me have it without a blush.

'Bertie,' she said, 'I've been thinking again about you and how necessary it is that you should get married. I quite admit that I was dreadfully mistaken in my opinion of that terrible, hypocritical girl at Roville, but this time there is no danger of an error. By great good luck I have found the very wife for you, a girl whom I have only recently met, but whose family is above suspicion. She has plenty of money, too, though that does not matter in your case. The great point is that she is strong, self-reliant, and sensible, and will counterbalance the deficiencies and weaknesses of your character. She has met you; and, while there is naturally much in you of which she disapproves, she does not dislike you. I know this, for I have sounded her – guardedly, of course – and I am sure that you have only to make the first advances –'

'Who is it?' I would have said it long before, but the shock had made me swallow a bit of roll the wrong way, and I had only just finished turning purple and trying to get a bit of air back into the old windpipe. 'Who is it?'

'Sir Roderick Glossop's daughter, Honoria.'

'No, no!' I cried, paling beneath the tan.

'Don't be silly, Bertie. She is just the wife for you.'

'Yes, but look here –'

'She will mould you.'

'But I don't want to be moulded.'

Aunt Agatha gave me the kind of look she used to give me when I was a kid and had been found in the jam cupboard.

'Bertie! I hope you are not going to be troublesome.'

'Well, but I mean –'

'Lady Glossop has very kindly invited you to Ditteredge Hall for a few days. I told her you would be delighted to come down tomorrow.'

'I'm sorry, but I've got a dashed important engagement tomorrow.'

'What engagement?'

'Well – er –'

'You have no engagement. And, even if you had, you must put it off. I shall be very seriously annoyed, Bertie, if you do not go to Ditteredge Hall tomorrow.'

'Oh, right-o!' I said.

It wasn't two minutes after I had parted from Aunt Agatha before the old fighting spirit of the Woosters reasserted itself. Ghastly as the peril was which loomed before me, I was conscious of a rummy sort of exhilaration. It was a tight corner, but the tighter the corner, I felt, the more juicily should I score off Jeeves when I got myself out of it without a bit of help from him. Ordinarily, of course, I should have consulted him and trusted to him to solve the difficulty; but after what I had heard him saying in the kitchen, I was dashed if I was going to demean myself. When I got home I addressed the man with light abandon.

'Jeeves,' I said, 'I'm in a bit of a difficulty.'

'I'm sorry to hear that, sir.'

'Yes, quite a bad hole. In fact, you might say on the brink of a precipice, and faced by an awful doom.'

'If I could be of any assistance, sir –'

'Oh, no. No, no. Thanks very much, but no, no. I won't trouble you. I've no doubt I shall be able to get out of it all right by myself.'

'Very good, sir.'

So that was that. I'm bound to say I'd have welcomed a bit more curiosity from the fellow, but that is Jeeves all over. Cloaks his emotions, if you know what I mean.

Honoria was away when I got to Ditteredge on the following afternoon. Her mother told me she was staying with some people named Braythwayt in the neighbourhood, and would be back the next day, bringing the daughter of the house with her for a visit. She said I would find Oswald out in the grounds, and such is a mother's love that she spoke as if that were a bit of a boost for the grounds and an inducement to go there.

Rather decent, the grounds at Ditteredge. A couple of terraces, a bit of lawn with a cedar on it, a bit of shrubbery, and finally a small but goodish lake with a stone bridge running across it. Directly I'd worked my way round the shrubbery I spotted young Bingo leaning against the bridge smoking a cigarette. Sitting on the stonework, fishing, was a species of kid whom I took to be Oswald the Plague Spot.

Bingo was both surprised and delighted to see me, and introduced me to the kid. If the latter was surprised and delighted too, he concealed it like a diplomat. He just looked at me, raised his eyebrows slightly, and went on fishing. He was one of those supercilious striplings who give you the impression that you went to the wrong school and that your clothes don't fit.

'This is Oswald,' said Bingo.

'What,' I replied cordially, 'could be sweeter? How are you?'

'Oh, all right,' said the kid.

'Nice place this.'

'Oh, all right,' said the kid.

'Having a good time fishing?'

'Oh, all right,' said the kid.

Young Bingo led me off to commune apart.

'Doesn't jolly old Oswald's incessant flow of prattle make your head ache sometimes?' I asked.

Bingo sighed.

'It's a hard job.'

'What's a hard job?'

'Loving him.'

'Do you love him?' I asked, surprised. I shouldn't have thought it could be done.

'I try to,' said young Bingo, 'for her sake. She's coming back tomorrow, Bertie.'

'So I heard.'

'She is coming, my love, my own –'

'Absolutely,' I said. 'But touching on young Oswald once more. Do you have to be with him all day? How do you manage to stick it?'

'Oh, he doesn't give much trouble. When we aren't working he sits on that bridge all the time, trying to catch tiddlers.'

'Why don't you shove him in?'

'Shove him in?'

'It seems to me distinctly the thing to do,' I said, regarding the stripling's back with a good deal of dislike. 'It would wake him up a bit, and make him take an interest in things.'

Bingo shook his head a bit wistfully.

'Your proposition attracts me,' he said, 'but I'm afraid it can't be done. You see, she would never forgive me. She is devoted to the little brute.'

'Great Scott!' I cried. 'I've got it!' I don't know if you know that feeling when you get an inspiration, and tingle all down your spine from the soft collar as now worn to the very soles of the old Waukeesis? Jeeves, I suppose, feels that way more or less all the time, but it isn't often it comes to me. But now all Nature seemed to be shouting at me 'You've clicked!' and I grabbed young Bingo by the arm in a way that must have made him feel as if a horse had bitten him. His finely-chiselled features were twisted with agony and what not, and he asked me what the dickens I thought I was playing at.

'Bingo,' I said, 'what would Jeeves have done?'

'How do you mean, what would Jeeves have done?'

'I mean what would he have advised in a case like yours? I mean you wanting to make a hit with Honoria Glossop and all that. Why, take it from me, laddie, he would have shoved you behind that clump of bushes over there; he would have got me to lure Honoria on to the bridge somehow; then, at the proper time, he would have told me to give the kid a pretty hefty jab in the small of the back, so as to shoot him into the water; and then you would have dived in and hauled him out. How about it?'

'You didn't think that out by yourself, Bertie?' said young Bingo in a hushed sort of voice.

'Yes, I did. Jeeves isn't the only fellow with ideas.'

'But it's absolutely wonderful.'

'Just a suggestion.'

'The only objection I can see is that it would be so dashed awkward for you. I mean to say, suppose the kid turned round and said you had shoved him in, that would make you frightfully unpopular with Her.'

'I don't mind risking that.'

The man was deeply moved.

'Bertie, this is noble.'

'No, no.'

He clasped my hand silently, then chuckled like the last drop of water going down the waste-pipe in a bath.

'Now what?' I said.

'I was only thinking,' said young Bingo, 'how fearfully wet Oswald will get. Oh, happy day!'

Chapter 6 – The Hero's Reward

I don't know if you've ever noticed it, but it's rummy how nothing in this world ever seems to be absolutely perfect. The drawback to this otherwise singularly fruity binge was, of course, the fact that Jeeves wouldn't be on the spot to watch me in action. Still, apart from that there wasn't a flaw. The beauty of the thing was, you see, that nothing could possibly go wrong. You know how it is, as a rule, when you want to get Chappie A on Spot B at exactly the same moment when Chappie C is on Spot D. There is always a chance of a hitch. Take the case of a general, I mean to say, who's planning out a big movement. He tells one regiment to capture the hill with the windmill on it at the exact moment when another regiment is taking the bridgehead or something down in the valley; and everything gets all messed up. And then, when they're chatting the thing over in camp that night, the colonel of the first regiment says, 'Oh, sorry! Did you say the hill with the windmill? I thought you said the one with the flock of sheep.' And there you are! But in this case, nothing like that could happen, because Oswald and Bingo would be on the spot right along, so that all I had to worry about was getting Honoria there in due season. And I managed that all right, first shot, by asking her if she would come for a stroll in the grounds with me, as I had something particular to say to her.

She had arrived shortly after lunch in the car with the Braythwayt girl. I was introduced to the latter, a tallish girl with blue eyes and fair hair. I rather took to her – she was so unlike Honoria – and, if I had been able to spare the time, I shouldn't have minded talking to her for a bit. But business is business – I had fixed it up with Bingo to be behind the bushes at three sharp, so I got hold of Honoria and steered her out through the grounds in the direction of the lake.

'You're very quiet, Mr Wooster,' she said.

Made me jump a bit. I was concentrating pretty tensely at the moment. We had just come in sight of the lake, and I was casting a keen eye over the ground to see that everything was in order. Everything appeared to be as arranged. The kid Oswald was hunched up on the bridge; and, as Bingo wasn't visible, I took it that he had got into position. My watch made it two minutes after the hour.

'Eh?' I said. 'Oh, ah, yes. I was just thinking.'

'You said you had something important to say to me.'

'Absolutely!' I had decided to open the proceedings by sort of paving the way for young Bingo. I mean to say, without actually mentioning his name. I wanted to prepare the girl's mind for the fact that, surprising as it might seem, there was someone who had long loved her from afar and all that sort of rot. 'It's like this,' I said. 'It may sound rummy and all that, but there's somebody who's frightfully in love with you and so forth – a friend of mine, you know.'

'Oh, a friend of yours?'

'Yes.'

She gave a kind of laugh.

'Well, why doesn't he tell me so?'

'Well, you see, that's the sort of chap he is. Kind of shrinking, diffident kind of fellow. Hasn't got the nerve. Thinks you so much above him, don't you know. Looks on you as a sort of goddess. Worships the ground you tread on, but can't whack up the ginger to tell you so.'

'This is very interesting.'

'Yes. He's not a bad chap, you know, in his way. Rather an ass, perhaps, but well-meaning. Well, that's the posish. You might just bear it in mind, what?'

'How funny you are!'

She chucked back her head and laughed with considerable vim. She had a penetrating sort of laugh. Rather like a train going into a tunnel. It didn't sound over-musical to me, and on the kid Oswald it appeared to jar not a little. He gazed at us with a good deal of dislike.

'I wish the dickens you wouldn't make that row,' he said. 'Scaring all the fish away.'

It broke the spell a bit. Honoria changed the subject.

'I do wish Oswald wouldn't sit on the bridge like that,' she said. 'I'm sure it isn't safe. He might easily fall in.'

'I'll go and tell him,' I said.

* * *

I suppose the distance between the kid and me at this juncture was about five yards, but I got the impression that it was nearer a hundred. And, as I started to toddle across the intervening space, I had a rummy feeling that I'd done this very thing before. Then I remembered. Years ago, at a country house party, I had been roped in to play the part of a butler in some amateur theatricals in aid of some ghastly charity or other; and I had had to open the proceedings by walking across the empty stage from left upper entrance and shoving a tray on a table down right. They had impressed it on me at rehearsals that I mustn't take the course at a quick heel-and-toe, like a chappie finishing strongly in a walking-race; and the result was that I kept the brakes on to such an extent that it seemed to me as if I was never going to get to the bally table at all. The stage seemed to stretch out in front of me like a trackless desert, and there was a kind of breathless hush as if all Nature had paused to concentrate its attention on me personally. Well, I felt just like that now. I had a kind of dry gulping in my throat, and the more I walked the farther away the kid seemed to get, till suddenly I found myself standing just behind him without quite knowing how I'd got there.

'Hallo!' I said, with a sickly sort of grin – wasted on the kid, because he didn't bother to turn round and look at me. He merely wiggled his left ear in a rather peevish manner. I don't know when I've met anyone in whose life I appeared to mean so little.

'Hallo!' I said. 'Fishing?'

I laid my hand in a sort of elder-brotherly way on his shoulder.

'Here, look out!' said the kid, wobbling on his foundations.

It was one of those things that want doing quickly or not at all. I shut my eyes and pushed. Something seemed to give. There was a scrambling sound, a kind of yelp, a scream in the offing, and a splash. And so the long day wore on, so to speak.

I opened my eyes. The kid was just coming to the surface.

'Help!' I shouted, cocking an eye on the bush from which young Bingo was scheduled to emerge.

Nothing happened. Young Bingo didn't emerge to the slightest extent whatever.

'I say! Help!' I shouted again.

I don't want to bore you with reminiscences of my theatrical career, but I must just touch once more on that appearance of mine as the butler. The scheme on that occasion had been that when I put the tray on the table, the heroine would come on and say a few words to get me off. Well, on the night the misguided female forgot to stand by, and it was a full minute before the search-party located her and shot her on to the stage. And all that time I had to stand there, waiting. A rotten sensation, believe me, and this was just the same, only worse. I understood what these writer-chappies mean when they talk about time standing still.

Meanwhile the kid Oswald was presumably being cut off in his prime, and it began to seem to me that some sort of steps ought to be taken about it. What I had seen of the lad hadn't particularly endeared him to me, but it was undoubtedly a bit thick to let him pass away. I don't know when I have seen anything more grubby and unpleasant than the lake as viewed from the bridge; but the thing apparently had to be done. I chucked off my coat and vaulted over.

It seems rummy that water should be so much wetter when you go into it with your clothes on than when you're just bathing, but take it from me that it is. I was only under about three seconds, I suppose, but I came up feeling like the bodies you read of in the paper which 'had evidently been in the water several days.' I felt clammy and bloated.

At this point the scenario struck another snag. I had assumed that directly I came to the surface I should get hold of the kid and steer him courageously to shore. But he hadn't waited to be steered. When I had finished getting the water out of my eyes and had time to take a look round, I saw him about ten yards away, going strongly and using, I think, the Australian crawl. The spectacle took all the heart out of me. I mean to say, the whole essence of a rescue, if you know what I mean, is that the party of the second part shall keep fairly still and in one spot. If he starts swimming off on his own account and can obviously give you at least forty yards in the hundred, where are you? The whole thing falls through. It didn't seem to me that there was much to be done except get ashore, so I got ashore. By the time I had landed, the kid was half-way to the house. Look at it from whatever angle you like, the thing was a washout.

I was interrupted in my meditations by a noise like the Scotch express going under a bridge. It was Honoria Glossop laughing. She was standing at my elbow, looking at me in a rummy manner.

'Oh, Bertie, you are funny!' she said. And even in that moment there seemed to me something sinister in the words. She had never called me anything except 'Mr Wooster' before. 'How wet you are!'

'Yes, I am wet.'

'You had better hurry into the house and change.'

'Yes.'

I wrung a gallon or two of water out of my clothes.

'You *are* funny!' she said again. 'First proposing in that extraordinary roundabout way, and then pushing poor little Oswald into the lake so as to impress me by saving him.'

I managed to get the water out of my throat sufficiently to try to correct this fearful impression.

'No, no!'

'He said you pushed him in, and I saw you do it. Oh, I'm not angry, Bertie. I think it was too sweet of you. But I'm quite sure it's time that I took you in hand. You certainly want someone to look after you. You've been seeing too many moving-pictures. I suppose the next thing you would have done would have been to set the house on fire so as to rescue me.' She looked at me in a proprietary sort of way. 'I think,' she said, 'I shall be able to make something of you, Bertie. It is true yours has been a wasted life up to the present, but you are still young, and there is a lot of good in you.'

'No, really there isn't.'

'Oh, yes, there is. It simply wants bringing out. Now, you run straight up to the house and change your wet clothes, or you will catch cold.'

And, if you know what I mean, there was a sort of motherly note in her voice which seemed to tell me, even more than her actual words, that I was for it.

* * *

As I was coming downstairs after changing, I ran into young Bingo, looking festive to a degree.

'Bertie!' he said. 'Just the man I wanted to see. Bertie, a wonderful thing has happened.'

'You blighter!' I cried. 'What became of you? Do you know –?'

'Oh, you mean about being in those bushes? I hadn't time to tell you about that. It's all off.'

'All off?'

'Bertie, I was actually starting to hide in those bushes when the most extraordinary thing happened. Walking across the lawn I saw the most radiant, the most beautiful girl in the world. There is none like her, none. Bertie, do you believe in love at first sight? You do believe in love at first sight, don't you, Bertie, old man? Directly I saw her, she seemed to draw me like a magnet. I seemed to forget everything. We two were alone in a world of music and sunshine. I joined her. I got into conversation. She is a Miss Braythwayt, Bertie – Daphne Braythwayt. Directly our eyes met, I realised that what I had imagined to be my love for Honoria Glossop had been a mere passing whim. Bertie, you do believe in love at first sight, don't you? She is so wonderful, so sympathetic. Like a tender goddess –'

At this point I left the blighter.

Two days later I got a letter from Jeeves.

'...the weather,' it ended, 'continues fine. I have had one exceedingly enjoyable bathe.'

I gave one of those hollow, mirthless laughs, and went downstairs to join Honoria. I had an appointment with her in the drawing-room. She was going to read Ruskin to me.

* * *

Now, if this is classic storytelling, and I believe that it is, then my theory is that it is probably packed with lots and lots of knowledge gaps. We can measure the extent of subtext by looking at the knowledge gaps between the audience and all the main players. Let's see who is where just before Bertie shoves Oswald into the lake.

1. Honoria thinks that Bertie is proposing to her. Bertie doesn't realise this, but we, the audience, do. So Honoria knows more than Bertie, and we know more than both of them.

2. In the second plot strand, Bertie thinks he is setting Honoria up for a relationship with Bingo. She is oblivious, so in this context Bertie knows more than Honoria and again, we know more than both of them.

3. Oswald is blissfully unaware of anything. Bertie knows Oswald is about to get a swim, and so do we, so we know more than Oswald (and Honoria) in this thread.

4. In amongst all this privilege information, Bingo is not hiding in the bushes awaiting his big moment as we expect. He's forgotten all about his love for Honoria and is out at the front of the house energetically falling in love with another girl altogether. Bingo alone

knows this, and nobody else does, so this revelation gap is planted to top everything off with an unexpected surprise at payoff.

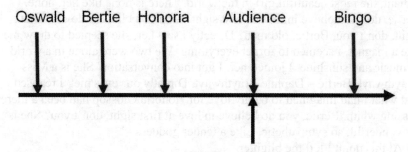

Oswald   Bertie   Honoria   Audience   Bingo

Story over time
(total knowledge available)
Is up to here...

Brilliant. Whilst Bertie trots happily along in thought and deed on one agenda, we are taking on board a completely different story, delivered entirely in subtext through these knowledge gaps. That is why we love it.

4.1.4   A Note on Comedy

Most theories of story, particularly those based on structure, fall over when they get to comedy. They end up concluding that comedy is just 'different', and their theories fall apart once humour is a factor.

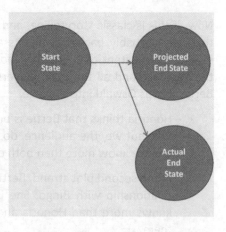

But look at the relationship between comedy and subtext. Knowledge gaps are fundamental to all forms of comedy and it is useful to look at this area. Comedy is basically simple, blatant knowledge gaps. Gags and jokes are a scenario deliberately built in one direction and then paid-off in another. Our brains are suddenly jerked from the surface text to the revelation, and we laugh at the new picture or implication that is delivered. When the joke begins, we get one picture: 'There are these two fish in a tank...' we naturally imagine two goldfish in an aquarium. But what we have really been delivered is one end of a knowledge gap. We don't know what the teller really means until we get to the next line.

'...one says to the other, 'do you know how to drive this thing?'' and after a few seconds of interpretation we get hit by a different picture, of two goldfish in a Chieftain out on Salisbury Plain and the interpretive jerk makes us laugh. We were set up with a knowledge gap concerning the true situation. Underneath the image we initially projected was a second interpretation that we didn't see coming. The sudden switch from one to the other (revelation) is the cause of the laughter.

Longer humour – as in a novel or a film story – relies upon knowledge gaps and misdirection on a grander scale, usually on the basis of characters not being who they say they are. The main plot events arrive in the form of revelation concerning who is really whom. Rather sad, really, that this is almost exclusively the plot basis for delivering humour in a full length work. (Fortunately, there is character as well as plot.)

This pattern, of setting up a start state, inviting an audience to reach their own conclusions in a projected end state and then paying off to an unexpected end state is well exemplified in a joke and in humour, but is also the main pattern for all story telling.

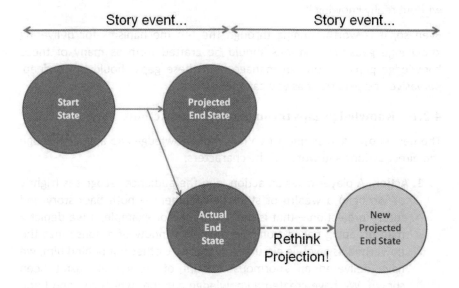

Story event by story event, the audience perceives an existing current state, uses current knowledge to project possible next and final states, and then the writer pays it off in a different direction, causing the audience to rethink the current state and reconfigure their projections to new envisaged states. This is your job, as a writer: endlessly work to build gaps in knowledge and tease the audience into constructing mental story states that are then proven to be wrong. Keep their brains busy asking and answering questions and you will have an absorbing and successful story.

When you hear from the theorists that stories must be written in subtext, this is slightly wrong. What this really means is that you must write your stories with as many types of knowledge gap as you possibly can, so your story can be *delivered* in subtext. Open the knowledge gaps and keep them as deep, extensive, pervasive and intriguing as you possibly can.

Knowledge gaps create a story in subtext: An underlying story created through the assumptions and projections the audience make to fill the knowledge gaps.

OK. So what does this mean for our writing? How do we create knowledge gaps?

4.2   Mechanisms for the delivery of knowledge gaps

As we mentioned earlier on, knowledge gaps are part of the human psyche and are a relentless part of our everyday lives. As storytellers, we tend to find it quite natural to create them without really thinking about them at all. The resultant subtext is just there, like the action and the characters, and you are likely to be creating and using knowledge gaps all over the place without really knowing it.

Even so, it is worth running through the ten mechanisms for delivering knowledge gaps. Your stories should be crafted from as many of these knowledge gaps as you can manage, and these gaps should be as deep, pervasive and persistent as you can make them.

4.2.1   Knowledge gaps through words and actions

The best known and simplest two forms of knowledge gap appear through the direct actions and words of the characters.

1. **Action**. A player takes an action, and the audience recognises (rightly or wrongly) a wealth of story development – both back-story and future projection – that is not spelt out. For example, if we depict a man dropping naked from the upstairs window of a house into the flowerbed as a young girl urgently throws clothes out behind him, we have delivered an enormous amount of story that hasn't been shown. We have created a knowledge gap into which you and I and everybody else who has ever heard a story promptly fills in the same interpretation. The same story told explicitly might start with newlyweds moving into a new home in the suburbs. But the girl becomes unhappy with a housewife's lot. Whilst hubby is at work in the city all day, she begins an affair with the local plumber. One day, the husband comes home early. The wife's afternoon plumbing is hastily curtailed and a leap from an upstairs window is required. None of this exposition is necessary. From the ten seconds of given

scene, the audience will fill this knowledge gap for themselves with the bored housewife whose husband works too hard, and the search for excitement and all the rest of it. And the audience can be trusted to fill in these blanks. Of course, they may be completely wrong, and there may be a different – perhaps perfectly justifiable – explanation for the action seen. Maybe this *is* the husband and wife. The house is on fire, and they are escaping together. You can use the audience tendency to fill in the blanks to mislead them. Alternatively, the audience may be precisely right, in which case you haven't wasted precious audience attention on unnecessary back story. You have delivered your story in subtext; the strongest way to deliver a story.

2. **Words**. In story as in life, people rarely say exactly what they mean. When Biff asks George: 'Do you realise what would happen if I turn in my homework in your handwriting? I'd get kicked out of school. You wouldn't want that to happen, would you?'

There is a pause and we leap all over the subtext: George would love for Biff to be thrown out of school. He'd be delighted. The words he says are: 'No, no, of course not, Biff. I wouldn't want that to happen...' But we know the truth.

We all lead a dual life. We rarely even know what we genuinely want ourselves, so if you create a character who not only knows exactly what he wants but is able to verbalise that need succinctly, nobody will believe that character for a moment. Characters must be real. They are misguided, uncertain, lack confidence, or are over-confident. They have false information, or secret motivations. And that means they make bad decisions, often against their own best interests, and mislead everyone around them with their words, either deliberately or by accident.

The vast majority of actions must have implications beyond the presented action, and the vast majority of dialogue in your story must not mean what it says. If your characters can be disingenuous (to themselves and others), the chances are much higher that the story will be interesting and the characters credible. Let's take a look at these two forms of knowledge gap in a short example from the Science Fiction author, Philip K. Dick. These are the opening words of the story *Minority Report*.

4.2.2   Extract From: Minority Report
By Philip K. Dick

The first thought Anderton had when he saw the young man was: I'm getting bald. Fat, bald and old. But he didn't say it aloud. Instead, he pushed back his chair, got to his feet, and came resolutely round the side of his desk, his right hand rigidly extended. Smiling with forced amiability, he shook hands with the young man.

"Witwer?" he asked, managing to make his query sound gracious.

"That's right," the young man said. "But the name's Ed to you, of course. That is if you share my dislike for needless formality." The look on his blond, over-confident face showed that he considered the matter settled. It would be Ed and John: Everything would be agreeably cooperative right from the start.

"Did you have much trouble finding the place?" Anderton asked, guardedly, ignoring the too-friendly overture. Good God, he had to hold on to something. Fear touched him and he began to sweat. Witwer was moving around the office as if he already owned it – as if he were measuring it for size. Couldn't he wait a couple of days? A decent interval?

"No trouble," Witwer answered blithely, his hands in his pockets. Eagerly, he examined the voluminous files that lined the wall. "I'm not coming into your agency blind, you understand."

Anderton winced, but outwardly he remained impassive. It cost him an effort though. He wondered what Witwer really knew…

* * *

In this way and in very few words, the reader is delivered an enormous amount of information. We have two characters, we know who they are, we know their relative ages, we know their relative situations, we know a good deal about the environment and, most importantly, we are given the basis of a fine conflict between the old, established Anderton, and the young, ambitious Witwer. And guess what, Philip K Dick didn't describe anything at all. Not overtly. All that back-story, exposition and character information was delivered through the actions and words of two men meeting for the first time and exchanging standard pleasantries. The reason it zings with excellence is because, from the very first sentence, a knowledge gap is opened up between us, the audience and Witwer. We know everything that Anderton is thinking, and from that we receive the real story in subtext. Anderton says he feels old and bald. That's not what we take on board. We instantly gather that he is insecure about the youthfulness and dynamism of a lad called Witwer, and he sees him as a predator towards his job. The conflict is presented through the knowledge gap that we are aware of between the thoughts we know to be lodged in Anderton's mind and the surface cooperation, professionalism and politeness of the way he presents himself to Witwer. The dialogue appears to be irrelevant – take a look at any delivered line, none of it delivers the real story. The 'real' story is the one we built for ourselves by filling the knowledge gaps Philip K. Dick offered us so masterfully.

4.2.3 Knowledge Gaps through Promise

One of the most important types of subtext, also readily evident in the beginning of *Minority Report*, is subtext through promise. This is, in a sense, both privilege and revelation, in that we are not given specific knowledge gaps, but we are made a promise, through our understanding of how stories work, that there will be incidents involving the material we are given. When we set ourselves up for a story, we enter into an unwritten agreement – a bond of trust between writer and audience – that the author will play by certain rules. One of these rules is that when a person, event or object is given some focus in a story there will be a good reason for it. Philip K Dick has made us a promise in these first few paragraphs that there will be meaningful conflict between Witwer and Anderton. If the story goes forwards without this conflict, we will be dissatisfied with the story. Subtext through promise is a critical tool for the writer, most useful in the setup phases of a story or event. We can show objects and characters, events and emotions, and trust that the audience will be interested to know how those elements will be used to deliver the story.

In *Back to the Future*, there is a great deal of subtext through promise, particularly in the setup stages, and it is well worth noting, when talking about best practice, that absolutely everything is relevant. Simply everything you see, hear or understand is there for a reason. The camera drifts across a wall of different clocks. They set us the 'time' theme and set us an environmental context (we are in a house at 7.53am); one of the clocks has a man hanging off the minute hand; another is an alarm with a tea-maker – it has activated but is unattended and pours tea all over the floor; between the clocks are some newspaper headlines framed on the wall, telling of a destroyed mansion in a fire; the bed is not slept-in; a television is on, and the newsreader tells of a plutonium theft; a home-made contraption selects a can of dog food, opens it, and automatically decants dog food into a bowl on the floor (surrounded by lots of other plops of previous automated dog-food deliveries); a boy arrives with a skateboard; he calls for 'Doc', and 'Einstein' – no answer – and he is a little taken aback by the mess; his skateboard rolls under a chair where there is... the stolen plutonium. Everything we see and hear relates to the story.

Next the kid plays guitar and another invention malfunctions. Then the phone rings. Doc urgently asks Marty to meet him in the middle of the night in a parking lot. To bring a camcorder and not to tell anyone. All this and we're barely at the end of the intro credits sequence.

The vast richness of relevant information in this first few minutes is quite staggering when you think about it, and yet we don't 'know' anything at all. But we trust – as we suck up the masses of information being conveyed and our brains seek out everything that is put in front of us – that all of these words, events, characters and items have significance. They are all used at some point somewhere in the story delivery. In a word, they carry genuine 'promise'.

Generally speaking, it is a heinous breach of that trust if you as a writer draw attention to interesting people and things, and then never involve them. And it is a huge benefit to us as writers that we can present relevant content and know that the audience will accept it because of its 'promise' rather than screw their noses up and wonder what on earth the story is about.

4.2.4   Questions are knowledge gaps

Any form of question raised in the mind of an audience represents a knowledge gap. Many of the types of knowledge gap discussed here actually raise a question in the mind of the audience, but this is a separate type of gap, because, as we shall see, not all gaps in knowledge are questions as such. The fact that Marty is a time traveller from the future as far as his parents are concerned in 1955 puts a huge knowledge gap into the story – but no actual question is raised or answered directly as a result of this gap.

We have already looked in detail at the main example: the inciting incident, raising a key question that provides the overarching knowledge gap that defines the nature of the overall story, so I shall not go into further detail. Refer back to **Chapter 3.1.3 – The inciting incident** for details and examples on the key question. Suffice to say that questions raised, directly or indirectly, in the mind of the audience cause them to make assumptions and project future states.

4.2.5   Knowledge gaps through subplot

When we set up a key question and foreshadow to our audience the possibility of a future scene at climax when this question is answered, we set the imagination racing in our audience's mind. Every event is absorbed in the context of, firstly, this key question; secondly, the current state of the story; and, thirdly, the projected possible state(s) that could transpire between this point and the desired end state at resolution. As the story's complexity develops, further subplots are set up, further key questions are raised and an array of potential developments is layered in. Thus through the main body of the story every event is interpreted not only at the beat and scene levels, where the real-time action is taking place, but the action in each event is also abstracted to assess the impact in other subplots, sequences, acts and the main story spine itself.

Hmmm. That was rubbish. I don't understand it, and I just wrote it. Let's go for an example.

Two-thirds of the way through *Back to the Future*, the story is at its most complex and, as we have seen, we have many key questions raised. At the main story level, we are asking: how will Marty manage to get back to 1985? In subplot we are wondering: how will he get his father to ask his mother out when she has expressed her desire for a 'strong man' and he is so weak and unassertive? And in another subplot we are told that his parents must kiss on the dance floor of the 'Enchantment Under the Sea Dance' in order to get history back on track – how is Marty going to make that happen? Will they kiss on the dance floor? Will Marty exist in the future? In some of these plot lines we have privileged information, and in others we are being set up for revelation.

When George punches Biff's lights out to rescue Lorraine and she looks lovingly into his eyes as he lifts her into his arms, we are not only enjoying the surface, textual conflict of the scene as George overcomes the bad guy Biff (and simultaneously answers the scene level key question – 'Will George win the fight with Biff?'). Our brains are also flying back and forth through all the other questions we have in our minds trying to get a grip on what this means for the bigger picture. We realise instantly that George has now finally managed, in somewhat unorthodox fashion, to effectively ask Lorraine out. They could easily become a couple from this point. And he's taking her into the dance, which means they are right in line for a kiss on the dance floor. This, of course, means that we can project a scenario by which Marty might be born and exist in the future. If he gets his skates on, he can also now coincide with the lightning bolt that will take him back to 1985. We're watching George help Lorraine up from the floor, and at the same time we're reconfiguring our projections on all these other levels as well.

Meanwhile, the story continues to be delivered in real time, so our brains are endlessly occupied and we don't get enough time to think about the subconscious plot (i.e., one huge chunk of revelation subtext waiting to hit us through the character development strand). We have recognised some of the implications for ourselves, but fail to realise that when Marty does get back to 1985, one huge knowledge gap still exists (a revelation gap) and things will have changed.

When Marty returns to 1985, we are surprised (as is Marty) to find that his parents are slim and healthy; his brother and sister are professional and successful; his home and life exude status and prestige and we don't instantly understand why. Once again, our brains are flying back through the information we have absorbed and we realise – as the revelation hits and the knowledge gap closes with a bang – that it was that punch that did it. It changed the manner of George and Lorraine's meeting and George's confidence and assertiveness over Biff was a feature of his life from that moment in 1955 onwards. Marty was therefore born to a strong, confident father, not a weak downtrodden one, and his life and family were different as a result.

This is 'knowledge gaps through subplot'. An action in one plotline delivers knowledge towards, and has an impact upon, the progress of another plotline. Similarly, a character who learns and changes will have an impact on their future actions and reactions to events. The key to successful delivery through subplot is to ensure that:

- All plot and subplot story lines are interdependent, so that a change in one has an impact on another. This is why subplots work best as 'deviations' from the main plot – dependent variables, if you like – not as separate stories that are disconnected from the main plot.

- All plotlines are set up with a good strong key question. A strong key question causes the audience to project clear future states for that plotline. An audience member with a clear understanding of where he expects the story to go can be more easily delivered subtext in terms of the knowledge gap between any current position and the expected and projected future state he can imagine because the key question foreshadows the resolution; i.e., what we see at the surface level is George fighting a bully. What we understand in our projections is how this will affect the chances of Marty getting his parents hooked up and getting back to 1985. The real story is arriving in our minds in subtext.

So, in summary, knowledge gaps through subplot are introduced when events in one plotline cause the audience to autonomously reconfigure their knowledge and expectations in another plotline. We use this audience behaviour to deliver information, but also, of course, to mislead and to set up our audience for future revelations, (they may or may not be right in their assumptions of what action in one plotline means to the development of another. I won't expand on this here. See the advice on using audience preconceptions from John Sullivan in the next section).

4.2.6   Knowledge gaps through implication and suggestion

This type of gap refers to the knowledge **derived** from an action or event, rather than directly from an action or event itself. A simple example would be the monster terrifying the occupants of the spacecraft in *Alien*. The monster doesn't actually make a physical appearance until three-quarters of the way through the film. Ninety percent of the time, its presence and awesome powers are all implied rather than spelled out, and we create in our own minds a perfect, totally terrifying monster as a result. Our own imagination, coupled with our personal insecurities, will do a far, far better job of building a monster that genuinely unsettles us than any purveyor of computer generated mayhem and teeth. For most of the film we see nothing but ceiling tiles rattling and images on radar screens, and because the knowledge is so lacking, we receive huge subtext through implication and we make the monster larger than life for ourselves.

These types of subtext are far more important for novelists, for whom direct access to the thoughts and true feelings of a character add a whole extra dimension to the writer's palette. A visual medium can work only with the actions of the players, and the thoughts and words must be interpreted. This is why the film of the book rarely satisfies – a great book gets us into the heads of the players and a film cannot easily do that.

As most of my examples are quite blatant in order to exemplify a point, let's use a subtle one to demonstrate knowledge gaps through suggestion. Picture the scene:

> A large, formal dining room in a well-off family home. Moroccan throw rugs on a parquet floor. Large bay window with velvet curtains. Tasteful lighting picks out antique wood furnishings.
>
> It is evening and the father, his wife and three children sit around the large oak dining table. They eat in tense silence. There is no sound but for the portentously slow tick... tock... tick... tock... of the grandfather clock. Nobody speaks. The cutlery clinks on the plates.
>
> Clink, chink. Tick... tock...
>
> The kids avoid eye contact. They look studiously at their plates.
>
> Nobody speaks until...
>
> "Potatoes," says the father brusquely. "Please."
>
> There is a pause whilst the rest of them look at each other to see who will fulfil the request. The potatoes are passed. The father serves himself. Silence descends once more. Tick... tock... tick... tock... Clink, clink. Swallow...

Unbearable, isn't it? Our brains are screaming that this isn't right. Normal families with kids don't act this way. Something is wrong, and we are desperate for a single clue – something – to which we can lock on; something that we can use to develop the story. We are so used to information gaps like this – in life and in story – that we know something is going on and we scour everything to get a handle on this wrongness and to fill the knowledge gaps. There *must* be something there. And we find it. Let me ask you a question about the above scene. Answer it in your mind before you turn the page... Don't think twice – don't read it again – just your first answer. Who is the bad guy around this table?

Don't turn the page until you've said the answer out loud...

That's right. The father. I drew your attention to him in the tiniest of ways. He did nothing wrong and there is no reason beyond this tiny focus and yet you locked on to him immediately and thought, 'that's our boy. There's something going on with HIM!' You may accuse me of cheating in the way I wrote it to take you towards him, but that's the whole point! You are the writer, and these tools are available to you. The father didn't do anything. None of them did. And this is the power that expert storytellers exploit. The reader or audience will be going wild to find the clues. If you give out the tiniest crumb, they are on to it like a shot and leading themselves up the path. And as consumers of story, we love it when a writer does this to us in such a way that we don't even know it is happening. Writers who expertly use the power of knowledge gaps through implication and suggestion create the stories with the greatest literary merit.

Whatever we show in the next scene the audience will instinctively connect the negative side of it to the father. A dead body. Stolen money. Whatever – they will link it to him. And don't forget, there are plenty of tools of implication and suggestion. The clothes someone wears could imply their honesty or piety or profession, riches, recent likely behaviour or criminal nature. The soundtrack or lighting can tip your audience towards a mood or characteristic. We know when we need to prepare to be scared because the music (or 'sound design', as they call it these days) tells us to. In the Wallace and Grommit adventure, *A Close Shave* we expect that Preston the dog is to be feared because he is sinister and surly – he looks like a Rottweiler – with a spiky collar; the mood darkens when he is on screen and the music becomes threatening. And of course, this doesn't have to be the truth; it can be a tool to mislead, and to cause your audience to project false impressions and project inaccurate future states.

Audience Preconception

Here is what John Sullivan said to me on the subject:

> In my stories I like to play on audience preconceptions a lot. The audience overlays an expectation on just about everything, so you can use this. For example, if you make your character really proud of his white suit and smart white shoes, then show a puddle outside on the road, the audience adds two and two... then of course he heads outside... directly towards the puddle... But you don't do what the audience expects, of course. You make him successfully step round the puddle and not get his suit all muddy. He walks on, very pleased with himself... and walks straight into someone and gets a coffee spilled all down it. People relentlessly try to put themselves one step ahead, and you can use that to keep the audience guessing.

This is using 'suggestion' as a tool of comedy. But he goes on:

> This doesn't apply only to comedy. Audience preconception works in any genre. Alfred Hitchcock said, "the monster isn't half as scary as the build up to the monster." A girl walking alone in a dark old house. The camera goes into close-up as she looks to the left and Hitchcock would deliberately put her off-centre, leaving the camera angle a tiny bit wide on the right so we subconsciously assume a hand is about to come in and grab her from behind her head on the right. Just in time, she'd swing round to the right and scream... and we scream... and there'd be nothing there. The girl breathes a sigh of relief. And we all breathe a sigh of relief with her... and a hand rushes in and grabs her from the left. Brilliant use of audience preconception to frighten six bells out of 'em.

So knowledge gaps are available not just in terms of what is genuinely happening and evident, but also through using the audience's innate tendency to project ahead and make assumptions about the future based on what they have already been fed. This tendency can, of course, be used to misdirect them.

4.2.7 Subtext through misinterpretation

Misinterpretation is another tool of comedy, but is equally used elsewhere, and is effectively the very definition of a knowledge gap, in that it highlights the exact moment at which a classic, character-driven subtext is driven in.

An event takes place, and through, for example, a misunderstanding on the part of the protagonist or misdirection on the part of the author (or indeed, any participant), the audience takes one interpretation and the protagonist takes another from the same event.

Subtext through misinterpretation is a common feature of P.G. Wodehouse humour. In the extract above from *The Inimitable Jeeves*, Bertie Wooster is having a conversation with Honoria about a chap who finds her attractive and would like to make a romantic approach to her. From that same conversation, as it is going on, we have three participants (Bertie, Honoria, the audience) and three interpretations. On the one hand, Bertie thinks that he is priming Honoria to be receptive to the advances of Bingo Little. On the other, Honoria believes that this conversation is a romantic overture from Bertie himself. We, the audience, know the truth – or at least, we think we do – and that puts us in a third position.

4.2.8 Knowledge gaps through subterfuge

Knowledge gaps are automatically a part of any form of subterfuge. They are implicitly achieved by ensuring that knowledge of a character's true agenda is denied to other characters who will be impacted by that agenda. In my children's story, *Clonk and the Birdman*, I have a sequence objective for a husband to build a plane. I made this plane's creation a subject of conflict, so the husband chooses not to tell his wife that he has lost his job and is now secretly building the plane when she thinks he is out earning money. This subterfuge means they can have actions and conversations that deliver the real story in subtext. When the husband says to his wife:

'No, no, no! You get yourself off to work. I'll sort the kids out some breakfast and get them off to school.' We know that he is really saying, 'Please leave soon so I can continue work on the flying machine I have hidden in the shed...'

Most people have secret agendas that they try to deliver without upsetting their loved ones or entering into confrontations if they can avoid it. This is the easiest way of creating a deep and long-lasting knowledge gap. Under such circumstances, subtext is unavoidable.

However, 'subterfuge' in these terms doesn't necessarily mean lies and deceit. It is just as likely to be implicit to the way we naturally proceed. In *Back to the Future*, Marty cannot tell anyone he meets along the way that he is a time traveller from the future. Similarly, whenever he is interacting with his parents, he cannot say that he is their future son. So, the story carries an ever-present knowledge gap – permanent subtext that pervades the whole story because of this subterfuge. Maybe this is one reason why *Back to the Future* is such a classic story. Whatever happens always happens in the context of this ever-present knowledge gap through subterfuge.

Many other classic stories have a pervasive element of subterfuge: every superhero has his mild-mannered alter ego, from Batman and Spider-Man to Captain Underpants and Billy the Cat. We know it, but the people he meets don't. Danny Wallace's *Yes Man* is always going to say 'yes' to any question or request. We know that, but the people he meets do not. In the film *Liar Liar*, we know that Fletcher Reede (played by Jim Carrey) is compelled always to answer truthfully. We know it, but the people he meets do not. In the book *Wise Guys*, by Nicholas Pileggi (who also co-wrote the subsequent screenplay for the film version, *Goodfellas*) we know throughout that the protagonist, Henry Hill, is a violent gangster. The people he meets around the town generally do not... In Ira Levin's *Stepford Wives*, we know that the husbands of the town of Stepford are turning all their womenfolk into submissive zombies. Newly arrived and independent-thinking Joanna does not know this – or of the danger that is approaching... In the story *School of Rock*, Dewey Finn (played by Jack Black) is an unemployed rock dude desperate for a job. He pretends to be his landlord, Ned Schneebly (played by the story's writer, Mike White), and takes on the teacher's job offered in a posh school. We know that he is not really Ned Schneebly, and as he teaches his class inappropriate rock dude principles, we know he is not a real teacher. The people around him, including the kids and the staff, do not. This knowledge gap through subterfuge makes for a classic and fascinating story.

The subterfuge is, in a sense, reversed in *The Truman Show*, in that it is only Truman who is lacking knowledge. Everybody else – all the other characters, the audience – the whole world – knows the truth. Only Truman himself is behind the curve.

Stories premised on a basic and pervasive 'knowledge gap' of this nature are almost always going to attract the right sort of attention from the business side of the creative industries. Anyone with a secret is an interesting subject for a story.

4.2.9   Subconscious aims

By the end of a good story, our protagonist will have perhaps gained more than he set out for, or got something different from that which he set out for, and changed or grown as a person as a result of his experiences.

Hercules was born half mortal. He set out on his labours in order to gain immortality and join his father Zeus in the kingdom of the Gods. However, having succeeded in all his tasks, when he was finally ready to take his reward and ascend into deity, he chose instead mortality and an earth-bound existence. He fought against Hades, Hydra, Gorgon, Cyclops and the rest of the gang, and when he finally got to the doorstep of immortality – the ultimate aim and the purpose of the quest – he turned it down. Why? Because the journey taught him that love is more important. He turned his back on all he had worked for – in order to live and die with the mortal woman he loved, Megara.

Granted, this is a Disney version of events, but this fact simply serves to show what a film company is looking for. Their interpretation delivers a classic story pattern whereby a protagonist has both a clear and stated target encapsulated in the key question, but also has a hidden or subconscious aim to which his drive for success in the presented world renders him blind. This is a form of subtext, whereby the entire subtextual story delivers a different resolution from that towards which the conscious or presented story was heading (i.e., the audience projected ending is whipped away at the last minute and replaces with an unexpected one, that can cause a re-evaluation of everything that has gone before).

When the protagonist is on the brink of the success he has fought against massive odds to achieve, the learning and growth he has undergone has changed him and he foregoes the goals he originally targeted because the process of getting there has caused him to re-assess his own values. In most cases, the original value is perfectly acceptable (in fact, often an aspiration we might share, such as the accumulation of wealth) but is forgone for a value that takes the protagonist up the hierarchy of needs. This is known as a Redemption Plot, and it generates a high quality ending and an extra dimension to the story and the protagonist. As we have discussed, most good stories show a clear character progression from one level of Maslow's hierarchy towards self-actualisation, and when this progression shifts from the subconscious aim through the telling of the story to the outcome at resolution we are greatly satisfied with the story.

4.2.10 Plot and character in subconscious aims

Most commonly, the primary plotline is 'event-driven'. It is more evident and conscious and deals with practicalities. The secondary plotline that nips in and becomes the overriding plotline at resolution is more 'subconscious'. It results from the character growth and the results of attaining higher principles from the learning gained through the events.

I am planning such an ending in my children's story, *Clonk and the Birdman*. George sets out to win the Birdman competition (practical target through events). However, through the difficult course of getting to the point where he could win, he learns a great deal about himself, his obsession and his feelings for the people closest to him. When he is within seconds of victory in the Birdman competition – a victory readily within his grasp – he forgoes his victory to fight for the woman and family he loves. Looking after our genes is more highly valued than looking after our selfish ambition, so deep audience satisfaction with the story is more likely.

This is just one component of an important structural element of a good story – the hidden or subconscious goal. Even *Back to the Future* – which has a very direct plot despite its complexity – has a hidden story delivered in subtext behind the presented one. As we know, Marty's aim was to get back to get back to 1985 – a practical, event-driven aim. What he achieved through the learning and character growth of his father, was self-actualised parents and a family (gene pool) that is superior to the one he left. *Back to the Future* has an ending with both the conscious plot (return to 1985) and the subconscious plot (improved quality of family) finishing in the positive, which is why we feel uplifted at conclusion.

Dickens' *A Christmas Carol* has fascinating events (a visitation on Scrooge by three ghosts) but the real story is about his character development into generosity of spirit. *Groundhog Day* has fascinating events (reliving the same day endlessly) but is ultimately about his character development into altruism and consideration for others. This pattern can be seen in many of the finest stories.

4.2.11 Knowledge gaps and metaphor

The Children's story, *The Ugly Duckling*, by Hans Christian Andersen, is apparently about a duckling that turns out to be a swan. But it is a masterpiece because it causes us to think about racism and segregation; self-image and confidence; pride and equality; kindness and cruelty. All that evocation in such a few words in a simple children's tale. Pure genius.

When we reached the end of *Lord of the Flies*, by William Golding, we had followed the textual adventure of a group of British schoolboys trying to survive on a desert island. However, when we completed the story at resolution, we realised we had actually learned important lessons about the fragility of civil society. The boys' experiences could be related to the problems between nations, and stern lessons learned for how society must control itself.

The 2005 French film, *Cache*, by Michael Haneke is, on the surface, about a French television presenter and his family being secretly watched and filmed by unknown persons. It focuses on the discomfort they feel from being watched, the impact this has on the family and how they deal with it. And yet, in metaphor it is a strong political indictment against French foreign policy and colonialism.

H.G. Wells' *The Time Machine* is (another) time travel adventure. But in metaphor, it carries a strong pro-socialist political message about the rise of capitalism and the exploitation of the workers.

George Orwell's *Animal Farm* is a story of animals taking over a farm and forming their own society. In metaphor, it shows us how a utopian society is made impossible by the corrupting nature of the very power necessary to create it. Wonderful.

Even the lightest of good stories will carry some form of deeper philosophical teaching sometimes over and above a life lesson for the protagonist, from *The Hare and the Tortoise*: 'slow and steady wins the day', to *Back to the Future*'s theme: 'if you put your mind to it you can accomplish anything'. *Back to the Future*'s metaphor is powerful enough to have us go forward from the adventure feeling that we, like George McFly, can take control over our lives, and not feel that we are simply victims of fate.

4.3 Knowledge gaps – any other business

Before we move on, I'd just like to touch on a couple of other points surrounding knowledge gaps and subtext.

4.3.1　Subtext and poetry

Now, I am not going to pretend for one second that I have any knowledge of poetry beyond the level around 'There was a young lady from Ealing…'. I can't trot out extraordinary and wonderful examples of the kind of amazing abstraction and allegory that goes on in the best poetry. All I do know is that it happens, and when it does, poetry provides us with the very finest examples of subtext through suggestion, implication, and metaphor. I would go as far as to say that the planting of knowledge gaps by suggestion, implication and metaphor is the very definition of great poetry, and those best able to deliver subtext in verse also turn out to be the best poets, but I really ought to talk to a poetry expert before making any strong statements.

I do know enough to give a small example. The following famous words by John Donne talk about bits falling off Europe and bells ringing:

> No man is an island, entire of itself;
> every man is a piece of the continent, a part of the main.
> If a clod be washed away by the sea,
> Europe is the less, as well as if a promontory were,
> as well as if a manor of thy friend's or of thine own were:
> any man's death diminishes me,
> because I am involved in mankind,
> and therefore never send to know
> for whom the bell tolls; it tolls for thee.

And this magic makes us think. And we somehow deeply understand, firstly, that each of us is an important component of corporate humanity, and, secondly, that it isn't just other people who die… our time on this earth is limited too. When one person dies, a little piece of us dies too.

Or something.

Even static art can do this. Envisage a painting of a large park in glorious summer sunshine. Playground. Jumpers for goalposts. Ducks on the pond. Café. Cyclists. Frisbee. Picnics. It seems like a standard sunny scenario, until you notice a young lady in the tennis court. She is dressed for tennis, but she is a lone figure. She leans on the fence of the tennis court as if trapped by it, racket down to the side, and she looks wistfully across at the children in the playground. Now you have found her in the picture, can you tell me about her life? Can you invent an entire back-story that is all about her? I'm sure you'll come up with the same as I did. She has no kids, and she desperately wants them. There's only so much tennis you can play in an unfulfilled life, and despite the money, time, parties – she wants children. Or is it just a painting of a park? Now do this for everyone you see in your day. The man sitting alone in the coffee shop. The girl on the bike. The woman at the chemist. Build their backstory, then ask yourself what it was about them that made you think the things you did... Then think of the power you can put into every image you project with your words – because your audience will fill in every knowledge gap you offer them with their own assumptions.

4.3.2   Does anyone really like Shakespeare?

No book on story principles would be complete without reference to Billy S, and for me, this section is where he can be explained and understood in ways that might mean something to you, particularly if you don't quite get him.

You might not particularly like Shakespeare, and you might wonder why he has such a reputation when his words appear to be gobbledegook and his stories so inaccessible. Well, actually, that's exactly why. He is known as a playwright, but his delivery is closer to poetry. His words need to be interpreted in order to make sense of them. In other words, there are knowledge gaps all over the place between what he says (the narration), what we make of it, and what he ultimately intends us to think and feel; i.e., the story is delivered in subtext. That's why people who put in the effort to work him out find him amazing. Everything has a hidden depth. Wandering around the works of Shakespeare is akin to being invited to take a walk in the Sahara Desert. No fun at all, until you make some effort, and discover entrances to underground caves full of hidden treasures. And the caves get lighter and richer the further in you go. Shakespeare's is the only writer who builds his stories this deeply in subtext. His genius is recognised as a playwright, but is actually for creating subtext.

So the answer to your dichotomy over how Shakespeare can be so lauded down the centuries, and yet feel like tripe is that if you put the effort into interpreting his words – if you look for the subtext – you will be rewarded in spades. Similarly, if you put the effort into great works of poetry, you will find rewards you could never have expected from skip-reading it. Shakespeare takes us to the edges of subtext in the sense that if he went any further, different people would interpret the content in vastly different ways, and the stories would fail. Some feel he has crossed that line, and perhaps the teams of academics, producers and directors who devote years to interpreting his meaning and intent are evidence of this. I disagree, because most people who put the effort into Shakespeare's work inevitably receive the same storylines. It is only in the detail that message and meaning are up for dispute.

4.3.3   Subtext and actors

A good technique for testing your writing for subtext is to imagine the time when you will have to work with actors. One look at any of the examples in this section and an actor would be rubbing his hands with glee. Good, solid subtext to deliver behind misleading words and indirect actions; three dimensional cause, effect, implication and suggestion.

Delivering knowledge gaps is what actors do that is special and difficult.

When actors assess a script in order to decide if they should take the role, the main thing they need to see is the subtext. Subtext is what brings characters to life; delivering subtext is what makes actors look good and they will give you a very hard time if your scenes – and particularly your dialogue – are 'on the nose'. Which would you prefer to act – a scene where you take your partner's fingers in your hands, look him/her in the eye and say, 'I love you, darling', and mean it sincerely, or a scene where you take your partner's fingers in your hands, look him/her in the eye and say, 'I love you, darling,' and the audience's mouths drop open because they know you are about to leave her for another woman? Clearly, the latter is packed with acting meat and story potential.

If your writing is surface level and predictable, it makes them look one dimensional and predictable and they never work again. They simply won't put up with it. Look at every scene and imagine having to act it. Would you be happy with the material you are asking them to work with? It's not a comfortable experience to have an actor come barging through the door and, in an emotional diva's tirade, accuse you of trying to ruin them. Prevention is definitely better than cure in these cases. Make it a part of your writing method to act the parts and speak the dialogue yourself at home. Don't be shy – get out of the chair, imagine you are the actor for the part, and go for it. If it is a novel, march around and speak it out loud, as you would read it on the radio. If it fails to satisfy and you can't work out why, it will be the lack of subtext, and you need to work on introducing the knowledge gaps that will give your dialogue and actions this third dimension. It is amazing the insight you will gain into your own abilities and the improvements you will make to your whole story as a result of this activity.

4.3.4   The shift to privilege

It is worth noting specifically that most new and aspiring writers find revelation subtext easier to write. Indeed, I think we have an instinctive bias towards revelation. Secrets are kept from the audience and the bangs come on revelation. This is fine, and works. However, the best stories have a balance of privilege and revelation, or even a bias towards privilege – i.e., telling the audience a lot more about what is coming up than an aspiring writer would naturally feel is correct.

If you look back at the Woodhouse extract, you will see that the audience is in a privileged position relative to Bertie Wooster throughout, and of the half-a-dozen subtexts, there was only the one revelation embedded in there to surprise us at the end (that Bingo wasn't around at all anymore – he was off falling in love with someone else). The main story was all in privilege form. Similarly with *Back to the Future*, we in the audience know about all of Marty's intentions the whole time. He plans to find the Doc, then they plan together to hit the bolt of lightning (they even make a working model and enact it – then they plan together how he will get his parents back together, then he plans – and even role plays – with his future father how George will win Lorraine's heart… It's all in privilege. It's not where the characters are trying to get to that makes the story interesting – we know exactly what is going to happen – it's how they get there.

It is very important to your maturity and authority as a writer than you find a balance of privilege and revelation in your stories.

4.4 Postscript

And finally on subtext, more for a laugh than anything else, I would like to present another wonderful scene. It didn't get a deal, it wasn't written by an acknowledged master, but it is delivered entirely in subtext. I have no idea who to acknowledge and thank for this masterpiece, but here it is for all to enjoy. This is a small ad from the classifieds section of a newspaper somewhere:

FOUND. DIRTY WHITE DOG. LOOKS LIKE A RAT.
IT'S BEEN OUT A WHILE. NO COLLAR.
BETTER BE A REWARD. TEL: 555 452596.

Masters of English devote decades of their lives to implying a subtext like that, and there it is delivered to perfection in twenty words. We have a character torn between his hatred for the dog and his urge to do the right thing and get it back to its owner. We have a mangy hound causing bedlam around his rescuer's house. We have a guy who is simmering with anger towards the original owner for not looking after the dog properly – he wants to give him a piece of his mind. We have a situation laden with conflict and emotion in twenty words, we can envisage what went before this ad was placed, and we can envisage interesting, conflict driven scenes when the ad is answered; and every bit of that underlying story is delivered in subtext. Brilliant.

Work hard on understanding knowledge gaps, how they deliver an underlying story and ensure subtext is present at all levels and in every scene of your story. Your stories will be fundamentally flawed without it, and will grip, engage and intrigue when it is there.

PLOT AND CHARACTER

A writer is a person for whom writing is more difficult than it is for other people.

Thomas Mann (1875 – 1955)

5   Plot and character

Most fine stories intertwine interesting events with a character's growth, and for most stories it is the character growth that is the more important. Story events are a vehicle for a character's journey. A story will often be described in terms of the events – *Back to the Future* is about a kid who goes back in time; *A Christmas Carol* is about a man visited by ghosts – but the real power of the story lies in the growth and learning of the characters *through* those events.

So this section is about character, but there is a critical link between the story events and the genuine character of your player(s), so we will also focus strongly on the ways in which plot and character are interlinked; specifically, arriving at the surprising conclusion that these two apparently separate criteria, plot and character, are actually one and the same thing. First, some background.

5.1   On raising emotion

Stories work when they stimulate our emotions. Combining a couple of dictionary definitions for 'Emotion', I have come up with this:

Emotion is a psychological state that arises spontaneously rather than through conscious effort. Feelings associated with aroused emotions include joy, fear, anger, hate, sadness, disgust, curiosity and surprise.

Every day we act out scripts in our lives. From the mundane: 'Getting Breakfast' script; the 'Journey to Work' script; the 'Going to the Supermarket' script, to the more interesting: 'First Date' script; 'Out on the Town With Your Mates' script; the 'Going on Holiday' script. Some scripts last decades ('The Relationship'), others a moment or two ('Using the Toilet'), others something in between ('The Holiday'). Every day is a potential adventure unfolding: the story of your life.

If you think for a moment about your daily scripts they are all largely predictable. If everything goes to plan, nothing in your 'Getting Breakfast' or 'Going to the Supermarket' script will be much different from how it was yesterday or last week, and no different from how we imagined it would be when you woke up this morning. Life is mostly like this for all of us. Everything we do follows a script and at every moment we are at different points through the cycle of any number of predictable scripts – routines – that do not surprise us. But... every single script carries the *potential* to depart from that predictability. And that's when it raises our emotions... and that's when it becomes a story.

Routines

Life 'scripts' that are highly predictable are called routines. We have an expectation for how every script will run before we embark upon it. On our daily commute we have a current state (at home) and our predicted goal state (at work) and we are very familiar with the actions we must take to get from former to latter. If we know the script very well and can follow its path accurately then this is a 'routine' which does not arouse emotions, either positive or negative. A routine is, in this sense, the opposite of a story.

However, if the script is new to us, or if the script deviates from the expected course, then our brain is set to work and we become aroused. We feel emotions for the whole time our brain is out of its routine groove... and this gives us a story to tell. We can recount to others what it was that stimulated an emotional response, and if we tell the story well, and if the listener can relate to the emotional experience, they will become engaged and will vicariously feel the same emotions.

I travelled on a commuter train recently. Lots of us were acting out the same 'Catching the 07.17 Brighton to London Train' script, but it meant different things to different people. For some it was a familiar script, enacted without the slightest emotion as the daily routine followed its usual course. These people read or worked at their laptops or dozed off, dribbling on the shoulder of the person next to them. The standard, daily grind. At the same time, for other passengers, this was not a part of their normal routine. One person I saw was starting a new job. Her brain was working hard as this new script unfolded. Her experience of the 'Catching the 07.17 to London' would be a story she would recount to her friends and family in the evening. It was an exciting, new script for her.

When we stopped at Gatwick Airport, a family of large Americans got on to the train with their luggage. They were simply ecstatic to be on the 07.17 to London. They were buzzing! Full of questions and interaction, they were absolutely thrilled by everything, from the look of the newspapers and the shape of the tickets to the passing cows in the fields. Whilst the commuter wouldn't tell his wife there were cows in the fields of Sussex, the Americans were full of it. They had a story to tell, because they expected London to be a big city, and here they were at London's Gatwick airport, and it had green fields with cows and countryside all around it. I listened in on their conversations and they were packed with excitement and even fear ("Y'all sure we're on the right train, Paw? This sure as hell don't look like no London I never saw!")

Even though you and I might know the 'Catching the 07.17 to London' script, we can relate to the emotional position of the Americans. I loved their presence and greatly enjoyed their emotional take on the journey; their 'story'. The thing to note here is that a story can only get a grip if it can get to the audience's emotions. My recounting of it to you now is only of interest because the emotional position of the Americans resonates with you.

There are three main ways a story separates itself from the normal routines and becomes potentially emotional:

An established script, but which the protagonist has not experienced before.

The audience may have experienced this script themselves, in which case they enjoy the recall of their own emotions (positive and negative) as the protagonist follows a known emotional path. This is why we love to lend a friend a book we've read, or take a friend to a film we have already seen, to enjoy it again through their eyes (and to enjoy it in a form where ALL the subtext is switched to privilege form, because we know it all in advance). Alternatively, even if it is an established script, the audience may not have experienced this script for themselves, in which case it works for them like a new script (see below). The emotion in any retelling of an established script comes from the characters, their reactions to what are new experiences for them, and the uniqueness in the personal detail of an otherwise well-trodden course. For example, how many stories are about the establishment or breakdown of relationships? Audiences love an original telling of a familiar, well trodden path.

An established script which takes an unexpected deviation from the normal course.

This is the most common source of 'new' stories. Many, many stories begin with a normal day and a normal person setting about their established everyday routine, until it takes an unexpected turn for the protagonist. When we set off on a normal shopping trip, and find at the checkout that our credit card is being refused, we have a deviation from the normal, established routine and a story to tell that evening about how we felt like a criminal, what the people around us thought and how it resolved in the end. At the fictional extreme, a deviation from the norm can take us to other worlds. Marty McFly begins *Back to the Future* as a young lad heading off for school. How far from the 'Going to School' script one can deviate is then demonstrated. The key point here is that the normality of the Act I setup allows us to relate to the protagonist and lock on to him in order to experience vicarious emotion on his unearthly journey when the script departs from the routine. We also know from the nature of the deviation from the norm, the protagonist's quest; what he has to achieve to get life back into balance.

A new life script. An event which is new to both protagonist and viewer.

There are very few genuinely new 'life scripts', and if it is a script that is so new that nobody has ever experienced it, an audience is unlikely to relate to it and feel emotional. A 'new' script works best when it takes people on, for example, a space adventure or to a sci-fi world where the rules are different. In these cases, it is important to maintain human elements that people can relate to, so you will find that the protagonist – even though he is battling aliens or reduced to miniature size or taken back in time – has a beating heart, faces human dilemma and is desperately trying to establish good human values over evil. A good story will reflect a character's learning and growth irrespective of how unearthly the story events are. *I-Robot* is a fine example of this working well.

In each case, the emotions of the viewer will be aroused as they relate to the experience of the protagonist.

5.1.1   The Grand Canyon effect

When people look over the edge of the Grand Canyon for the first time, their response is purely emotional. They cannot stop themselves from being absolutely staggered by one of the most powerful and memorable experiences of their lives. Bammo! Take that between the eyes, you small, pointless person! We've all seen a view before but... just, wow. And yet, within a few short minutes, these same people are looking at their watches and wondering what's for lunch. What on earth has happened?! The same staggering panorama, which only seconds ago made these people wet themselves, is suddenly no more powerful than the view across Hackney Marshes. What has changed?

The reason is that when our emotions are aroused, our brains are not entirely in control, and are working hard, sucking up information, desperate to gain full understanding of the new phenomenon that is unhinging us. We process new material very, very fast as a result of emotional circumstances, and as the brain begins to piece everything together and gain that understanding, the emotion recedes, until the point where the brain has a complete handle on matters. Once this has happened, the emotion is gone... and the situation has lost the mystery and wonder that disorientated us for those wonderful few seconds. This is why people find life gets more boring as they get older, because they find most circumstances no longer arouse their emotions as their brains become increasingly experienced. Sad, really, isn't it? Look at the veterans of the 07.17 Brighton to London train in the morning; crying out for retirement to rescue them from the early rise and this desperate commute. Then imagine what they were like when they were kids, the first time they ever had the excitement of getting up at 6.00a.m. to go catch a train...

Interestingly, then, in story (as in life) we are constantly gathering and interpreting information using our instincts to understand the current position and project to a desired future position. If the story is doing its job properly, this brainwork will arouse emotion. Even tiny gaps in knowledge have our brains casting around looking for answers. And don't forget, our brains are beyond supercomputers in power here, and we are working with feelings and ideas. The processing that our brains do in emotional situations is phenomenal. And it gives us a buzz, particularly if new understanding comes from the process. We've had an 'experience'. We love it. Every small gap in knowledge can work on us – what is the dice going to do? What's going to happen next in this football match? Why is that guy with all the tattoos crossing the road towards me? Everything that opens a key question that resonates with our emotional self is a driver for our lives at that moment. As story tellers we must use this to access emotion in our audience. But how?

Well, if we are putting all the right things into our events, we should be doing it anyway. Creating gaps in knowledge through characters taking meaningful decisions under the pressure of conflict and dilemma is the very essence of story, so we will take a closer look at conflict and dilemma in the next chapter. For the moment, in order to access emotion:

1. Events should create empathy with characters through the dilemmas they face and the knowledge they lack in order that their plight arouses vicarious emotions in the audience. Note that it is not the emotional *response* of the protagonist, screaming or crying, for example, that arouses our emotion. If we see someone crying, we don't start crying too. We ask, 'Why are you crying? What is the problem?' When we understand the emotional triggers – the events that caused the tears – then we can empathise with the response and can feel emotional ourselves.

2. Conflict is critical to story. Events must depict a change in the protagonist's fortunes from positive to negative, or negative to positive, to carry an emotional charge. This should be achieved by the protagonist taking action under pressure and through conflict with antagonistic forces ranged in opposition to the protagonist's desires.

5.2   *Plot-driven or character-driven?*

If you are like me, then at some point quite early on your journey to becoming a writer, you came across a discussion concerning whether a story should be 'plot-driven' or 'character-driven'. And if you are like me, you thought about it for a while and decided: 'what a pointless discussion! You need both! You can't have characters without giving them things to do and you can't have events without characters to act them out. You have to have both – it's bloomin' obvious!' And you wondered why the question ever came up.

Then you realised that the discussion doesn't go away. It is endlessly scrutinised in high places. And you asked yourself if there was something more to it. So you dug a little deeper, and next found a discussion amongst the egg-heads, telling you that character *is* plot, and that plot *is* character, or that the plot is a framework in which the characters climb around, and the actions of the characters build that framework (which is plot) and so on like this. And if you are like me, you didn't understand that either.

I honestly didn't understand what the fuss was about for years and years. It drove me nuts trying to make out why it was so deeply discussed and what it was the world was struggling to get across to me. But I think the penny has finally dropped now, and I hate to say it, but character *is* plot, and plot *is* character, and yes, it is important —critical, even —that you understand this relationship, so let me see if I can explain it any more clearly than those who tried to get the thing across to me.

So you are unlikely to understand the next two paragraphs, but by the end of this chapter, you *will* understand these two paragraphs. I promise. Here we go, then:

> **Plot is character, and character is plot, because as soon as a character takes a meaningful action, they are driving your <u>plot</u> *whether you like it or not*. Conversely, as this linkage works in two directions, as soon as an event happens which elicits a meaningful reaction from your protagonist, then his <u>character</u> is developing in the eyes of the audience *whether you like it or not*.**

Note that it is not the event which reveals a protagonist's character, but his reaction to the event. The action he takes defines his character. Similarly, it is not the event which drives the plot (as you might expect), but the action taken by the character that defines the event, and drives the plot.

Confused? Let's step through some explanation, and then come back to these paragraphs at the end. If we take the two extremes, we get actions detached from characters and characters detached from actions. Let's begin from these extremes and work our way towards where they join in the middle.

5.2.1   Action without character

There are three levels of action without character, all of which are bad for your story.

1. At the blatant end, we have a plot event with no character involvement whatsoever. Lightning strikes a tree in a remote area of the Australian outback. So what? It's not a story because no reaction is required of an emotional protagonist. This is the starkest example of action without character. This is not a story. This is a screensaver.

2. In the middle ground, we have an 'emotionally detached' action. If you watch the news and see that someone was killed in New York yesterday, you are unlikely to lose any sleep. This is surely a dramatic event, with high emotional potential, but it will not generate much of an emotional response. Why is this? Someone's personal script has taken them to a death that made the news, and yet it remains largely meaningless to you. The reason it washes over you is because you are running your personal 'Watching the News' script, not your 'Death and Grieving' script. The event is meaningless because you are not emotionally connected with the individuals on the news; they have no character in your eyes. We haven't been part of the 'Act I setup' before the tragic event, so we don't empathise. It is an action without

character. We must develop the character of the individual before his death for it to become emotionally meaningful. For a story event to work, the audience must have an emotional connection with the character involved.

3. If we increase the known character, we increase the emotion. Let's say we find out that John Lennon has been shot in New York. This is a person we 'know'; he has affected our lives; we have been through his Act I and Act II, and now relate to the tragedy at climax. We see him as a peace-lover and artist. We feel strongly that this is a terrible event. We turn up the television to hear the details and we will talk to our friends about it and discuss how we feel. Suddenly, our emotional connection raises our interest. If we increase the known character further, we increase the emotion. Look at the emotion on the faces of the friends and relatives of the deceased in New York as they experience the same death we are experiencing, but with a different level of emotional involvement.

4. The most subtle example of action without character actually happens rather a lot. A character takes an action, but it is not a <u>meaningful</u> action, because there is no dilemma riding on his decision to act. For an action to be meaningful, it has to bring out the genuine character of the player. Failure to recognise this is certainly one of the most common mistakes writers make. They provide their characters with challenges – car chases to win, love lives to agonise over and bad guys to overcome – but their decisions to drive recklessly, leave their husbands and shoot up bad guys are not difficult decisions to make. Because if the character is, for example, Rambo, we know he will 'decide' to kill the next enemy soldier to come storming over the hill, and the one after that, and the one after that, but these are not difficult decisions for him to take – they involve no dilemma – so these 'actions' carry little or no emotional charge for the audience. Yes, there is conflict, but that isn't enough if the response to that conflict is one-dimensional, obvious, and involves no dilemma. In order for his actions to be meaningful, the character must face difficult choices. He must be tested and a decision must be made that could have severe consequences if he gets it wrong.

We will return to this later in **Chapter 6 – Conflict and antagonism**. For the moment, take it that meaningful actions are those taken by characters under pressure of conflict causing dilemma.

5.2.2   Character without action

From the opposite end of the argument, if you have a character without any actions, you have a pointless scene and a crying need for a dustbin. For instance, let's say we are shown a picture of a man. So what? Until he does something, we don't know anything about him. Let's dress him up as a policeman. OK, so now we have some *characteristics* as our brains overlay stereotypical presumptions about what makes up 'Policemen', but beware: this is still an individual without *character*.

Characteristics do not equate to character

Characteristics are just the wrapping. We have dressed our player as a policeman, but we don't know if this person is courageous, slovenly, extrovert, alcoholic or a good father. We don't even know if he is a criminal or not! Come to think of it, we don't even know if he is truly a policeman... (or even truly a man!). Only his actions can reveal these things. What he does will define his character. And guess what: what he does – the actions he takes – instantly becomes the plot (whether you like it or not).

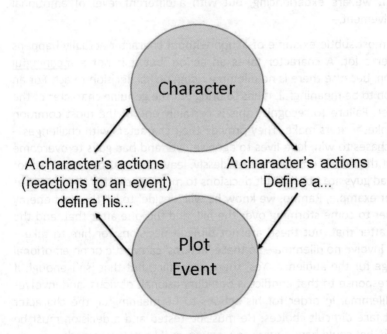

So we have a circular definition that shows that the actions of the characters define both the plot and the character.

A player's character is only defined by his actions.
The plot is defined only by the actions taken by the players.

The plot is defined by the actions taken by the players whose true character is defined by these same actions which define the plot which is defined by the actions taken by the players whose true character is defined by the same actions which define the plot which is defined by the actions taken by the players whose true character is defined by the same actions which define the plot which is defined by the...

Both character and plot are defined by the actions taken by the players.

Why is this important to you?

Creative writing classes often focus on descriptions. Endless exposition and prose that is totally devoid of character or plot. This is all well and good, as long as the teacher is sure to tell his victims that this is worthless as far as story is concerned. Its only validity is as an exercise that is not part of genuine story development. It's rather like doing scales on a piano – it has technical value, and it's great exercise, but it's not the same thing as playing a song, and it certainly isn't composition. Do it, of course, because it is good for you and your ability, but be warned: description for its own sake contributes not a jot to story.

Similarly, writers are advised to make a list of their characters and what they are like. The literature tells you to 'know them' as if they are family. To define them from birth – their childhood experiences, their schools, their house moves, their siblings – everything. For each one we must think long and hard about what these people are like as 'characters', and list their traits and attributes, from their physical characteristics to their likes, dislikes, allergies, toughness, weaknesses, ancestors; how they feel about the other characters around them, what their pose is towards life events, what they eat, what sort of sex they like and so on. Again, this is useful, and I'm not saying you shouldn't do it, but these activities should come with a health warning: characters that are fixed in advance can badly damage your plot!

You cannot possibly define your characters before you know what they are going to *do*.

Only the actions your protagonist takes – specifically those actions taken under pressure and when facing dilemma – will define his character, so basing a character on the hilarious bloke at work or the eccentric Greek at the kebab house simply will not work. It will serve only to frustrate you when the character doesn't naturally lend himself to the actions required and vice versa.

The problem writers stumble into here is that they have a character they have grown to know and spent a year defining. They also have a plot they have mapped out to the finest detail. They then find that the way the character wants to behave, if he's true to himself, is not helpful towards a plot which needs a different character to drive it believably. The story is compromised from the outset because the character is not credible in taking the actions the plot demands.

So, returning to our starting point, plot is character, and character is plot, because as soon as a character takes a meaningful action, they are driving your plot *whether you like it or not*. Conversely, as soon as an event happens which elicits a meaningful reaction from your protagonist, then his character is developing in the eyes of the audience *whether you like it or not*.

Note that it is not the event which reveals a protagonist's character, but his reaction to the event. The action he takes defines his character. Similarly, it is not the event which drives the plot (as you might expect), but the action taken by the character that defines the event, and drives the plot.

So, yes, do map out the character of your players, and yes, do map out the sequence of events that comprise your plot, but do this as an ongoing and, as far as possible, retrospective and background exercise, allowing both plot and characters to change and grow as each influences the other.

The practical point of all the above is that we effectively have to develop both plot and character *at the same time and as the same thing*. The starting place can be either plot events or character arcs, depending upon which is the subject of your inspiration, and we will look into both of these things shortly. If you have plot events that do not elicit character actions, ask why they are there. If you have character actions that do not move your plot forwards in the direction the plot must go, ask why they are there.

I would go further and say that I now find that it is only when my stories have plot and character that are one and the same thing that they really work. It's essential. And the key lies in conflict. Conflict forces your players to take action under pressure. Conflict forces the characters into actions which define both their character and the plot. So let's take a closer look...

6   Conflict and antagonism

The life blood of story is conflict. I do not exaggerate here – the term 'life blood' is chosen carefully. Because without conflicts that force our characters to make choices under pressure, we simply do not have a story. Characters have to make difficult decisions if your story is going to grip, and conflict is what makes these decisions intriguing.

Conflict is defined, for our purposes, as the placing of two sets of aims in opposition to each other, only one of which can win out. Commonly, this places the aims of the good guy in opposition to the bad guy, but, as we shall see, there are several other places to find usable conflict. Before we talk about what conflict is, let's have a few words on what conflict *isn't.*

Writers often confuse 'conflict' with a 'really tough challenge', and it's very important to distinguish between the two. If we offer a mountaineer the challenge of climbing a mountain, we are not surprised when they enthusiastically take up that challenge and we don't fear for them daily on their journey. We know they are professional, and we find no anxiety in their decision. Yes, it is a dangerous journey, and yes he is risking his life to take up the challenge, but there is no dilemma here in the decision. A mountaineer *chooses* to climb mountains and we recognise the joy for them in taking this course of action. It's a really tough challenge and there is apparent conflict – man against mountain – but, for him, it's a no-brainer. He may face lethal dangers, but he will approach the task professionally, and feel thoroughly fulfilled when he comes out the other end. To create real conflict, we have to extend the decision to ask ourselves, 'what is the cost of making this decision?' 'What are the alternatives?' And, 'what risk does he take in making a choice?' This is not the risk that is associated with the choice he takes. This is the cost involved in taking one action over another. Let's introduce some triangulation.

6.1   Conflict triangulation

As we are, then, the mountaineer has to choose to climb the mountain or not. If he does, he must risk death on a mountain because the weather is atrocious, conditions are impossible and he will almost certainly die. If he doesn't...? Well. He'll stay safely at home and put his feet up. There is no choice of evils. No dilemma. He may be a mountaineer but he's not a fool. It's too dangerous, so he'll leave it a couple of weeks whilst the weather clears up; then it will still be a challenge, but there's no real conflict. But how about this: 'the mountaineer has to choose to climb the mountain or not. If he does, he risks death on a mountain because the weather is atrocious, conditions are impossible and he will almost certainly die. If he doesn't... his climbing partner, stranded near the summit and with a broken leg, will certainly die.'

Now we will learn something of the true character of our mountaineer. Will he listen to the weathermen telling him that the conditions are so bad out there that he will die before he gets near his partner? Will he listen to his wife, who says she can't stand it anymore, and will leave him if he doesn't recognise his duty to her and his children and turn away from risking his life on a futile rescue mission? Will he heed the solemn pact he had with his climbing partner that each will leave the other and save themselves if one becomes a life-threatening liability? Or will he risk his own life and the wellbeing of his wife and children to save his friend because he couldn't live with himself if he didn't at least try?

Now both options have a cost and both have a benefit. And he has to make a choice between them – one or the other. Risk his own life or let his buddy die. It is this triangulation of the conflicts – the cost involved in making one choice and thereby being unable to take another – that turns a challenge into a conflict which demands the true character of the individual to come to the fore, and for <u>meaningful</u> action to be taken.

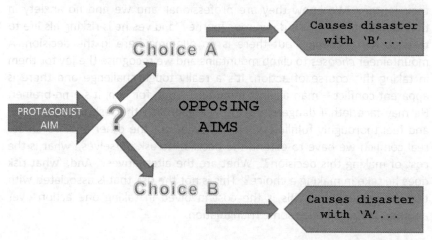

A sports star takes drugs to improve his performance in the final of a competition (a moral dilemma). If he is insecure about whether he can win without drugs, and confident he will get away with it, this might be an easy decision for a mildly dishonest man to make. So the writer triangulates this by ensuring there is a drugs committee in the mix who will be testing him as soon as the race is over. The sportsman is faced with making a decision – to dope or not to dope? – but whichever he chooses will prove to be a catalyst in another area. Salve his moral self by resisting the drugs – and lose the race. Take a gamble and a mouthful of luminous pills to win the race – and he's in trouble with his moral self and the drugs authorities. Now let's give character to this triangulation. Say the sports star takes the drugs because his girlfriend works for the drugs test committee and it is she who will perform the drug test. Would he put her under this pressure? If he does, what will she do? She now has a relationship conflict to set against her professional integrity. Will she be professional and honest and nail him for his cheating... and probably lose the relationship? Or will she falsify the results, secure his love and their financial future by ensuring his victory? Now she is worried about their relationship. Does he really love her, or will he cast her aside as soon as he has his gold medal? And so it goes on. It's suddenly a lot more interesting than the simple decision to cheat or not, and notice how the true characters come to life. The (re)actions of the players (to cheat or not, to show loyalty or not, to be subservient to the demands of the other or not, to be professional or not...) define their characters, because these actions are taken under pressure of conflict. And don't forget that the actions the players take also define the storyline. Suddenly, fascinatingly awkward choices have to be made by players under pressure, and our story springs into life in front of us. Now we are really writing a properly motivated story...

Stories result from characters being forced to take decisions under pressure.

Example

The series of slasher/horror films, beginning with *Saw* in 2004, directed and co-written by James Wan and co-written and starring Leigh Whannell, are entirely built on wonderful, awful, terrible, fantastic conflict triangulations. A protagonist will find himself, for example, invited to rip open the body of a living but drugged person in order to find a key to a padlock in their intestines. Clearly, nobody in their right mind would do this. They would just find some other way of getting the padlock off. So the writers triangulate. The padlock secures a bomb to the head of the protagonist. If he doesn't get it unlocked and off within a time limit, his head will be blown off. The decision must be made: kill another, fillet their stomach and rummage around for a key... or accept imminent death by cranial explosion...? As the story develops, it transpires that most of the players are entangled in similar extreme triangulations, requiring them to engage in the goring of others to save themselves. The entire story is built on these types of unbearable conflicts. A truly fantastic story, the power of which lies primarily in the ability of the writers to triangulate conflicts. You possibly don't like gory horror, but I have to say, the *Saw* series of movies are great stories.

So where can we find conflict? Let's take a look at all the areas where we can find conflict and run through some more examples.

6.2   Levels of conflict

Conflict exists on four levels. Most stories focus on one or two of these, the very best stories include inter-related plots on ALL these levels. Such stories keep our minds working overtime; a plot line on one level is impacted by the actions resulting from the plot line on another level, and our brains are constantly challenged to try and assess the consequences of one choice against the consequences of another for our hero (i.e., we feel emotional. It's a winner).

The conflict levels are:

6.2.1 Internal (Accessible)

The protagonist has inner conflict. Perhaps he is deluded, riddled with guilt, or racked by self-doubt (like George McFly). The decisions such a protagonist has to make are in conflict with his own actions and inner beliefs. Often a character is struggling with his head over his heart, or, like our druggy sportsman, with the likelihood of gaining a benefit in life but having to go against his own morals to do it.

In the film story, *Brick Lane*, Nazneen (played by Tannishtha Chatterjee) is frozen into stasis by her internal daemons. She struggles to reconcile the guilt she feels as a result of her upbringing in Bangladesh and her Muslim religion against the prevailing western culture in her imposed home town of London. The British cultural tide is sweeping her children along and offering her temptation and opportunity. She wants what she sees other women have in this culture – a job, independence, romance, freedom. She must establish her place in her new world without losing everything she holds dear (including her mind). And her husband is strongly against the prevailing culture and she will anger him if she doesn't remain subservient. Is she strong enough (weak enough?) to choose to hold true to her cultural standards from Bangladesh, or succumb to the temptations on her doorstep... Something has to give...

These are also known as 'accessible' conflicts, because they are entirely within the control of the protagonist.

6.2.2 Relationship (Partially controllable)

Relationship conflicts are conflicts in which the protagonist is able to have a strong influence on events because the conflicts are between him and someone with whom he is directly involved on a personal level. Again, the basic 'head on' conflict might be between the protagonist and the forces of opposition, but this should be triangulated to create dilemma, so, for example, taking action to address a conflict with your boyfriend might worsen matters with your husband. Similarly, addressing a conflict on one level can have an unexpected impact in another. Our druggy sportsman might take a decision to obey his moral self (internal conflict) and not take the performance enhancing drugs. His girlfriend might not like this. She could unexpectedly dive in and rant, 'you'd better take those drugs buddy, or I'm off. I'm not marrying a loser, and I can fix it for you to win.' (Relationship conflict.) Now what is he going to do?

In *Brick Lane* it is clear to see how, when Nazneen is required to make a decision in terms of her relationship with her husband, Chanu (Satish Kaushik), the stakes are high. The family and all the family relationships will be thrown into turmoil if her actions compromise her cultural values. This triangulates beautifully with the conflict that we know exists for her internally. If she takes the desired action in her relationship conflict she compromises herself in her internal conflict, and vice versa. What will she do?

This is a 'partially controllable' conflict because the protagonist has a fifty percent stake in the relationship at the centre of the conflict, and therefore has a level of control over the outcome.

6.2.3 Institutional (Little control)

Often conflict is found in the relationship between an individual and the wider world beyond their close relationships and, most importantly, beyond their direct influence. The corporation you work for or a hospital treating your loved one might have such an influence. Equally, a policeman, doctor or judge. Or beyond this to the decisions made by the taxman or the courts, a publisher (one close to my heart, there) or football team, a betting shop (another there, I think) or school, a TV show or pub – any number of individuals or organisations with which you are not 'close' in terms of the control you can exert over their actions, but from which there are consequences you might suffer, can throw horrible problems your way which cause dilemma and conflict. Once again, it is clear to see how these factors can overlap with both Relationship and Internal factors. Nazneen is in constant conflict with the UK culture, which offers her opportunity and yet tears her apart internally. She gets work (against her husband's wishes, and the dictate of her culture) and this leads to an affair with a man who turns out to be a leader of a radical Muslim group. Her conflict with and through this group is an example of Institutional conflict, as is her conflict with UK culture and her workplace. Can she resist the passion that the group and the affair spark in her heart?

Think of the number of stories based on a protagonist fighting a faceless and relentlessly single-minded organisation that is unjustly damaging him: The invisible authorities in *The Prisoner*; Harrison Ford fleeing from the FBI as he tries to prove his innocence in *The Fugitive; No Way Out; Coma; Marathon Man; The Bourne Identity* and many, many more stories which use the relentless power of a remote institution to provide faceless forces of antagonism with which the protagonist cannot negotiate.

Often the resolution to such a conflict comes from the protagonist finding the tiny exposure the institution has left by which it can be accessed; the 'little control' that the protagonist has over events is targeted, found, prized open and used to win out.

6.2.4 External and coincidental (No control)

The widest level of conflict comes from factors over which the protagonist has no control whatsoever. In simple terms this means the impact brought to the story by, for example, the weather, disease, acts of God, accidents and the like. It also covers anything out of his control but slightly more subtle, such as acts by uninvolved characters or entities, such as a car crash or a robbery. A rule of thumb to bear in mind here is that plot lines that resolve because of some coincidence are generally unsatisfactory. Plotlines must resolve through positive character action or your audience will feel cheated, so be very careful not to let something random and out of the protagonist's control magically sort things out for him.

However, good use of coincidental factors can be very powerful indeed, particularly as part of the setup. The film *Meet Joe Black* had Joe Black (Brad Pitt) knocked down by a vehicle. It came out of nowhere and was completely unexpected; it took place near the beginning of the story in an amazingly powerful piece of cinema that shook us to our roots. This coincidental factor was a powerful and memorable inciting incident. (Shame about the rest of the film, though.) *Groundhog Day* simply couldn't have happened without all that coincidental snow. The entire film *Castaway* with Tom Hanks was built primarily on conflict at this coincidental, uncontrollable level – a plane crash, and remote island survival. Abrupt global cooling was the basis for the film *The Day after Tomorrow*. Note though, that these coincidental factors were not a part of the story resolution. Indeed, they are often the cause of the problem, and reaction to the coincidental conflict is a primary driver for the story action.

For the moment, let's take a look at *Toy Story* for examples of conflict at all levels. It's an interesting story to examine for two reasons:

- There is no bad guy. The conflict is all contrived with the additional limitation that you cannot terrify the under-5s with serious forces of evil.

- Conflict takes place on all four levels. Most 'classic' stories are found to have all forms of conflict, beautifully entwined. *Toy Story* is a fine example.

Did you say: "a story with four levels of conflict and no bad guy?!" How did they do that?

Good question. A fine story requires forces of good and bad. Nine times out of ten, we will find ourselves a protagonist and sling problems and dilemma at him through conflict with the antagonist. A good guy and a bad guy. The best children's films make a 'bad guy' out of a 'misguided' good guy, so they can learn their lessons and thereby banish the 'evil'. Take *Mary Poppins*. The 'bad guy' is made out of a totally benign and loving – but misguided – father; a city banker who has forgotten how to live in the here-and-now, enjoy his life and play with his children. He is in conflict with his own up-tightedness, and the house is on edge with the discipline and tension that accompanies the father when he is around. Mary Poppins, Gawd bless 'er, shows us the right way to be. She gets much better control and discipline but within a context of fun and happiness.

In climax, the behaviour of his children puts the father under massive pressure to explain himself to the grey suits at work, and show his rigid professionalism or lose his precious job in the bank. He makes his decision, casts off his boring banker's mantle, and goes dancing off with a street full of chimney sweeps to go fly a kite with his kids. They all live happily ever after. Brilliant. He was never really a bad guy – he was a misguided good guy – but he represented the antagonistic need of the story perfectly, until excellent character growth and learning took him to a new level of understanding and the story was complete. (It didn't show the subsequent home repossession, marriage breakdown and slide into alcoholism that led the father to become a homeless crack addict wandering joblessly round the streets drinking Special Brew, but there you are. This is a kids' film...) Anyway: *Toy Story*.

6.2.5   *Toy Story* – relationship conflict

In *Toy Story* the main conflict is at the relationship level between Woody and Buzz Lightyear. Buzz is a modern, attractive toy. His arrival on the scene causes instant conflict as Woody tries to maintain his position as leader of the toys, and Andy's favourite, in the rush by everyone else to admire Buzz and all his digital gadgetry. This is the key question raised: "Will Buzz replace Woody?" and Woody is under pressure. Their relationship is just like that between two children – argumentative, combative and full of visible relationship conflict. Can children and parents relate to this? Oh, yes.

6.2.6   *Toy Story* – internal conflict

Both Woody and Buzz have internal conflict. Woody is **insecure**; desperate to maintain his position as Andy's favourite and to remain the leader of the toys, and he is considering breaking his own moral code and 'being bad' to regain the status quo. At the turning point that launches us into Act II, Andy is going out with his mum. He is under instruction to 'bring just one toy'. He is coming upstairs and Woody only has a second to act to make sure it is he who is chosen. (He has to make a decision under pressure.) He doesn't want to do something morally wrong (internal conflict) but can't resist it. He will 'accidentally' push Buzz down behind a desk so Andy will not be able to find him, and will take him, Woody, instead. The ruse goes wrong. Instead of falling behind the desk, Buzz is knocked out of the window, falls twenty feet to the ground and disappears. Other toys saw what happened and suddenly Woody is not only losing his status as Andy's favourite, he also stands accused and mistrusted by his own gang. Far from respecting him as their leader, his friends now think he is a murderer. Woody faced internal and relationship conflict. He took action under pressure to fix it all, but it didn't work – it made life much more difficult indeed. This is the inciting incident that launches *Toy Story* from the setup of Act I into Act II.

Buzz also has internal conflict in the form of **delusion**. He believes he is a real space ranger, and despite all Woody's efforts to convince him that he is just a toy, his delusion drives events. Indeed, his delusion gives Buzz his confidence and superiority, his reason for existing, his motivation for all his decisive actions and leadership qualities (actions driven by character). The conflict comes when he starts to realise that maybe he is a toy after all. His entire world falls apart as he struggles mentally with the situation. His collapse from leadership and confidence comes at precisely the wrong moment for Woody, who needs those qualities for both of them to escape. Buzz's capitulation to this inner conflict has a profound, negative and unexpected impact on the Institutional conflicts Woody is trying to deal with (escaping from Sid's house). Suddenly, Woody can't get away – and not only that, he has to carry Buzz, whose confidence has left him now he realises he is only a toy.

6.2.7   *Toy Story* – institutional conflict

At the institutional level, Woody and Buzz are toys trying to get by in the human world, so institutional conflict is a rich vein of material for the writers. The toys find themselves up against a plethora of forces over which they have very limited control, requiring them to make good decisions under pressure. Examples include Sid and his dog; traffic; Andy and his friends – indeed, all human life; doors and machines; the other gang of toys at Sid's house, and so on.

6.2.8   *Toy Story* – external conflict

At the coincidental level, there is also major conflict. Woody and Buzz are lost in the big wide world and trying to find their way home to Andy's house, battling major problems with geography. Even when they find themselves close – inside the house next door – they have to battle principally against huge uncontrollable factors to get back home again. Andy's birthday party is a coincidental factor (indeed, it is why the conflict, in the form of Buzz, arrived in the first place), as is the house move (placing them in conflict with a time limit ticking down on them – that is also out of their control), so is Andy's visit to Pizza Planet (remember these are coincidental factors – out of control in Woody's story even if they are manageable in Andy's world). The house move provides a key component of the climax. Just as they are about to make it back home, they find 'home' is moving in the form of a removal van. It seems that, yet again, all their superhuman efforts to get back have been foiled because the place they have been striving to get back to is no longer the right place to be. They have to raise themselves to even greater efforts to finally overcome the problems railed against them. This 'quest to get home' is not the main story element, but dominates Act II. This is, again, very clever, because all children will relate to the 'evil' that is to be lost and unable to find the way home, and yet this is not in the pure sense a 'bad guy'.

Even the weather gets involved – the rain and storm cause Sid to delay exploding Buzz until the following morning, leaving all night for Woody and Buzz to take critical life-saving actions. There is also an inopportune gust of wind (caused by a passing car) that extinguishes the last match – the one that was about to save them.

In the end, positive protagonist efforts resolve all the conflicts completely. Woody was not replaced by Buzz, but Woody was not rewarded for his bad actions – he was rewarded when he became a good and loyal friend – a strong moral message invisibly driving the character growth and therefore the whole story and giving it a huge third dimension. Buzz is no longer deluded. He is reconciled with the idea of being a toy and values himself for what he is, not what he wishes he was; further great character growth and a valuable moral lesson. The quest to get home was successfully accomplished, but look how it happened. All the time that Woody and Buzz were in conflict – particularly in self-centred conflict which they tried to resolve in selfish ways by each trying to dominate the other – they couldn't get anywhere. As soon as they started to work together as a team, they got the success they needed. Their behaviour was the ultimate bad guy, and once they had overcome that, they won out magnificently. Again, strong lessons being learned through the **themes** of *Toy Story* – the life lessons: be comfortable with who you are; cooperation beats selfishness.

It is worth noting in the context of our 'psychology and stories' discussion earlier, that we said all bad guys are egocentric, selfish and driven by a clinical self aggrandisement to the detriment of wider society. All good guys are altruistic and fighting for a moral imperative and a greater good that will help all of us climb the hierarchy. In *Toy Story*, Woody and Buzz 'learn' (and implicitly, 'teach') this lesson as they grow from the selfish position to the cooperative. They are, themselves, effectively negative bad guys when they are selfish, and the world fixes up when they become more society-appropriate. This cleverly uses *the characteristic itself* as the bad guy, but placed into the character of a known good guy rather than having a big scary bad guy display it. The essential character growth that defines great stories is there in spades as the pair make their journey from self-centred and ego-centric to co-operative and generous of spirit.

6.3   Practical application

In summary, look for simple conflicts with which people can relate, then where possible, intertwine them with other story events to make them more complex, and triangulate them as often as possible to give your protagonist dilemma, consequences of actions and a choice of evils (or irreconcilable goods) wherever you can. When the protagonist takes action to resolve a conflict it should result in an unexpected outcome – not as the audience predicted or the protagonist planned – and one which, generally, makes life even more difficult, or at least different from expectation. Think beyond your first idea. The first solution to enter your head could be the perfect answer, but it might equally be a cliché that you are capable of topping, and topping again to come up with something truly fresh and original. This in turn will open up your story to whole new possibilities.

If your story is short, or you recognise that it is lacking in conflict, or you need other plot strands against which you might triangulate your conflict, look for conflict on all four levels to find ways of introducing some meat for you to work with. Take any event and try to see how it could be developed in different types of conflict. For example, something as simple as 'The Visit to Pizza Planet' sequence of *Toy Story* can be viewed from any conflict angle. It is an external conflict to Woody, who has no choice but to go there, it is partially controllable to Andy (if he didn't want to go, he would enter into a relationship conflict with his mum over it), and fully controllable to Andy's mum. If she didn't want to go, she would have internal conflict on her levels of assertiveness – go to keep her son happy, bowing to his pressure, or assert herself because, say, she can't afford it. To create institutional conflict with Pizza Planet, we could put into the story that they had been barred last time, but decide to go anyway and try to get in. Additional relationship conflict comes from the presence of Sid who is already there. It is that easy to find possible storylines by playing with conflict possibilities at the different levels.

This said, note the use of words above like 'where possible', 'might' and 'generally'. Not every conflict can be triangulated or made beautifully complex. Not every outcome can be unexpected or naturally make life worse. Don't force these things – look for *opportunities*, but these are not 'rules'. Don't bend your story out of shape just to crowbar these things in. Use your knowledge of these elements to spot the opportunities, to intertwine the events of plot and subplot, and to give your creative mind focused and directed food for thought. You will know when it is right.

6.4   The antagonist

If there's one thing novice writers get wrong more than anything else, it's the bad side of their story. Why? Because we are good people. We've never been murderers or rapists or global dominators or political underminers or manipulative psychopaths or any of the other species of evil that we end up writing about. I would go further: as writers, we are probably even more pacific and sensitive than the average person and even less capable of handling confrontation. We don't like evil in our lives, so we instinctively want to save our good guys from grief and give our bad guys a hard time even when they are fictional! We are taught to write from the heart, so we do. The result is that from page one, we are starving our bad guys of the oxygen they need for success... and instantly consigning our scripts to the bin as the forces of antagonism are reduced to nought in the eyes of our audience.

Unless you have suffered yourself, doing justice to the bad guys in your story is not going to come naturally and you will need to work ten times harder than the writers who have felt it for themselves and can bring that suffering to life in their work. So you must use all your energy and imagination to make your forces of antagonism convincing, and your bad guy bad. Get right into him and let him take you over. Somewhere in your pure heart is a little black spot. The bastard you could have been if your life had been different. Try to connect with it. You've been resentful. You have been jealous. You don't like to admit it, but you have manipulated. You've felt hatred. You know someone you could have murdered, even if only in your most secret and darkest moments. Try to scare yourself with your own characters. They all reflect you in some small way, so you must battle with your subconscious to imbue them with evil that has the same levels of integrity you will happily give your good guys. If you don't, your story will be weak.

Why put myself through that?

Put it this way: if you put your other hat on – the hat of the audience member in the cinema – we look forward to seeing a bad guy close up. It's an experience we avoid in the real world, but the cinema lets us get so close we can smell the evil and feel genuinely nervous and excited by the experience. But only if the scriptwriter has done his job properly.

If you still struggle to be bad yourself, look at the job you give yourself from the protagonist's viewpoint. Your hero can only be as heroic as the effort it takes him to defeat the bad guys, so you must give your bad guys all the power they need to appear unassailable, and from there you must make them even more powerful – apparently beyond defeat – and weaken your good guys to the point where it seems impossible for the bad guys to lose.

From there, your protagonist is going to have to be pretty damn special to win out – and I for one would like to see how he's going to do it.

Every cinema goer knows, from the moment they see the poster, who is going to win and who is going to lose. They've seen enough movies to take their seat feeling pretty confident, deep down, that things will end up fine for the hero. When things get a little tense for my children in the cinema, I whisper to them that everything is going to be fine. I promise them that the good guy will win in the end. And I am always right. Your job, as a screenwriter, is to make me squirm. Make me fear that on top of the amazing plot you are about to deliver, I've also just lied to my children, because maybe – just maybe – this is the time when the good guy isn't actually going to make it. And that is totally dependent upon your ability to deliver powerful, believable, convincing and (almost) unassailable forces of antagonism.

7   Dialogue

Within the novel, dialogue has a different and greater impact than it does in visual media. As we saw in the example from Philip K. Dick, the author takes us inside the mind of the character so that we can contrast the thoughts in his mind with the words and deeds delivered without having to search beneath for subtext. We often already know the subtext implicit to his thoughts, so we can simply sit back and enjoy the interactions between the characters and how they interpret the explicit subtext. In other words, dialogue in a novel often represents privilege knowledge gaps because we already know what the protagonist is really thinking.

The same dialogue in film, however, is delivered by people, and their true thoughts and feeling are hidden, just as they are in the real world, so what is said cannot be taken at face value. The audience is naturally looking for the visual clues that deliver the subtextual truth, so in film the dialogue is often used to mislead and create a contrast between the words, thoughts and deeds. This contrast gives three dimensional life to character, but makes dialogue a lot more tricky to write.

Dialogue carries more power in a novel because, in and of itself, the dialogue is on an equal footing with any other writing; by which I mean the reader takes on board the import of what is 'said' with the same attentiveness that he absorbs the action and exposition around it. In visual media, dialogue is given markedly less importance than visual information – around 80:20 in favour of the visual.

The expression is that 'actions speak louder than words', and there is no doubt that this is true in the context of script writing. If a particular stream of dialogue is very important, and you want to be sure your audience takes it on board, you need to be sure that there is little or no interesting action taking place at the same time, or you need to reassert the same message several times, or, best of all, find a way to deliver it through action rather than words.

Let me give you an example of how this works in practice. In *Back to the Future*, when Biff and his henchmen chase Marty from the diner, Marty fashions a skateboard from a passing kid's box cart, and uses it to make good his escape. I bet you a beer that you never noticed during this action, as Marty comes back past the diner having made a circuit of the square, that the following dialogue takes place between the people inside the diner.

Girl: "What's that thing he's on?"

Boy: "It's a board with wheels!"

The implication is, of course, that this was the embryonic moment at the root of the eventual invention of skateboards, but this dialogue is not only unnecessary in delivering the core purpose of the scene, but you didn't notice it anyway because of the intense visual action going on at the same time.

In one sense, this implies that dialogue is unimportant in film, but this is not the case. When the action allows the space for dialogue, it means that it has to be crafted extremely carefully, firstly, so that it can be acted in such a way as to deliver a correct subtext, and secondly, so the audience notices it. The audience will notice your dialogue if you suppress the action for the duration of the speech. There is a third line delivered in the sequence mentioned above, and this third line was formed in such a way that you *did* notice:

Girl: "What's that thing he's on?"

Boy: "It's a board with wheels!"

Lorraine: (Adoring) "He's an absolute dream!"

The reason you noticed Lorraine's line is because the action was suppressed for the two seconds it takes her to deliver her line. The first two lines are delivered anonymously whilst we watch the pursuit between Biff in his car and Marty on his skateboard. The camera then cuts to a close up of Lorraine for her line. We see her face and expression as we hear her words, and we momentarily shelve the excitement of the chase. Bingo, we take on board the words she says as well as the important subtext and plot point that we gather from them (she is becoming romantically interested in her own son).

The second technique in ensuring your spoken words are noticed is to ensure the sentences are punchy and structured in such a way as to leave the audience waiting until the end of the sentence for its full meaning. When we looked at beats earlier on, we said that each one should ideally have the audience questioning and jerked around by the unexpected content of each beat, and left surprised by the outcome. Your spoken sentences must work like beats. Leave the key word in the sentence to the end, so the audience are hanging on the outcome. Use unusual and interesting words as much as possible so they are more attention-grabbing. Lorraine didn't say, "Oh, my God, I just love him soooo much!" Is there any more clichéd line than 'I love you/him/it/her etc'? This would be a bland sentence that doesn't grab. No, what she says is, "He's an absolute dream!" This is perfect dialogue. It is short and punchy, it is interesting use of English in terms of the words chosen, but most importantly, we don't know what she's going to say until the last key word. "He's an absolute..." and we're thinking 'what?! He's an absolute what?!' This sentence construction draws us up from the visual and into the dialogue, making us listen to find out the answer to the question – an absolute what? It could be anything! She delivers the last word, we take it on board, then it's back to the action and we have the information the writers wanted us to get: Lorraine is infatuated with Marty – this is a key component of the main subplot, so the director crafted these two seconds carefully to be sure we got the message.

In novels, the rule I have for myself is to use as much dialogue as possible. It gives character to the words and allows the reader to build up a more human story. In film scripts, the rule I have for myself is 'dialogue should not be necessary'. It's a valuable enhancement to a story in the same way as the background music and sound design; it can enhance the emotions, but dialogue is not generally of much more value than that. By avoiding any first draft writing until a complete preparation has taken place, I make it a safer bet that the dialogue that does get in is doing the right job. Avoid writing any dialogue whatsoever until the very end. The rule is 'show don't tell', and that literally means keeping the characters' mouths shut for as long as possible. The characters do talk, of course, extensively, even, but by the time I allow them the power of speech I am intensely aware of the story events, so it is much less likely that their words will create wrong impressions.

Watch the first half of *Atonement*. This is a fine story, with close to perfect film-story delivery in that first fifty minutes or so. It is filmed in one location (an English country mansion), and in addition to its other virtues, this first half has excellent dialogue. Entire minutes pass with no spoken words at all – five whole minutes or more in a single wordless period – and what dialogue there is has been considered so that it is economic; allowing the actor to deliver the intrigue behind the words through pure acting expertise. We interpret every movement; every facial expression; every action, and build the story to our own perfect design in our minds as we idealise the characters to our mental image of what we want them to be. Dialogue instantly delivers us depth of personality and authorial design that won't match up with our own internal design – a design which is perfect for us. A picture paints a thousand words, and yet ten words remove 90% of that information from us. Too much chatter equates precisely with anti-quality.

The whole of the first half of *Atonement* is dripping with subtext and is an excellent example of how a film story should be delivered. (I keep specifying the first half because the film loses its way a little in Act II. The book is better.) A similar – perhaps even better – example is *No Country for Old Men*. Note how the extraordinary tension is built with no dialogue whatsoever. Think then how wrecked it would have been if these intense, beautiful characters were chatty!

The children's film *Wall-E* (2008), written by Andrew Stanton and Pete Docter, is literally wordless until two-thirds of the way through. Not a word. And it is interesting that this wonderful story loses some of its magic as soon as the dialogue finally arrives.

7.1 Ordinary People

Best of the lot, *Ordinary People* – the Academy award winning movie from the book of the same name by Judith Guest – opens with a family under tension. They all know why, and we, the audience don't. Even though they all know the problem none of them are talking about it openly and the tension this creates is unbearable. The knowledge gaps crack open and crack again in three dimensions as we discover the parents have trouble with the son, who is working with a psychotherapist. Through this, we realise that the family is coming to terms with the death of an older son. From each perspective we see the mother (played by Mary Tyler Moore), father (Donald Sutherland) and second son, Conrad (played by Timothy Hutton) attempting to handle the bereavement in different ways. In the final therapy session, the boy finally cracks and we learn everything. The knowledge gaps crash shut as revelation piles on revelation. We leave the story realising that Conrad, who started the story as the struggling one, the one who was 'ill', has ended up as the strongest. The mother, who tries to cope by pretending everything is fine, ends up leaving her husband. As so often happens in therapy, it is the 'sick one' – the one who tries to do something about it – who is actually the healthiest of all. He has learned, changed and grown. The ones who bottle it up and try to 'soldier on' are the ones who have the most serious long term problems. [4]

Which returns us nicely to...

7.2   Character growth and learning

We have talked about this a few times without getting right into it. One of the top three factors in great stories is a clear progression of character growth across the course of the story. Someone, somewhere in your story must change and grow as a result of the telling, as the son, Conrad, does in *Ordinary People*; as Scrooge does in *A Christmas Carol*; as Phil does in *Groundhog Day*; as Buzz and Woody do in *Toy Story*. Ideally, most of the main characters will have their own story that you could map out independently of everything else, but as long as someone palpably learns, then the audience will have learned with them and the story will satisfy. When we talk about the principles that lie beneath all good stories, this would be one of them: at least one character learning life lessons is usually present in a story that wins.

In *Toy Story*, Woody and Buzz can't get anywhere until they change and grow. They fail to achieve their aims until they learn to work together. Their movement from selfishness to co-operation is clear character growth and defines this excellent story. And, of course, by the time we get to Toy Story 3, there isn't a dry eye in the house, because all the characters have gone forwards about 12 years, and now it's time to change and grow into a whole new phase. All of them. Andy is leaving his mother's care and going to college. Mum is moving to a new phase of life without her son at home. The toys are in transition from being owned by a boy to... who knows where? The garbage? Donation? The attic? It is Andy that really demonstrates the key growth for the story. He begins by trying to store the toys in the attic, but he overcomes his sentimentality and realises that they are best off being played with by another child.

So who learns life lessons in *Back to the Future*? As we mentioned earlier, the characters are quite polarised and act very squarely within their stereotypical domain. Indeed, they specifically *don't* seem to change or

---

[4] *Ordinary People* was rejected by a couple of publishers before Viking Press picked it up. One rejection letter said Judith Guest's 'level of writing does not sustain interest'. This is the book that then sold 500,000 copies, and the film of the story won an Academy award and two Oscars. This is what you are up against in trying to become a writer. Even the greats get rejected. You will need to keep faith in yourself and don't weaken...

grow. Biff is a bully. Whatever is thrown at him, he will address it with a bully's mindset. Similarly, Lorraine is 'marriage-waiting-to-happen' girl. Every time she is on screen, she addresses all events with a romantic view and a racing heart. Doc Brown is 'mad inventor' man. Every time he features, he is in the mode of a crazy haired inventor. None of these characters particularly change or grow across the course of the telling. Even Marty, the story's protagonist, doesn't change or grow. He is just a normal kid – a very rounded individual representing us, the audience member and leading us through the story. [5]

However, there is one notable exception. **George McFly** is, for the majority of the story, stereotyped as weak and unassertive. That is all we get from him. That is, until he is pushed to the limit. True character emerges under pressure, and when he can't stand any more, he overcomes the bully Biff, laying him out with a haybaler of a left hook in the school car park. In doing so, he breaks out of his stereotype and changes and grows in dramatic ways that leap him and his family up Maslow's hierarchy. George is the one character in *Back to the Future* who changes and grows and learns life lessons. *Back to the Future* is a genuinely great story, and George's character growth is one of the key factors in the story's greatness. The fact that George is not really the protagonist doesn't matter. As long as someone changes and grows, the story will satisfy.

7.3   Some notes on plot and character

Key points: firstly, stories are all about **character actions**. The way a character under pressure reacts to a situation defines both his true character AND the plot at the same time, whether you like it or not. So ensure that everything that happens is connected to the protagonist and make all character reactions to the event significant to his progress towards his aims.

Secondly, for all that we are trying to avoid cliché, it is largely unavoidable that most good characters will have a certain degree of definition about them that will make them appear clichéd. This happens because we only narrate the events that are significant to the story, so we only define the character and plot that draw out those relevant aspects of that character.

---

[5] In this respect, John Sullivan maintains: "I try to have a character who represents the audience. He's the one who asks the questions the audience would ask and looks puzzled and gets enlightened and so on in tune with the audience. You talked about *Back to the Future* – no clearer example of a lead character who represents you and me and leads us through a story which really addresses the issues of other people."

If you watch *Back to the Future* analytically, the characters appear to be almost ludicrously polarised into these stereotypes. The Wimpy Nerd; The Incurable Romantic; The Bully; Inventor Man – and they never step out of character for a second. But it is part of the 'agreement' we have as consumers of story that we realise they do and feel other things – those things just aren't relevant, so they aren't narrated. A wimpy nerd can actually be quite strong and assertive at given points in the day – at his Sci-Fi Interest Group, in the Math's lesson. The Incurable Romantic still studies and has personal ambitions and interests beyond boys and marriage, but these things do not drive <u>this</u> story, so the characters only appear in those moments in their lives when they were relevant to driving <u>this</u> story, so they do, quite acceptably, appear to be polarised, almost stereotyped characters.

Don't be scared of this in your writing. Well defined characters drive stories more easily and naturally, and as long as your characters are true to themselves when put under pressure of conflict and required to make a decision, the fact that they respond in a 'typical' fashion is realistic. Archetype is not the same as cliché or stereo-typing. Hmm. Perhaps we had best draw a distinction.

7.4 Stereotypes and Archetypes

A cliché gives us something predictable and tired. Something we've all seen before. stereotype provides us with a caricature of the truth. For example, 'All football fans are hooligans' – and we can picture him, can't we? Skinhead with tattoos and a knife in his boot, looking for trouble at football grounds. Well, when I go to football matches, I never see anyone like this. They don't really exist, but we all carry the image and recognise the stereotype. Even those that indulge in violence don't look like that, and the vast majority of football fans are just normal people like you and me who are a million miles from that caricature. That's the stereotype, and is different from an archetype in that the stereotype is common to almost no members of the type.

An archetype is the underlying model that is fundamental to all members of the type. If you made a film about a football hooligan and the violence he brings to the world on a Saturday, not many people around the world would relate to his story. However, if the story addressed the factors that are common to all of us that motivate his lifestyle – loneliness, lack of confidence, paucity in parenting, a need to belong to a group – these are universal factors, by which we can relate to the character and his actions.

I recently watched the Disney Pixar film, *Up* (2009, written by Pete Docter and Bob Peterson). What a wonderful story. On the surface, it is a children's story about an elderly gentleman Mr Fredrikkson (voiced by Ed Asner) and his unwanted 8-year-old charge (Russell, voiced by Jordan Nagai) addressing the key question: will they successfully drag Mr Fredrikkson's floating house to the top of Paradise Falls in South America? But really, this wonderful story is about his loneliness following the death of his wife. It's about broken promises and unfulfilled dreams. It's about life and death, hope and fear. All these things are fundamental human values; archetypes. You don't need a child with you to love this story. I highly recommend it to you now as a truly excellent example of story-telling.

7.5 Creative constraints

Earlier in the book, we talked about how structural limitations actually force a writer to come up with brilliant ways of working within imposed limits, and how that can be a positive benefit. There are several other types of limitation that work in the same way and are worth mentioning, beginning with how quickly a writer allows a new idea to take root. I include this in the section on character and plot, because our first ideas for events and characteristics are often not the best.

Indeed, I make it a rule never to wave through the first sunbeams of creativity that come to me. The chances are that they are a conditioned response to the circumstances that provided the spark. I make a point of trying to rethink the idea, and then rethink it again; firstly, to make sure I have given everything due time and effort, but secondly, to make sure that I am not just trotting out clichés or repeating some work of others that my mind has sub-consciously handed to me. It may be that my first idea ends up being the best one for the job, but this is rarely the case. The first idea is merely the platform, and disallowing yourself the option of simply accepting the first idea forces you to build on this and come up with better things.

Other forms of limitation are beneficial in the same way. I am currently writing the story for a musical production, and am very, very determined that the story will be strong. Most musicals, and especially operas, are impenetrable at the story level; you have to buy and read the programme before you have any idea what the thing is going on about. (I saw the *Nutcracker Suite* recently. Great music, great ballet, but I *still* didn't know what the story was about even after watching the performance *and* reading the programme.) Of course, the limitations placed on the writer of a musical story are much greater. The story must be delivered entirely in song (or even in dance) and, in the case of opera, exclusively by large people shouting. A song can only truly present a simple emotion, not a complex dialogue; subtext is rendered ten times more difficult to imbue, so I have great limits imposed on me as a writer. Then there is the 'working with musicians' limitation. They have their new, hot favourite songs, and they want to crowbar them into the show at any cost. I therefore get regular visits from them excitedly telling me things like: 'we have a great new song!

We need a seven-year-old girl in the story, NOW, and she must be lost and alone in some snow.'

I tell them the story is too far developed *without* a small, lost, snow-capped girl. There's no place for one and it simply isn't possible to change things now to force one in. They get all emotional and next I have the management telling me that it is a great song and that I *have* to incorporate a seven-year-old girl into the story and cover her in snow by the end of the week. I go away and strain my brain and do you know what? There is a way – the lead lady, in flashback to the horrors of her childhood, recalls the time she was abandoned and sings this amazing piece of music in an empty dream-like stage full of dry ice and falling snow. It's fantastic. It opens up the character, enhances the story, provides a cute child, an enormously emotional context for the new song and there won't be a dry eye in the house. The creative limitations placed on me forced out new and wonderful material I would never have found without those limits.

Personal time

The other form of constraint which is most important and very hard to deal with is the Personal Time Constraint. The great majority of aspiring writers I meet tinker with their work for year after year, and nothing gets finished. There is no official completion date for a story, and a writer's brain can always find 'improvements' and dance around the thing forever. I was as bad as anyone for massively overworking my material. It is much safer to simply be 'a writer' for years and years without delivering anything, just in case it isn't actually perfect yet, or for fear that people won't like it. My output has quadrupled since I have had deadlines. When you know the date of the print run for your book; when dates are in the diary for marketing events; when the 'first night' date is set for a play; when the first day of principal photography is laid down for a movie, these things seriously focus the mind, and one becomes more skilled at getting above that bottom line and not aiming for some mythical perfection.

Willy Russell told me he simply cannot produce anything without a deadline. He accepts a commission, then can't come up with anything he finds convincing. Then the deadline starts to bite and he wishes he hadn't accepted the job. With no time left, he goes back to the businessmen and tries to give them their money back, but they wave the contract at him and tell him he had better get on with it. With nothing left to do but sweat and cry, he starts to write, and the most powerful, urgent drama emerges into being, driven by that pressing deadline. It goes to the stage and is hailed as a masterpiece, whilst Willy lies shaking and sweating in a darkened room, mumbling to himself 'never again...'

All the successful writers told me of similar dynamics behind their best material. The urgency of a deadline forces out good stuff. Non-professional writers feel privileged in having the luxury of years to complete their work, but the opposite is true. The final product – if it ever appears – lacks immediacy. The problem is: how do you impose false deadlines until you have genuine ones? My answer was always to work to the academic year. I set myself a specific list of tasks that I must achieve before the schools break up. Once the term is over, I do not allow myself to write for the duration of the school holiday (I only allow myself to plan for the next term and think deeply creative thoughts), so I work hard to achieve those targets before the enforced break. I know it is still only a paper tiger, but I find the academic year a fine working dynamic for writing, and that chunking the year up like that does impose good discipline.

Steven King reportedly forces himself to write 2000 words a day. Sunday, his birthday, Christmas Day – every day. 2000 words. Some days he's done before lunch. Other days he's still struggling with it at midnight, but 2000 words will emerge. They might all get thrown away, they might be solid gold. It doesn't matter. All that matters is that he makes it a rule to produce 2000 words every day. I guarantee that your writing quality and your productivity will go up dramatically if you could do a quarter of that, as will your chances of success.

When one is writing speculatively and without deadlines, it is far too easy to continue to mull things over for days, weeks, months... And this is the point of all the above; limitations and constraints are seriously good for you. Go looking for them. Impose them on yourself as hard as you can. And watch your writing go up ten points. Structure your story. Structure your routine. Structure is good. Remember:

There is no finish line with a story, so don't aim for it. But there is a bottom line. Aim to surpass it.

7.6   Genre and theme

In broader terms there are two other factors that impose creative constraints on story development: Genre and Theme.

Genre means the type of story – comedy, science fiction, horror, thriller, cowboy, mystery and so forth. A complete genre definition expressed within the film industry will identify the **target audience, the format, the setting and the mood**. For example, *High School Musical* is a Family film (audience). It is a Musical (format), the setting is 'Contemporary American Senior School' and the mood is 'Sentimental Candy Coated YouBetcha American Sickly Saturated Romance Cheaply Ripped From *Grease*'.

Seriously, the 'mood' expresses the vibe of the story. When you get a deal for a film, you will find yourself at some point describing your vision of the story to the Director of Photography. He will be trying to extract the mood from you in order that he can organise the lights and the feeling that the film should portray visually. *High School Musical* is bright and optimistic. The Director of Photography chose to film it in bright lights and slightly saturated colour in an affluent California neighbourhood. *Lord of the Rings* is dark and portentous. This is the mood, so it is filmed in grey light on bleak New Zealand rocks. Be conscious of the mood of your work in order to help you to pick the correct nouns and adjectives as you write. A word like 'chilling' suggests the mood is Horror. 'Bloodcurdling' is Thriller. 'Macabre' is Mystery. 'Disturbing' is Psychological Drama. 'Scary' is Comedy.

It is useful to think of a story mood in terms of the time of year or the specific location. For example, the film *Truly, Madly, Deeply* was filmed in the autumn in Hampstead, London. Big, blue days with homely Victorian houses and changing leaf colours set a golden mood. It can also be helpful to picture the lead characters as existing film stars; when people talk about stereotyping in actors, what they actually represent is the mood. Bruce Willis places us into Action/Suspense. Ben Stiller locks us on to Comedy.

Theme tells us about the 'topic' of the story; the emotional areas with which the story is primarily concerned. Examples would be acceptance, betrayal, greed, love, family, freedom, justice, friendship and redemption. The theme is often the subject of the overarching moral or subconscious subtext that lives with us once the story is over. The themes of *High School Musical* might be seen as 'Education', 'Growing up', 'relationships' and 'friendship'. *Toy Story* addresses the themes of co-operation and friendship.

How often have you come out of a movie with a new feeling towards life or thoughts about your own life? The theme of *Dead Poets' Society* is nutshelled by the new school master, John Keating (Robin Williams) teaching the boys the idea of 'Carpe Diem' (Seize the Day) and symbolised in his forcing his wards to stand on the desk in order to 'see life differently'. The main plot is about the students as they try to reconcile their own identity with the 'self' they must portray to fit into an authoritarian institution on one side and be accepted by their friends and feel comfortable in themselves on the other. But whatever we saw in the story, we all came out determined to enjoy life today instead of planning for some grand future that might never get here. Quite often, the theme is encapsulated not only across the entire film, but in one brief symbolic moment early in the story, like the *Dead Poets'* example when they stand on the desks.

A cohesive story is likely to fit only one genre, but may address multiple themes. The genre and theme are important, because they set audience expectation and they set boundaries on the writer for character behaviour and acceptable action. A writer must remain within the 'rules' of a given genre if the audience is going to accept the actions of the characters. For example, it is perfectly acceptable within a Fantasy genre, such as *Harry Potter*, for some previously unseen form of alien to float in through a wall and heavily impact the story line by flying about and performing strange magic. However, within a Cowboy film, the introduction of a strange character flying through walls and turning people into frogs would be unlikely to work. It would be outside the promised genre, and the audience would feel dissatisfied.

Set the genre and theme for your story. Go back to your story baseline and fill it in now with a paragraph along these lines:

My story is called <story title>. It is a <genre, location in time and space, setting, mood and theme(s)>.

7.7 Plot and character – summary

So far, we have seen four essentials to a great story.

1. We have an inciting incident and key question, leading to a resolution that addresses satisfactorily the key question raised.

2. We have knowledge gaps opened up between the different participants in the story, layering in subtext. The presence, depth and extent of these knowledge gaps are directly related to the quality of your story. The more subtext there is, the better your story will be.

3. We have conflict for your characters, which forces them to make decisions under pressure that reveal their true character.

4. And we have at least one character changing and growing as they learn life lessons through the events that comprise the story.

It is interesting in the context of the above list to map out a standard classical pattern to a story structure in these terms.

A character is delivered who has personal problems, hang-ups, difficulties that cause him or her to behave in society-inappropriate ways. For example, Scrooge is greedy, miserable, slave-driving and hates Christmas; George McFly is weak and unassertive; Phil (*Groundhog Day*) is anti-social and selfish. (This is the **character development** thread of the story.) There is usually a relationship that is suffering and bonds being tested as a result of their flawed character.

A key dramatic event takes place (Scrooge is haunted by ghosts; Marty is sent back in time; Phil is forced to relive the same day over and over). This is the story driven by **story events**, and is most probably built around the inciting incident/key question mechanism.

The character's response to the events is driven by their character flaw(s), and is therefore inappropriate. They try to use their society-inappropriate ways to solve the problem, but that just digs them in deeper. (Scrooge tries to bully the ghosts, then tries to blame the poor people for their plight. Phil responds to his day being repeated over and over by taking advantage of his knowledge of the day and being even more selfish and anti-social; George capitulates to his self-doubt at every junction). This is the story driven by the **character's reactions** to the dramatic story event.

When all seems lost, the character faces one last chance to win or lose all. But to win, they must conquer their flawed character and become society-appropriate. This is where the character is ultimately faced with impossible choices that will reveal true character. But a choice must be made. They do so and live happily ever after. (Scrooge becomes generous and Christmassy; Phil becomes altruistic, using his daily advantage to help others; George stands up to the bully.) And the problem caused by the dramatic event is solved as a result. (The ghosts leave Scrooge in peace; Phil breaks out of his repeated day; Marty makes it back to an even better 1985.) The character has learned and grown through the most extreme **conflict** and the story progressed through **character growth**.

At resolution, the world has changed. The character has grown through learning, and, as a result of his actions, the world looks a more balanced, society-appropriate and improved place to be. Scrooge has friends and laughter; Phil has love; George has self-fulfilment and a high quality lifestyle and family.

As ever, of course, this is not a formula for success, but it is interesting to see how many stories have a pattern along these lines, and to show the relationship between plot events and character events.

THE STORY DEVELOPMENT PROCESS

Writing is easy. All you do is stare at a blank sheet of paper until drops of blood form on your forehead.

Gene Fowler (1890 – 1960)

8   The seeds of a story

All stories start the same way – with a basic idea. This starting point and the reasons you found the idea attractive in the first place are really important, because it is often useful when you are deeply into the story and feeling that you can no longer see the wood for the trees to remember where your story started and the issues at its core. This is why we created our story baseline. It gives us that fundamental framework, and as we continue to add to and refine our baseline, we remind ourselves of the roots and core values of our story and keep ourselves on track.

Bob Gale said that *Back to the Future* began with this simple premise:

A kid goes back in time, meets his parents when they were young, and his mother falls in love with him.

That was it. One sentence, 21 words, and yet already intriguing. You can quite imagine being a studio executive and saying, "Tell me more..." whilst reaching for your cheque book. It's worth noting as a principle, even at this early stage, that a great story is likely to betray its power even in a brutally reduced form like this. Studios love stories that have a 'high concept', meaning that the story can be expressed and show promise in a sentence or two. Not just because it's a sign of a good story, but – much more importantly in their eyes – it's also a sign of clear and easy marketing. A writer generally knows he's onto something hot when the idea shows power in a paragraph, and our lives become a search for these nuggets. I also think it is interesting to note that the *Back to the Future* premise exhibits all three of the core values we have discovered so far, even in this high concept form:

- Characters with interesting conflicts.

- Dramatic story events.

- Subtext.

Once we have an idea, the challenge is to take the right steps to nurture this simple premise into a fully developed story without losing the beating heart that gives this premise its underlying power. How do we capture that power? What do we do with this premise to take it forwards?

Stories are all about those lovely **knowledge gaps**. As we know, great stories feature relative gaps in the knowledge available to all the participants in a story – the protagonist, antagonist, other players, author, audience – all the participants. At any given moment in a good story, each participant will know more or less than some or all of the others. At the birth of a story, the development process is about opening the main knowledge gaps that will pervade and define the longest arc(s) of the story.

Here is what Bob Gale had to say about the early development of *Back to the Future*. Note how many of the things he says translate into questions asked, or, creating or filling knowledge gaps:

Like any other writers, Robert Zemeckis and I started with an idea, and ours looked like this: a kid goes back in time. He meets his parents when they were young and his mother falls in love with him.

That was it. The idea. The starting point. We began to question this premise to see what it must mean. For example, some obvious things immediately spring from this premise: some characters, some obligatory scenes [inevitable events] and some more questions:

Firstly, we know we must have three characters – a son and his parents. What can we infer about these characters from the premise? Well, if his mother is going to fall in love with the kid instead of his father, we know that the mother is looking for a boyfriend. We also know the kid must have different qualities from his father that she will find attractive. So we said, what if, instead of his father being paternal to him and telling him how to behave, it was the other way around? After all, in 1955, his father is just a kid himself, so why should he be paternal? Marty from 1985 could be the streetwise, strong one, and his father is unassertive and he learns from his son. Excellent. So the character of George McFly takes its first shape (weak, unassertive), as does the character of his future son, Marty (smart, streetwise) and that of his mother-to-be, Lorraine (romantic – a marriage waiting to happen).

Secondly, many, many questions naturally drop out of this premise. How did he time travel? Why did he time travel? Deliberately or by accident? Did he get home again? What would a kid do in his parents' time? What dangers were involved? What happened when his mother fell in love with him?

And if you take any one of the basic questions and drill down into them, you get more characters, more events, more behaviours, more questions and more answers. Take the first question, for example. How did he time travel? Answer: there must be a time machine. OK, so what form did it take? Where did it come from? Who built it? What does it look like? Maybe a corporation is making it. But why? Maybe it is government property. Maybe the kid stole it. Maybe it's a product of a crazy inventor, and bingo, we knew that was right, and Doc Brown was born – our fourth character – a crazy-haired inventor.

How, what, where, why...? And for each answer we came up with, there was a set of implications that began to build the story. So, for example, we asked ourselves, what would a kid do in his parents' time? Wouldn't it be great if he invented rock and roll? What would this mean to the story? Well, it would set the timeframe – it meant that he had to go back to around 1955, and this in turn meant the mood and culture and attitudes of that time were given to the story. It also meant that, somewhere in the setup, Marty had to show he could play music, so his band in 1985 was driven in, as was his ability to play guitar and his musical ambition. All this had to find its place in the setup.

Similarly, we thought why doesn't Marty invent the skateboard? We decided Marty would invent the skateboard in 1955, so we needed to establish him as a skateboarder in the setup in 1985. You can see straight away from these two small examples that Marty's character is emerging all by itself – he's going to be a guitarist in a band and he's going to be a skateboarder – and this in turn affects his behaviours – he enters a Battle of the Bands competition and he gets about town using a skateboard.

We thought strongly about the ending early on. If you don't know where the story is heading, you can't aim towards it, so we focussed our interrogation of the premise on the ending. For example, we agreed that we wanted him to make it back to 1985, and we wanted him to come back to a better life than the one he left in the first place. We knew that much. Most time travel stories end up as salutary tales of how bad everything will be for you if you screw with time. We wanted ours to be positive and different, so we made Marty unhappy to find himself in 1955 – he never wanted to travel through time – and his basic aim was to get back to his girlfriend and his life in 1985. We also made him screw with time accidentally, and find himself obliged to fix things up before he could go home. This gave us excellent jeopardy and dependency – the main plot couldn't resolve until the subplots did, and the clock was ticking down – a classic device for building tension, of course. We also needed something more than simply his return to 1985 as the end-game. He had to come back for a dramatic purpose, which is why we came up with the idea of Doc Brown being killed in 1985 before Marty goes back. In 1955, Marty realises he can return to a point in 1985 earlier than he left in order to save the Doc's life, and suddenly the story worked beyond the simple drama of getting back to 1985.

All these plot events came from asking questions of the premise, and because everything was therefore linked back to the underlying premise, the story kept its integrity – its cohesion.

So stories begin with a simple premise, which naturally evokes big-picture questions that will need to be asked and answered in the main body of the story. These questions need to be raised and answered by characters and their behaviours, so these same questions implicitly help you to establish the right characters for the behaviours, and the right behaviours become the action.

8.1.1 Question – or knowledge gap?

All questions are, by definition, knowledge gaps, but not all knowledge gaps are questions. We can see, even at this early stage, several excellent knowledge gaps between the players that will give us the subtext a great story needs, but these are not questions that a character will ask or answer in the story. Throughout the time Marty is in 1955, we, the audience, along with Marty alone, know he is a time traveller from the future. Nobody else knows, until the revelation comes for Doc Brown's younger self when he finds out. At the same time, we, the audience, along with Marty, know that George and Lorraine will fall in love and get married. They are 17. They don't know this, and would be embarrassed (George) and horrified (Lorraine) for most of the story if you suggested such a thing to them. Two excellent, deep, pervasive and persistent knowledge gaps that define the story, grip and engage us. But these are not questions: nobody ever asks or finds out whether Marty is a time traveller. It's a knowledge gap, not a question.

The key question

Of the main questions that your premise evokes, one of them is likely to be your **key question**. The question that is answered across the full arc of your story, and which your audience will sense is the one that has to be answered before the story can be considered finished. Identifying your key question gives your story its ending, because your climax and resolution will answer this key question.

As we can see from Bob Gale's words above, one of the questions listed was: 'did Marty get back to his own time again?' This became the key question for *Back to the Future*, provides the key dramatic arc for the story, and leads us to a clear expectation for the climax and resolution. But they didn't start from here. They started from the premise. They worked out the natural implications of the premise. Later, they could see some events naturally wanting to take place before others and some ending after others. Some questions are 'bigger' than others. The events surrounding Marty being sent back in time became the clear and logical main storyline that would raise the key question and be the driver of the climax and resolution. Had they picked a different event to arc across the full course, they would have raised a different key question and written a different story.

Also note carefully that the basic story development technique is based around a creative, imaginative process, not some predefined structure or rule base. Yes, we use our experience to help us to guide our creative abilities to grow an optimal story from that premise, and when we choose events to narrate they will, of course, permeate our story with structure, but we are letting our creativity lead us, and from that the story will evolve into the shape it naturally wants to take on.

9 Sequences

As the process of asking questions of the premise is generating characters and events, behaviours and ideas, and these generate further questions, what do we do with the output? Back to Bob Gale:

What we did with the answers when we liked them was we wrote the event on an index card, and put it on the story 'map' as an event that would need to be there. The index card would say something like: 'Marty invents rock and roll'. This would drive out another index card, which we knew must come before this one. If Marty is going to get on stage and play rock and roll in 1955, we'd better establish he can play, so we wrote on another index card: 'Establish: Marty can play rock and roll', and we placed it chronologically ahead of the one saying 'Marty invents rock and roll'.

Over time the process of asking questions and finding answers puts out more and more index cards, and the story develops in front of you. I would recommend that you get off your computer and do the same. Get a pile of blank index cards, write the scene aim on each and further index cards that establish what needs to be in place to facilitate the scene taking place. When you lay the cards out on the floor you can see your whole story in front of you much better than you can see it on a computer screen. You can move things around and work with your creative instincts to see what goes where.

I must admit, I was personally sceptical about getting off my computer and working with index cards, but since meeting Bob I have done so and, I have to say, it's a very positive thing to do. It gives you a complete overview of your story in a way the computer cannot, and it seems to provide a much more natural, intuitive mechanism for working with a full-length work. I recommend it.

Bob talks above about each card representing a scene. In terms of this book, I would change that to 'event', as some of these things will end up being scenes, but many are actually sequences, that will break down into scenes later. It is also worth noting that once you have thirty or forty of these out on the floor, you probably have more than enough. Most new writers imagine you need a hundred of these events, but in reality, as few as a dozen may represent your entire story. Best of all is to come up with far too many, and strip away to leave only the meatiest, but the final story will probably comprise less than thirty.

9.1 Towards a step outline

It is worth noting at this point that, if you are following this book sequentially in writing your own story, you are still far from ready to write any first draft detail. We are building towards a step outline, which must be completed before a word of detail is written. Read this chapter with a view to thinking about how your ideas will actually convert into strong story events, but don't write the depth yet.

Let's say you have an index card that contains a sequence objective, like: 'Marty is sent back in time'. To develop this idea, on the back of that card, we put a sentence describing how we might deliver that sequence. So for example:

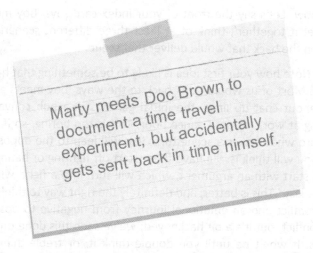

Marty meets Doc Brown to document a time travel experiment, but accidentally gets sent back in time himself.

And do this for every index card. The front of the index card presents a 'Sequence Objective' in the delivery of the 'big picture' story. The back of the index card presents a possible method for delivering that sequence objective.

Note that as long as the sequence's basic 'front' objective doesn't change, the method of delivery on the back for that sequence objective is infinitely variable. In other words, if you don't want to send Marty back in time using a time machine built from a DeLorean, then you can change it to a refrigerator (which was the initial idea!), or a flying horse, or a dream sequence, and it makes absolutely no difference to the delivery of the story at the sequence level. This is excellent for keeping control of your story at the high level as it becomes more complex later in the detail.

If you can write your sentence on the back of the card using a conjunction (such as the word 'but' in the above example) you are also making life much easier for yourself. The delivery is more likely to contain or accommodate the all-important turning point if it has a different outcome from the initial direction, and the 'but' tends to indicate the likelihood of such a dynamic. 'Protagonist A expected that X would happen, but Y actually happened'.

You can clearly see that we are beginning to impose some structure over our ideas, but that still doesn't mean we should stop the creative flow. Indeed, it is absolutely critical that we look hard at the sequence delivery sentences and force ourselves to be as creative and brilliant with our ideas for delivery as we possibly can. Your first idea for how to deliver any given sequence is probably not great – it will be a conditioned response from your experience of other stories. Your second one may be a clichéd opposite of the first. It may take three or more brain strains before you come up with something genuinely original and satisfactory, so do take your time and agonise over the words you write on the back of the index card.

Do it now. Let's say the front of your index card says 'Boy meets girl, and they get it together', think of at least three different scenarios you could write on the back that would deliver that scene.

Done? Note how your first idea is likely to be something that has been done before. Most of us would think back to the ways 'boy meets girl', and we'll think about chat up lines, the initial gambits in a pub conversation, or a meeting at work, or on a dance floor. This is too boring, so if you've taken on board what makes a scene turn, you will leap to the opposite. The next thing you will think is, 'I'll have them start off fighting or hating each other. They'll start with an argument, which will turn into a fight, which escalates into... a kiss.' This is better, and definitely the right way to think, because we have conflict and an emotional journey from negative to positive through that conflict, but it's a bit hackneyed; we've seen this done once a week on *Friends*. It won't be until you double-think it, or treble-think it, that you come up with something truly original. So where did you go next? My next thought on this would depend on the characters: how about a boy who is so shy he can't deal with girls at all, who meets a lesbian. He feels safe with her because they can be friends with no sexual tension in the air; no danger of a relationship. She feels the same way. Men are mates, not lovers, so they can both continue on their safe pathways... Then he does or says something crass and politically incorrect. She should be furious, but she laughs. She doesn't rise to it as we have come to expect from her character. Oh, my God... I think she finds him attractive...

See how far we have got from our first thoughts? From something horribly clichéd – 'Get yer coat, luv, you've scored,' at the pub – to something original, much more interesting and firmly character, conflict and subtext driven in three quick jumps.

9.2   Planning scenes

Once we have worked ourselves to distraction to ensure that we are happy with the story at the sequence level and with every single method of delivering each sequence objective, we are about ready to move forwards.

Note that, at the end of the last work on development that we did, I said that it might well be that you are ready to simply deliver each sequence in your own, natural voice from your own instinctive story-telling capability. This is absolutely valid. Each sequence represents a stand-alone story, and each is a short piece that you are more than capable of delivering with joy and creativity. If that's how you feel, just go for it. This chapter will present a method of further breaking down your 'sequence' short story into even smaller chunks of 'scene' level short stories. If this doesn't suit you, just go for it as you are. This said, it would be valuable for you to work through my prescriptive method here and then take or leave what you like from it in your future writing.

Note also that every time you choose to move to the next level of detail, you are also taking another step in the reduction of story flexibility. Every level of detail serves to nail areas of your story into place, so it is always – always – better to resolve any unhappiness with your story at the highest level possible. If you know, right now, that your story isn't right, there is no way that it will improve simply by thinking, 'sod it,' and moving on to the next stage simply for the feeling that you are moving forwards. Be tough on yourself. Look more deeply at the sequences and how you intend to deliver them. Look at the ending. This must be completely the right ending or the whole story is sunk.

If there are literally no further improvements to make at the sequence level, then you are ready to move on. You have probably spent weeks if not months or even years getting the sequences right. The aim now is to present your story as a step outline. This is achieved by taking each sequence and developing it from a couple of sentences into a few paragraphs. Each sequence, in theory, has a beginning, a middle and an end of its own, so it should be possible to imbue your sequence with a full set of story dynamics. It won't always be possible, and it might not even be desirable, but it would be unusual for a sequence lasting many minutes not to have a protagonist, antagonist, sequence aim, conflict, climax, resolution and a measurable turning point.

So we take each sequence objective and expand it for ourselves.

Sequence Expansion – example

To begin with then, you will have a sequence aim. If your sequence objective on the front of your index card says, for example, 'The Protagonist Must Find Dr Livingstone', and you know or decide beforehand that he must succeed in this aim through the scenes that comprise this sequence, then you know that the classic scene structure will be as follows:

1. **Setup scene.** The sequence must be set up in such a way as to deliver an inciting incident that will have the audience ask the right question: 'will the protagonist find Dr Livingstone'?

2. **Progressive complication scene.** Forces of antagonism must be clearly ranged in opposition to the protagonist's aim. In this scene the ability to

find Dr Livingstone will be brought into doubt or perhaps thrown off course altogether. The forces of antagonism are likely to be in the ascendancy. (Because we know, ultimately, that the protagonist will succeed, we make it look far more likely that he won't.)

3. **Progressive complication scene**. Further progressive complications are optional, and you can have several of them. (If you think about it, the entire hour or more of Act II of a story is just one big set of progressive complications in between finding out the story key question in Act I and paying it off in Act III.) This is also the natural space into which to bed in or pay off material in service of other sequences or plot lines.

4. **Climax**. The final confrontation takes place. The protagonist wins and Dr Livingstone is found (and the protagonist's fortunes, in terms of this aim, have swung to the positive).

5. **Resolution**. At this point, now we know the answer to the key question that we were given at setup, what does the world looks like? How have things changed? If we lift our eyes to the key questions in other plot lines, and particularly at the level of the main plot story line, what are the implications there? (This scene will be particularly strong if his victory in finding Dr Livingstone is outweighed by a larger swing to the negative in the main plot story line that he doesn't even know about. Think knowledge gap. Think subtext.)

Now, for each of these five scenes to achieve the sequence objective (i.e., to set and answer the key question) is one thing, but to do so in such a way that each individual scene carries power too, means that each scene itself must be given life. How do we do that? Well, we work carefully and diligently on EVERY SCENE to ensure that each one has a turning point. In other words each of these five scenes has:

- A protagonist.

- A protagonist's aim.

- An antagonist and/or forces of antagonism.

- Conflict. The antagonistic forces or aims of the antagonist are in direct opposition to the protagonist's aims.

- A value change in the fortunes of the protagonist across the course of the scene, from positive to negative or vice versa (i.e., a turning point).

- Story progression in subtext.

So, taking each scene individually in the search for Dr Livingstone, it might look like this. Let's assume we have a protagonist, Johnny, his brother, Ronnie, and a helpless maiden, Connie. The key question that we wish to raise is: 'will Johnny and Ronnie get Connie safely home to the city?' They are all tramping through the jungle trying to achieve the wider story aim of getting Connie safely to the city. She's worth a fortune and the baddies are trying to kidnap her:

Scene I

Setup scene. At camp, in the jungle whilst the three plan the next day's walk, which will get them to the city, Ronnie spikes Connie's drink.

The next morning they wake up to find Connie feeling seriously unwell. Ronnie pretends to know something about this particular form of jungle disease and says Johnny must rush as fast as he can to get Dr Livingstone, who lives down in the jungle valley, or Connie will die. Johnny trusts his brother, of course, leaps to his feet and sets off heroically.

This scene has its own protagonist (Connie) whose aim it is to get home safely. Johnny is the story protagonist, but she can sensibly be this scene's protagonist, because:

1. it is her values that are at risk;

2. She is the character in conflict with the scene's forces of antagonism;

3. Johnny, the 'big picture' protagonist, is still affected overall by the action centring on Connie.

The scene's antagonist, Ronnie, has an apparent aim (to kill Connie) in opposition to Connie's aim (to get home unmolested), therefore conflict exists. We also have subtext in that we now realise Ronnie has an evil plan that we see proceeding behind hero Johnny's back. (We, the audience, and Ronnie, the antagonist, know more at this point than Connie and Johnny.) We will also hear Ronnie's words of false medical care to Connie and his lies to Johnny, so there will be orthodox subtext in the dialogue as well. The scene has its own setup, complication, and a turning point which works as a sequence level inciting incident, setting the sequence key question: **will Johnny manage to get Dr Livingstone?** The wider story includes the key question, **'Will Connie get home safely to the city?'** The scene has its own turning point in that the helpless maiden's fortunes have gone from negative (poisoned) to much more negative (her hero has galloped off on a wild goose chase to get Dr Livingstone, leaving her in the clutches of the bad guy). With all these elements in place, it's probably a pretty good setup scene.

Scene II

As soon as Johnny is out of sight, Ronnie tells Connie that Johnny is really a bad guy who tried to kill her and he got rid of him. She was lucky Ronnie was there to save her. She must come with him quickly before Johnny returns. Grateful to Ronnie for saving her, she agrees. They get their stuff together and head off in the opposite direction towards Ronnie's lair where he will mercilessly administer his own nefarious plan.

This scene has its own protagonist, Connie, with her aim (to get home unmolested), Antagonist Ronnie, and conflict (Ronnie's aims oppose Connie's). Things have gone from bad to worse for her. She's been poisoned and had her hero removed; not only that, but she now thinks the hero is the bad guy and the bad guy is the good guy, and is willingly going to the bad guy's lair to suffer unspeakably at his hands. She doesn't know what we, the audience, know, and neither does Johnny, so the story is naturally moving forwards in subtext. Another good scene.

Scene III

Hero Johnny gets down to the bottom of the hill. There are crocodiles in the river, and a horribly rickety bridge. It's nerve-racking for him to get over, but he makes it, and sees a sign to Dr Livingstone's house. He rushes forwards towards it.

This scene has its interest, but it doesn't feel right. Why? Let's see if it has all it needs. The scene has a protagonist, Johnny, with a clear aim (to cross the river). There is antagonism in the rickety bridge and the crocodiles, but they don't really get properly in opposition to his aims. The croc's might look fierce, but they are irrelevant, because Johnny doesn't go up against them. The bridge is a bit of a challenge, but it's not a tough choice to make – cross a rickety bridge to save a girl's life? And the bridge held fine, so there was no real antagonism there – in fact, the bridge helped. Looking at the conflict, the bridge and croc's are not properly opposing Johnny's aim. This is classic poor writing where I have mistaken a tough challenge for genuine conflict. This scene doesn't work. We need to rewrite this with some stronger, more genuine, conflict. Let's try again:

Johnny gets down to the bottom of the hill to find that the bridge has been cut down. A sign says the next crossing is 25 miles downstream. He doesn't hesitate. He will risk his own life to save Connie. He takes off his shoes and heads for the fast flowing water. He doesn't notice as the crocodiles slide ominously into the water from the bank opposite...

Protagonist, Johnny. Aim: to cross the river. Antagonism – crocodiles and fast flowing river in direct opposition to his aim (to cross the river), so we have conflict. Values have changed for Johnny as he came to the river optimistically and suddenly his mission appears impossible. Turning point is nice in the scene as his fortunes have gone from promising to unlikely-to-succeed. Subtext shouting at us from our privileged knowledge of the presence of the crocodiles. I would also bolster the subtext with a view of the progress of the bad guy during this scene to accentuate the subtext at the sequence and act levels (Johnny is risking death on a wholly pointless journey). Now it works.

Scene IV

Climax scene. Johnny fights the fast flowing river and wishes he'd learned to swim when he was a kid. Even so, he's doing all right until the crocodiles show up. He is too late to go back, so he wrestles them manfully and makes it to the far bank where he emerges in long focus and in slow motion looking pumped and gorgeous having lost his shirt and defeated three crocs on the way over. All the while, Ronnie cackles and twirls his moustache as he ties Connie to the railway line. Johnny emerges, finds Dr Livingstone and implores him to come and rescue Connie, and Livingstone agrees. Meanwhile Connie is tied to the rails and the City Express is 10 minutes away...

The climax scene has a clear protagonist, Johnny, with a clear aim, to cross the river. There are clear forces of antagonism ranged in direct opposition to the aim of the antagonist. His value changes from negative at the outset to achieved beyond doubt at the resolution (he crossed the river). At the sequence level, his key question is answered: will Johnny find Dr Livingstone? Yes, he did. Again, the subtext is present in the knowledge that Ronnie has entirely fooled Johnny into all this risky action, whilst Ronnie, as the bad guy, progresses nicely with his dispicable agenda towards Connie, so the 'real' story is moving forwards in subtext. So despite Johnny's apparent success at this scene level, the wider story has gone from positive to negative across the course of the sequence, with the bad guy doing very well indeed, and across the course of the act, with the story level aim of getting Connie safely to the city also going significantly to the negative.

Hopefully you can see the ease with which scenes can be thrown together against a clear sequence aim. We then test each scene to be sure it has all the elements one would expect to find in achieving its higher level aims, and yet grip and intrigue within itself on the way through.

Also absolutely critical to the success of this sequence is the duality of the presented 'textual' action and the background or 'real' story moving forwards in subtext (subtext through subplot, to be precise). We are following Johnny through his successful aim to find Dr Livingstone. He is brave and dynamic and thrusting and decisive and is achieving what he is setting out to do... and all the while we know that the wider, more important aims of rescuing Connie, getting her to the city and apprehending the bad guy, have all become less likely to succeed.

The key point to remember in terms of the relationship here between creativity and structure is that your creativity within a scene must generate a turning point. Every time. Scene after scene for the duration of your story, some small, some medium and some large, but turning point, turning point, turning point. If you think about it, all the turning points we talked about throughout the discussion on structure are actually delivered at the scene level, because story delivery is ultimately the work of a scene. So every scene must encompass either a minor, moderate or major turning point, and your creative challenge is to ensure that the scenes link to become the sequences, acts and ultimate story, scene by scene by scene. (And, of course, if you are a novelist, this still applies just the same. We are only using the *terminology* of the theatre, remember. If you want to see a novel delivered 'scene by scene', read anything by Michael Crichton.)

I must say at this point, I use fairly strong language here to push you towards always searching out turning points and always crow-barring in conflict, and so on. I do this, because as soon as I make it optional, you have the disastrous opportunity to give yourself an excuse not to make your story the best that it can be. Of course, not all story events can turn, and not all should turn. So let me reassert that this is not a rule book. Remember what we said: If a scene works for you, who cares what the structure is? Who cares if it has an antagonist or conflict? Don't forget, we only even begin to look at structure when we perceive a scene doesn't work properly. We don't care a jot how we did it *if it works*. So, if you don't feel your scene needs all that push and dynamics, then don't force it. Some scenes probably will need to lay back a bit and draw back the pacing.

As Bob Gale points out:

> In writing scenes, the primary question is to ask whether the action does its job in delivering the big picture. Not all scenes need to carry conflict and antagonism and 'turn' and so on. If all scenes carried that much power throughout your story, I think it would be hard to watch. The scene where 'Marty invents rock and roll' carries none of the things that the rule book guys would tell you a scene has to have. There's no antagonist. There's no relevant conflict. The scene doesn't even deliver towards any sub plot or even the main plot, but does it work? Judging by what people I meet tell me, it's the single most identified and best remembered scene in the whole of *Back to the Future*.

So we're back with your instincts. We only look at the structure of a story event if we perceive there is a problem with that event, and we want some clues as to why that event is troubling us. That is when we measure out the turning points and see what is missing. Then we can hope that looking at the structure will swiftly lead us to identifying the bug that we sense is there.

On the other hand, the other factor in learning about turning points is that if we have a sequence objective and we miss a great opportunity to create a turning point that would naturally have worked well for our story, we are potentially weakening our story. Spotting these opportunities not only increases the power and grip of that given event, but it brings into focus the conflicts that are available, and that helps us to identify more plot possibilities.

9.3 Scene dynamics

Don't forget that scenes deliver turning points through the *meaningful* choices the characters make. I stress the term meaningful here, because the choices they make should ideally involve dilemma. In general, a scene sets up to offer the protagonist a choice. The key question is raised: which choice will he make? The choice will involve paying a price; choose A and give up B. Choose B and potentially lose C. Choose C and trigger D. Stakes are high, but the choice must be made. Often, whilst we are still assessing the implications of A, B, C and D, our protagonist chooses Z, leaving our brains scrabbling around for what this means as we project forwards. Let's look a little deeper at what we mean by 'meaningful'.

When a Jedi knight decides to laser a storm trooper's head off with a light sabre, we gain little from it because it is the decision we fully expect from a Jedi knight every time he stumbles across a representative of the dark side. It's a challenge, of course, because these storm troopers can be tricky johnnies, and if you don't get them, they will get you, but it is not a dilemma, and it's not great story, because deep down we know who will emerge from the conflict on top. However, when a Jedi knight is faced with the decision to laser his *own father's* head off because his father is a representative of the dark side, we have a genuine dilemma for our character and a decision to make that will cause us to grip the armrests just that little bit tighter. Luke Skywalker (played by Mark Hamill) was put into this position in *Star Wars*. Choose to offer his hand to his father and allow him to live – and be colluding with the dark side and laying himself open to slaughter at his father's hand; or choose to take the path of righteousness – and be responsible for the cold blooded killing of your own dad. Ooooo. Tough one...

When a player is faced with difficult choices to make as part of his challenges, then his inner self is revealed, and suddenly the genuine character (and therefore his actions and therefore the plot) springs into 3D and we have a winner. In short, these are exactly the moments where the story jumps into life, inspires, grips, intrigues and engages. The scene and the story will turn on his decision and we all rush forwards in our minds to try to get a handle on what could possibly happen next.

Our minds work on many levels as we absorb a story. We build a 'configuration' of the story as it develops in our mind, with the events building on one another like a tree structure as we project from the current state (as we understand it) through a range of possible outcomes, and ultimately to some future desired result where the protagonist with whom we empathise gets to where we would want him to be. The beats build scenes, the scenes build sequences, the sequences build acts, and our brains fly backwards through the delivered knowledge to build our understanding of the current position and fly forwards through imagined coming events to build the story forwards.

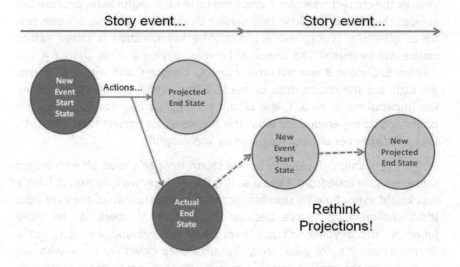

Each turning point generates new insights that we count into the sum of our knowledge, and each time the information is not quite as we expected it would be, we have to go back and reconfigure our story from the earliest point that the latest insight impacts. By the halfway mark an audience might have accumulated in their minds the information from thirty scenes. They are subconsciously looking ahead to where the next scene is likely to take them, and what that might mean for the direction of all the story lines. In their minds, they speculate as to the story direction for where the characters must go next towards answering key questions, when a new turning point they didn't expect provides such an insight that they are sent reeling back through half the story, and are forced to mentally reconfigure the meaning of the dozen or more major, minor and moderate turning points they've already taken in. Breathlessly, they reconfigure their mental picture of the story so far – every root and branch from the point the insight impacted – and speculate anew on where on earth the story is likely to take them next.

It is this speculation that the writer works with. The information he has delivered means his audience should naturally be led to an expectation, both in terms of the truth of the existing story 'state', and their belief about where it is going next, only for it to pay off another way and leave them reeling once more. Audiences love a story that does this. It is extremely pleasant brainwork and is the essence of emotion. This is why we so love a story with a twist in the tail. It gives us the unique experience of (re)building an entire story, from start to finish, all by ourselves, from the point in the past that the twist impacts, through to the total meaning of the climax and the nature of the resolution.

At climax in *Back to the Future*, Marty hits the lightning conductor in 1955 just as the bolt hits the clock tower and he is transported through time back to 1985. He wakes up the next morning exactly as he woke up at the setup of the whole story in act I. Marty is relieved when he wakes to find that everything is fine; he did manage to put history back on track and get home safely. But as he absorbs his home and environment, he realises that things are not the same. The house is tastefully decorated, his sister is eating healthy fruit for breakfast and discussing her many suitors with her brother, who is all suited-up for his professional career. His parents are 'self actualised' and their relationship is strong. And Biff is subservient to George McFly, waxing his cars and addressing him respectfully.

In a rush of insight, we realise that Marty failed to fix just one of the historical events that changed because of the actions he took in 1955. Yes, he got his parents to meet and fall in love, and that put his future birth back on track, but in doing so, he changed the mechanism of his parents' meeting. Originally, George was hit by the car and taken in to Lorraine's house as a victim. Lorraine felt sorry for him, and they were brought together through her taking pity on him – the 'Florence Nightingale effect', as Doc Brown called it. In the new course of events, as altered by Marty's presence, they met when George arrived in Lorraine's life as a knight in shining armour to punch Biff's lights out and win her hand and adoration through strength of character. This single punch changed George's view of himself, as well as other people's perception of him. From being bullied and dismissed, he became known and respected, giving him self-assurance and pride that carried through the next thirty years to pervade George and Lorraine's marriage and careers, and therefore the characters and the self-esteem of their children.

The skill of the writer is to continuously exercise the mind of the audience through new information, payoffs, surprises, revelations, insights and changes of direction. A scene must change the world view of the audience. It must change the sum of knowledge on which they are building new insights and projections.

10 The step outline

Rounding up the position, we now have at our disposal our **premise** – the story in a sentence or two; we have the inciting incident, key question and climax, which, if written out, would explain the story in a paragraph or two. This is **the high concept.** We have the list of **sequences** – the fronts of the index cards – which portray the main beats of the entire story, which, if written out, would provide a **story synopsis** (perhaps around 500 words). And the sequence events – the backs of the index cards – which, if written out, will portray the story in a series of steps at the sequence level – probably in around 2000-3000 words. Fleshing these out into scene events as discussed above, delivers us the step outline at the scene level; if written out this is likely to convert into a **treatment** of the story of around 5,000 to 20,000 words (the variation in word count is more about your personality and what feels right to you than any laid-down criteria. I have 'treatments' from 3,000 to 40,000 words. Whatever works for you is fine, however as a sales tool, the shorter the better).

By the time we get to **Chapter 14 – The commercial world**, in which we shall put our salesman's hat on and get out there in the market place, you can see how, in addition to the final manuscript, we might have converted the above acumen into a presentation pack that can handle any requirement.

For the moment though, we continue to get increasingly detailed in our delivery. The step outline is the critical bridge between your fine ideas, your structural and design preparation and a completed script. It is the first full representation of the whole story, and yet, critically, it remains flexible. As we develop our step outline, we will find new ideas and interesting opportunities. We will learn more about our characters, we will begin to find hidden depths to the story and confirm to ourselves the events which work well and those which are weak. We may even change or discover whole new components which will have a wide impact on the final story, such as finally finding the perfect ending that has eluded us or a new tweak to the inciting incident or a new subplot idea that will change or colour the entire work. I have known stories change out of all recognition through the ideas that come to mind from this point forwards, so keep your wits about you. Fine new ideas can even trigger entire new stories! This is the value of the step outline – it is a vehicle that facilitates story development and change, at the same time as focusing in on the final product.

10.1 Writing by writing

Look, I'm getting fed up with all this preparation. Why not just start at the beginning and write the damn thing?!

I have sympathy with this question. Starting at the top of page one and just going for it was how our natural ability to write took us down the path towards becoming a writer in the first place: we wrote short stories and we just did it. We started at the beginning, wrote it until the end, cleaned it up and then sent it around to an amazed and admiring audience.

Some people do pull off this same approach in delivering longer pieces too, but I don't believe it is sustainable. What we really need before we can confidently deliver the final draft of any length of story is the ending. Until we know the ending, we cannot line everything up so the story spine leads towards that ending, and if we start on page one and just write, we don't get to the end... until the end. Once we finish the story for the first time, and then discover the ending through the writing process, if that ending is a surprise to us (and I promise you, it might well be very different from the sketchy beliefs you had about it when you wrote 'Once upon a time...'), we have to go back and rewrite everything that is not in line with this newly discovered ending.

So you set off on a rewrite. It's mildly painful, because you have to change things you liked the first time round, and the occasional new element has ripple effects that make it tricky to be sure you haven't left in old stuff that is now flawed, but you are still full of optimism, because knowing the ending gives you a boost... and some new ideas. Indeed, this first rewrite, with this new ending, opens up a fascinating new twist and a wonderful possibility for a subplot. You desperately want to incorporate this wonderful new turn of events, but the thought of picking through and rewriting the relevant sections of your 100,000 word novel to gain that improvement might be too much to face. A full length work is a marathon, not a sprint, and if you do have the guts to get stuck into a second or third rewrite, you certainly won't by the fourth or fifth revision. It is at these junctures that we give up or make do. We become jaded with the story and lose sight of its original beating heart. Energy fails us and the story dies in a drawer.

However, with the step outline, change is easy. In fact, it's a delight. Rearranging the events in a new order, standing back and taking another look, experimenting with possibilities, dreaming through new ideas in the night and then building them in as well is a fantastic way to inspire creativity and squeeze the best out of our ideas in ways we simply couldn't contemplate when faced with changing the fourth full draft.

So avoid going into detail or writing a full draft, and value your step outline. I like to work with the step outline for weeks or even months before moving on; indeed, I keep on and on working it until the step outline stops offering up new possibilities. Once the step outline stops finding new ways to arrange itself, the chances are very good that you have found the version that will become your first full draft. There will still be a good deal of room for further creativity and fresh ideas, but once your main story has found its structure, these tend to have an impact limited to the detail and cleverness of individual scenes rather than at the sequence or act level.

As a hint at this point, you will endlessly come up with ideas and snippets for character action and dialogue, gags and events that you cannot wait to put into your story and desperately do not want to lose. Start a file now – I call mine TheDump – where you put all these ideas in enough detail that you cannot possibly forget them. However, do **not** write out full pages of actual draft dialogue and action. Resist the temptation. Defer your pleasures. Just make a good solid note of the event or action you mustn't lose in TheDump, and move on. I promise it is the right thing to do.

10.2 What information goes into a 'step'?

The step outline is your story represented at the 'event' level – it's the backs of your index cards. It doesn't really matter whether this is a sequence, act, scene, paragraph, beat, chapter – you will find the level that works for you – just a logical event. This said, I seem to make two types of 'step'. In the first, an 'event' represents a sequence; as we have seen, a relatively high level representation of story progression. The second one goes deeper, with each event representing a scene in the final story. At this point, do not worry too much about whether an event is a sequence or a scene or anything else. Just let it logically chunk itself out into the steps that come naturally in delivering the story. For the moment, the aim is to list **significant** events, not analyse or structure them beyond loose linkage.

Step outlines are distinctly personal – indeed, they are not ever intended for anyone else to read – so over time you will discover what works best for you. It is also worth noting at this point that story development is not a sequential list of jobs to do. You will not just be working on the step outline drawn from the backs of the index cards. Although this is your focus, you will also be working forwards – changing the method of delivery of a sequence objective; putting ideas for detail into TheDump – and backwards – revisiting sequences and higher story events to change or tweak or delete or replace them as you build knowledge and work into the detail. You are endlessly working on your story now at all the different levels, from beginning to consider detail right up to the bird's eye view.

In addition to the story content, each step additionally contains a level of technical information that allows you to keep track of what the scene or sequence is achieving in the wider context, so every step <u>can</u> include information concerning its structural purpose, for example, you might note in the corner of your index card: **'Main Plot Inciting Incident. Act I climax'**. Again, this doesn't work for everybody – I tend to only do this if I feel there are problems with the story – but if you are worried about the structure of your story, it might be helpful to see it in this context, as shown in the example coming up next.

10.2.1 Example – plot step outline

This example is taken from a children's story of my own, entitled *Clonk and the Birdman*, and you will quickly get the idea. Below is the step for the first sequence.

The front of the sequence card says: 'The Bird family loses in Robot Wars'.

The back of the sequence card says: 'The bird family enter their robot in Robot Wars. George Bird is optimistic that it will prove him as an inventor, but they fail to win'.

The step outline says:

Sequence 1. Act 1 – Main Story Setup

Our story opens as the hyped audience count down for the start of a battle in an episode of Robot Wars. Three home-made robots and four house robots clash in a last man standing, to-the-death battle. Three... two... one... Activate! Off they go! In amongst the house robots, the smoke, the flying metal, the hyped crowd and dramatic commentary, one of the battling robots looks like a conical tank being driven by a determined-looking, humanoid mini-robot (CLONK). Two children – MAX (13) and VICKI (10) are working Clonk, the tank he is driving and the weaponry via remote controls as the robots whack chunks out of each other, the crowd wince and scream and the sparks fly. The kids' dad (GEORGE BIRD, 36) gives urgent advice behind them as their mum (HATTIE BIRD, 33) jumps up and down behind them and watches through her fingers.

The kids do really well – one by one, by hook and by crook, they defeat the other robots until there is only one other robot left. It's a fast, metal wedge of aggression, and it's really annoying. Eventually, Clonk (remotely controlled by Vicki) gets out of the tank, runs across the pitch and angrily breaks the cheesy robot's aerial off. It spins in circles out of control and into the pit where it explodes in flames. The kids win!

In the televised interview afterwards, their victory interview is interrupted. The judges deem that they had two robots in play, and they are therefore disqualified. The family goes home defeated. George is particularly dejected – as an inventor, this was going to be the making of him.

Sequence 1 – Checks (optional):

Don't bother with these checks if you are not worried about this content!

    Is there a Protagonist? Bird Family

        Protagonist aim – to win Robot Wars

    Is there Antagonism? Other competitors in the Robot War

        Antagonist aim – to win Robot Wars

Protagonist/Antagonist aims in conflict? Yes

Sequence has an inciting incident? Start of Robot War

Sequence Key Question raised? Will the Birds win the Robot War?

Protagonist value under threat: Success

    Value at start – Optimistic. Potential win

    Value at end –Dejected losers

Sequence has a turning point? Yes – they go from winners to losers

Sequence key question answered? Yes – they lost the robot war.

Rather pleased with this opening – it carries all the signs of an effective event, which is particularly pleasing with the difficult opening slot. Good structure in itself; good introduction to the story's overriding theme of robots and gadgets; good introduction to the family members in their roles and yet plenty of action; decent turning point and unexpected twist in the climax. The sequence is also highly representative of the story as a whole – it's about a family, its focus is on George as a wannabe inventor, with Clonk as a significant part of the action. The sequence manages to encapsulate the theme and mood of the whole story: George loses the battle, but he still has his family; this 'foreshadowing' of the main messages is often a facet you find in an early sequence in a good story – it helps to orientate the audience and makes the story gel. All quite promising. [6]

---

[6] Just as an aside, in an example of what happens in the commercial world, once I got a deal for this story, the very first thing the production company did was remove this Robot Wars sequence. It was too expensive for a location setup that was only used the once (actually, it was used twice, but they didn't want to discuss it with me). So I was required to write a different beginning. Typical. I got something half decent, and was obliged to scrap it for something cheaper.

So each sequence is documented in the manner shown above, and each can be subjected to the checklist following the sequence. At the end of the first act, I add in an extra set of the same checks, but at the story level, in order to ensure that the other elements that should probably have been delivered have indeed been accounted for; e.g., the story level's inciting incident and key question; a mid-act turning point at the end of Act II.a; a climax turning point at Act III and so on.

If you find that you have problems there are three common issues with the step outline:

Back-story

If you have entire sequences that are necessary to the story, but which just don't carry the power you would like to see from them, the chances are that they are delivering back-story. Take the information in that sequence and embed it into other sequences. Often the 'progressive complications' sections of a story event spend a good deal of their time bedding in back story or preparing the ground for future events.

Relevance

I am certain – 100% certain – in your first draft step outline, that you have material in your story that should really be removed. You keep it because you love it, but it won't work. Other people *won't* love it if it isn't relevant to the story; even if the material is brilliant, hilarious, iconic, glorious – if it isn't relevant to the story, it will not work. Store these puppies away for another day, but in terms of this story, they need to be shot like dogs in the street.

Once you get the self-belief that you can always come up with new creative ideas to fill a requirement, there is huge satisfaction in cutting material that should be cut. I get a perverse enjoyment from chopping things these days, safe in the knowledge that it's ready and available for another story, and its removal will benefit *this* story. At least 80% of the ideas we come up with will need cutting. Once you become reconciled to a level of quality control that expects to discard 80% of what you write, your output becomes much more authoritative.

Subplots

It is important to recognise that a subplot is not the same as a 'separate plot'. Yes, a subplot, more often than not, is a mini-story in its own right, but it must still impact the protagonist on his main plot journey. Subplots are purely different forms of conflict facing the hero on his existing journey.

For example, in *Back to the Future*, the main plot is concerned with if and how Marty will get back to 1985. The subplot is the story of how Marty disturbs the course of past events when he prevents his parents from meeting in 1955, and therefore removes the likelihood of his own birth. He must get his parents back on the path towards true love to ensure his own future existence. But notice, the resolution of this subplot is directly connected to the main plot. It is a separate story in the sense that it stands alone rather well, and has its own inciting incident, key question, complication, turning points, climax and resolution, but it is, most importantly, tightly linked to Marty's main plot progression. If this one can't be resolved, the main plot will fail to resolve as well. A classically structured story will be a series of causally linked events, so when you move into subplot it must still evidently impact the overall progress towards the main plot goal. When you watch *Back to the Future*, note how many significant scenes have Marty McFly as the protagonist. I'll tell you how many: all but one (the one in which George punches Biff's lights out). Every single scene moves the main plot.

One last point on the step outline. Remember that it is your own personal tool, so it doesn't have to be nearly the same as mine. Adjust it to your purpose over time. The main thing is that it will be used as a totally reliable template for writing the first draft without having to think about whether you are remaining faithful to the main events. They are already fixed and decided, so the step outline 'contains' the big picture events. You can focus on the entrance and exit point to the scene or sequence you are writing, so you don't have to think about the bigger picture.

10.3 The story pitch and treatment

Before we move into the first full draft, we have one more job to do.

Whether you are an author or a screenwriter: sit a few individuals down over the next few weeks, and pitch your story out loud to them. Do not simply give it to them to read – you can't – it's a step outline and you should show it to no-one. Pitch it aloud. You are still developing your story, and it is aloud that you learn more about it than at any other time.

Don't just think, 'Sod that,' and skip to the next chapter. I know the pitch process is uncomfortable, but there's huge value to be had. As soon as you've done it once or twice, you will realise just how important the pitch is to the writing process, so please trust and believe me. It has to be done. Do it on your own for practice and refinement – even alone it will be revealing – then get someone in front of you and put yourself through the pain.

Up until now, being a writer has been a solitary, hidden process. You can tell people you are a writer, and they take you at face value and find you interesting and ask you lots of questions about your writing and your story. From today onwards, when someone asks you what your story is about, you take them somewhere quiet, sit them down, and you tell them your story.

Pitching your story is, at first, a difficult process, because you are laying your creative self on the line and setting yourself up for a public failure of some sort. It's the first time you deal with people who will be genuinely assessing your creation, and if your story is weak, the problems stick out like a sore thumb and it is no fun. But it is also the single most valuable event in the development process. Precisely because it is mercilessly revealing; it tells you everything you need to know about your story... if your story is flawed, it will show you what needs to be done to fix it. If your story is simply pants, it will save you from the months or years of writing and rewriting it. If your story is good, you will go forwards with massive confidence that you are on to something worthwhile.

Interestingly, as you tell your story, most of the discoveries you make will come from you, rather than from the person sitting opposite. During the pitch, you will be amazed at how many changes your instinctive ability to tell a story will demand as you go along. You can see and feel how your story plays out in real time. And as you do so, you will notice yourself automatically changing the story to get the right sense across, or making a change to the pace or even rewriting material as you go in order to keep the story vibe right. You will find yourself missing out sections – sections you've already spent hours on in step outline, and now discard because out loud you simply *know* they don't work – changing events, reordering things. Pitching your story out loud is naked exposure, and it is unbelievably valuable.

After each pitch, go back to your sequences and your step outline, introduce the changes your instinct demands, then pitch it again. Keep pitching it until the story you tell grips and turns and satisfies and you no longer miss sections out and make changes afterwards.

Ignoring your friends

For the most part, the pitching process is **not** a mechanism for getting comments from someone else. Most of your nearest and dearest wouldn't tell you their true feelings anyway, and – to be brutal – their comments are mostly worthless. Friends and relatives are not ultimately your target audience, and your relationship with them skews your likelihood of objective insights, but you listen to your own story through their ears and you react through their expressions, and you simply know where changes need to be made. I suppose there is some value to be found in a trusted opinion, but what's more important is to watch body language and notice the way **you** respond to the affect your story is having on that person.

I often argue with myself after pitching: 'I just love this sequence on paper, then when I'm pitching the story, I skip over it. Why on earth is that?' But I love it, because it reads well and is hilarious, but the next time I pitch it, I miss it out again. It's clearly not right, and it has to go.

Working with constructive criticism

If you do want to get value from people's comments, you need to force people to be honest with you. Most people won't look you in the eye and tell you what they really think. They can only be trusted to tell you that what you've achieved is amazing and that the story is amazing and that you are amazing. You have to thank them very much for being so positive, then chivvy them to tell you what was their least favourite bit. Even if they loved every minute there must be a weakest point for them. Try to force them to be constructively critical. Once they get the idea, there's no stopping them, which can be a bit of a pain, but it is necessary.

Next, you take what they say and assess it in your own mind. Do their comments ring a bell with you? Is this person representative of your target audience? I pitched *Clonk and the Birdman* at my kids and it went over well. They stayed listening to the end, which is quite an accolade, and they want me to tell them the Clonk story again, so I take that as a thumbs up. I did perceive some weaknesses in my own mind (I don't mean weaknesses in my mind, I mean weaknesses in my story in my own mind – oh, you know what I mean), and found myself cutting to the chase once or twice, which I will watch for in the next pitch.

The pitching process is merciless. It finds out the weak stories and leaves them dying on the floor. It's a great process if your story is strong, but horrible if it is weak. Either way it tells you what you need to know: that your story is a winner that people will truly love, or that there is no point whatsoever in investing the blood, sweat, tears and years in a full draft and marketing exercise. Give it up, learn your lessons, bank the good bits, and move on to a new story.

If you are scared to pitch it to people; if you are not going to and are at this very moment moving on to the next section, the chances are this is your subconscious talking to you. You know, deep down, that the story sucks. Be honest with yourself. Why don't you want to pitch it? You could be wasting your life on this story... maybe now is a good time to think about a new story. Either that, or you lack personal confidence. So many of the writers I work with I just *know* will never be successful because they simply lack the self-belief to push on with their ideas and deliver their stories in their own way irrespective of what the world thinks. They come to seminars by people like me hoping to find other people who will magically turn their ideas into winners for them. It doesn't happen. Editors and producers do not descend from heaven and fix up half-arsed stories. If they could do that, they would be writers themselves. Delivering a complete and excellent story is YOUR job.

Have confidence in your abilities and go for it your way. If you think about it, there's actually no other way to tell your story exactly right – apart from your way, so you might as well get used to the idea and get pitching...

On the positive side, if you come out of the pitching process with confidence in your story, you can be as sure as you can ever be (at least, before you ask someone to part with some money for it) that the story has genuine strength. And if you are looking for people to pitch at, book clubs and writer's clubs are a fantastic platform, because they are strangers, and because they are sympathetic to your plight in pitching. This will prove even more difficult, and yet much more valuable, than pitching at friends and relatives.

Once your pitch is complete, write it up as a short version of your story. It doesn't matter how long it is; it will be as long as your pitch has naturally shaped it to be. This will become your 'treatment' to send out as part of your presentation pack. Many, many deals are done on the basis of a treatment rather than a fully fledged script, so keep it carefully for future use.

11 Writing the first full draft

OK. What I do now is copy my step outline into my scriptwriting software (more on software in a while) in one huge chunk. I then begin addressing it one scene at a time. I start with sequence one, put line breaks between the logical separations of scene I, II, III, IV and so on that make up that sequence, then begin writing the scenes. Each time I finish a chunk, I delete the steps from the step outline and begin work on the next one. It's as simple as that.

I try to treat each scene as a standalone short story; as if there is nothing else in the world that I must do in my writing but turn this scene into a short story and deliver it to perfection. I must perfect the beginning, middle and end as if this single event IS my entire story. If I can get every single moment right, I have half a chance that the whole beast will be right when I get to the end.

This is our chance to be purely creative. The preparation all pays off, and it's the most wonderful and powerful process. And it's all down to you. Each step is a short story to be written, and is a joy, so you will find yourself fairly cracking along. I like to take two or three weeks away at a retreat for this bit, to really immerse myself in the world I am creating and try to give each scene every ounce of life I can.

And here's the great news: I'm not going to get involved. This is pure writing, and it's all yours from here. If your steps deliver the scenes, and your scenes deliver the sequences, then your sequences will deliver the acts and your acts will deliver the story. Simple!

The best advice I can give as you launch into your first full draft is, don't be scared to go back and make further changes to your steps, sequences and even premise. Delivering the detail is bound to generate new ideas and great additional material that you must integrate into your story. If this happens, stop, go back to the top and redefine everything to ensure the new material is firmly bedded in. So don't switch off the creative juices and don't be scared to go back around the loop to get the step outline right.

STORY ANALYSIS AND PROBLEM RESOLUTION

There are no writers. Only re-writers.

Anon

12 Story analysis

The tips and techniques in this chapter are really of value in improving a completed script or fixing problems in a troublesome one, but at this stage of our story development, if we can get our defence in now, it could save a good deal of time and Paracetamol later, so knowing this stuff in advance might help with prevention.

When analysing a story I know nothing about, I read it through in one go, trying to absorb it simply as a consumer of story. I try to resist developing thoughts about it, but just let it happen to me as a story should. When finished, I make a page of notes on how I *feel*. Stories are not made for analysis, and people can always – always – find problems with things, so it is really important to take off the nitpicker's hat, look for the positives and see what the story does for me as a person. I then try to encapsulate the inspiration. What is it that the writer was on to when he decided to devote a proportion of his life to this creation? That inspiration will be the heartbeat at its centre.

Once I have an idea what the writer is trying to achieve, I will usually have a vibe for what is wrong straight away. Later we will look at solving amorphous and frustrating problems with a story. However, in my experience, the chances are that the problem lies in the big picture.

12.1 Common story problems

It's not as hard as you might imagine to generalise story problems. More often than not, story problems fall into the same categories, so let's run through the usual suspects.

12.1.1 Problems and subtext

A good many stories read more like diaries, with real life problems exaggerated and multiplied in order to pump up the drama. The author has grasped the idea that stories must reflect truth, and so they present a slice of life where the angst-ridden protagonist bounces from one challenge of life's grim reality to the next, the victim of first a lack of money, then a bastard of a boss, then a bastard of a boyfriend, and then the car breaks down. Then *after* lunch, the company goes into liquidation, the brother steals from mum and blows the money on his drug habit, the best friend loses the court case, Auntie Betty's husband leaves her and mum is diagnosed with... and so the long day wears on. The author can point at conflict, 'real' characters, at least one truly nasty, authentic bad guy hurting good people, drama, and real world truths. How can it possibly be that it doesn't work?! It's a common problem and surprisingly difficult to explain to the author why it doesn't work.

From a theoretical viewpoint, the problem here is almost certainly with subtext. There isn't any. Using the brutal truth of grim daily life as a stick to batter us with does not tell a story. A diary is not a story. Whatever potential a manuscript of this nature has will not be realised until the writer moves away from a personal perspective and introduces intrigue and suspense through subtext and the inter-relationships between the characters. There are many, many true-to-life stories that started off as diaries of extraordinary life events and genuine personal experiences. The trick is to look for ways to present the material using the different types and mechanisms of subtext discussed in depth earlier.

Life truth

A story lives in the events that do *not* happen every day; in the events that change the daily script and take us somewhere new. When you read a 'true story' the key events that separated that person's story from normal life are the events the writer should choose to narrate, not the other 99% of his life that was rather ordinary. Yes, we want a story to reflect a truth about life, but not through showing us the streets, people, office work, bitchiness, anger, joys and disappointments we can see every day. The story of the *Three Little Pigs* presents us with a truth about life, and yet as those piggies build houses and the wolf huffs and he puffs it has no clear real world elements whatsoever. This is the kind of truth we are after; the kind that resonates with life archetypes and our subconscious conflicts, not with our daily grind.

Knowledge gaps

As we know, subtext equates to knowledge gaps, and the biggest knowledge gap is the one that drives the entire story; namely, the key question. A story lacking subtext will often betray itself at this fundamental level, with a vague or no key question, and therefore no inciting incident and therefore an undermined ending. We will look further at subtext-related problems in a minute, but you can begin to see that subtext underpins everything that goes on in a story, and its absence is fatal. Often writing which is authoritative, clever and really quite attractive is let down by the lack of subtext.

12.1.2 Baseline analysis

Given that the problem with a story is not obvious (or, more likely, is multi-dimensional) I begin my analysis from the good old baseline.

Analyse all the key elements of your story baseline. Answer these questions again:

> What is the title, genre and setting of the story?
>
> Who is the protagonist?
>
> What is his problem?
>
> What is his goal?
>
> What opposes him in achieving this goal?
>
> What is the inciting incident?
>
> What is the key question raised?
>
> Who is the antagonist?
>
> What is his goal?
>
> What happens in the end? Does this address the key question raised?

There are many possible anomalies that this process might raise, and I couldn't possibly cover every scenario here. But clearly, if any of the above basic elements are not clear and present, there is a good chance that the problem areas are revealing themselves.

If your story baseline is not easy to populate and if every question is not answered easily, then your story is likely to be unclear, meandering or confusing. You have issues that must be addressed before you move on to the first full draft.

13 Structural analysis

Generally speaking, stories work with a surprisingly similar and limited number of underlying structures, Lots of theorists have proposed new underlying structures and 'anti-structure' approaches to story, but they are misguided or, if you want my honest opinion, simply wrong. I'd love to see something new and brilliant that works through someone doing something different with structure, but it hasn't happened in the last 2,300 years, and I doubt it ever will, so until it does, in my own stories, I work exclusively with a modest range of structures.

One of the benefits of this is that it gives us two reasons why structure is an excellent analysis tool:

- Where most issues to do with character, plot, subtext and so forth are amorphous and subjective, structure can be objectively analysed, and is directly revealing of creative flaws.
- Structure is often the source of the problem.

So for a story consultant looking to fix story problems, structure is the low-hanging fruit. Beginning with the biggest structural components, one of the most common 'fixes' for a story is to rework it into a 'classic' three act structure. Remember, structure is a function of the events you choose to narrate, and the order in which you narrate them, so simply re-positioning the key events can deliver, as if by magic, an appropriate inciting incident, turning points, progressive complication, climax and resolution. I am endlessly amazed what good it does for the telling of a story when it is arranged in this way. An inexperienced writer often knows instinctively that something isn't right, but can't put his finger on it. We re-arrange it in classical form and two things happen: firstly, the problems become clear (because we find these problems get in the way of the desired structure), and secondly, the very same story suddenly delivers. We all need guidance, particularly given the enormity of a full length novel or screenplay, and a classic structure provides a good deal of the guidance we need. It just works, and if a story has all the elements of a *good* story, it is likely to lend itself readily to this structure.

Now, I know this is cynical and that buying into a predetermined structure sounds fairly uncreative, but the truth is, *it works*. Like your skeleton works for you, the structure of your story will allow it to function. For me, the rule you should apply is this: if you want to be successful and make any money, use the brilliance that came up with your story in the first place to make sure it fits a proven, orthodox structure. That way the story editors can see clearly that they are dealing with a writer who knows what he's doing and gets the basics in place. It makes them feel more comfortable in working with you.

Of course, there are stories which don't want or need a classic three act structure, but we are talking about analysis of *problem* stories here, and in my experience, a problem story often has issues relating to the events chosen for narration and the order in which they are placed. Going back to a classic structure is very revealing. It doesn't mean you have to stick with a classic structure, but knowledge is power, and this process often provides the knowledge of where the problems lie.

13.1.1 The major turning points

To define the boundaries between the main structural events, a full length story is most likely to have at least 1) and 3) of the following major turning points:

Act I Turning Point. An event that propels the protagonist on his quest. This will orientate the audience, who will understand from this what will represent a successful – or failed – outcome to the story for the protagonist when we reach the end.

Act II Turning Point. Although not an inevitable, necessary structural plank like the other two, the dynamic of story often requires a turning point around the halfway mark if interest is not to flag. Usually, this is a serious blow to the progress of the protagonist and a setback against his achieving his quest.

Act III Turning Point. Act III is characterised by a major turning point at which the protagonist enters into the final conflict with the forces of antagonism. The outcome of this ultimate battle will definitively tell us if the protagonist succeeded or failed in his quest.

13.1.2 Key question

And of course, your inciting incident, perhaps coupled with the Act I turning point, must raise the correct key question in the mind of your audience. I won't go through the principle again – you know this stuff – but we do need an inciting incident that raises a key question: The flag drops to start *Wacky Races*, the key question is...? Exactly. Who is going to win the race? The referee blows his whistle to kick off a football match. The key question is...? Who is going to win the match? A plane comes down in the mountains. The key question is...? Will the passengers and crew survive?

Many people will look at their story and think, 'that's fine, but my story simply doesn't lend itself to a big, clear key question. It just wouldn't be right to try to force one in!' And, of course, it mustn't be forced. We have been talking throughout this book about what defines a down-the-middle, mainstream story, and I've used examples with obvious key questions in order to demonstrate the principle. But as I mentioned before, most stories that win the highest acclaim are off to one side of the mainstream, and the key question is not necessarily delivered on a plate with neon signs pointing at it. In the highest quality stories, the key question is usually part of the subtext – a knowledge gap divined by the audience through thinking about the events they have seen – so if you are writing a subtle story or one of high complexity and high literary merit, the key question might take time to evolve from the material delivered, and will grow over a period in the mind of the audience. But have no doubt: however subtle the key question and its method of delivery, in any good story it is likely to be there. Yes, there are exceptions. *A Christmas Carol* is a story without a clear key question, and yet it is an absolute classic. It has. Instead, half-a-dozen sequence event questions. It's quite possible your story is an exception too, in which case I would find it hard to advise you without seeing your story. Contact me via the web and I'll discuss it with you (I'm really very good, far too cheap and seem to get more attractive with every year that passes...). Seriously, stories without one overarching, clear key question, tend to have very definite character growth and/or comprise a number of smaller story events that do have key questions.

If your key question is subtle or ethereal or deliberately unclear, I can't help you to gauge if you have it right. I know what you are going through: endlessly worrying that you haven't given the audience enough to 'get it', but on the other hand, you don't want to ruin the beautiful subtlety by overstatement. The only clue I can give you is never to underestimate the intelligence of your audience. Remember the dining room scene discussed earlier? The audience is massively busy pulling apart everything you give them for clues as to where the story is going. You only have to sling them the seeds and they will envisage the trees for themselves. And secondly, you must trust your instincts. It is something that must feel right to you, and you will deliver it correctly more through instinct than by science.

If you are a fairly inexperienced writer grappling with a subtle and complex novel plot, it might be worth practicing on a couple of more mainstream storylines, to develop your experience, as you grow the complex masterpiece into its ideal form in the background over the longer term.

13.1.3 Foreshadowing

It often amazes me that we all know, long before we even take our seats in the cinema, the basic beats that a story is going to take. We see a poster showing our hero looking tense, with an extraordinary monster of doom looming behind her. Before the movie begins, we know that these two will go into conflict and, in the end, the good guy will overcome the monster, and good will win out over evil. We are right every time – and that is what we *want*! Even so, we are still interested to watch the journey. We want to know what will happen.

Now, this dynamic is extremely important to writers. Here is what Willy Russell said to me:

> I deliberately tell the audience at the very beginning basically what will happen in the end. I know it sounds odd, but knowing where the beacon is that we are heading towards is not only vital to the writer in knowing where the plot is going to go, but it heightens the tension in every single scene, because the audience understand the implications far more when they know where we're trying to get to than they do if I had kept it all secret and we'd had a revelation at the end. As it is, the emotion builds towards the inevitable with far more power than it otherwise would. The audience shouldn't be asking: 'where is this story taking me?' it should be, 'I know where the story is taking me – how on earth are we going to get there?'

A fine example of this is, as ever, *Back to the Future*. In each of the plotlines, we are told what the plan is right up front. We then watch the characters try to fulfil those plans. Doc and Marty make a detailed plan to hit the bolt of lightning and send him back to 1985. Marty and George make a detailed plan for how George will ask Lorraine out on a date. They also subsequently make a detailed plan – even to the point of acting it out in a role play – for how George will assertively save Lorraine from Marty's inappropriate advances to make George appear strong and dynamic. All these plans are given to us in detail and, in every case, the end goal is achieved, but not in the way they planned or in the ways we expected.

This aspect is really important. Most new writers want to build their story in secret (i.e., structure all their knowledge gaps in the form of revelation subtext), because it is easy to imagine the power of the revelation when it eventually explodes into the mind of the audience. As writers mature, they discover the power of privilege subtext, and although it doesn't make a lot of intuitive sense to give your audience advanced knowledge of what lies ahead, I think you will have realised by now how privilege subtext works. I urge you to think about how to strike a balance between privilege and revelation in your own work, and force yourself, wherever you can, to err on the side of privilege.

Incidentally, this is why we greatly enjoy taking a friend to see a film we have already seen. Because we have watched it already, all of the revelations are known to us, so we are enjoying it the second time with the same subtext now delivered in privilege. We enjoy the same plotlines from the new 'privilege' perspective, but also enjoy the difference in knowledge we have over our friend as they take on the same storylines in revelation.

13.1.4 Climax and resolution

Is your key question answered at resolution? It may be that you deliberately want to leave the key question open or unanswered; to have your audience finish your story deep in thought and without a clear, closed ending. That's fine, of course, as long as the ending at least addresses the key question. An open ending is much harder to pull off successfully than when dealing with the purity of down-the-middle stories, in which the ending simply answers the key question raised.

See Chapter 3.10 – Structure and non-classical form for hints on successfully stepping away from the mainstream.

13.1.5 Turning points and sequences

The next level down takes us to the structure at the sequence level. Here we are still looking for turning points, but now we are looking for indications that key design factors are missing. You will recall that a turning point is essential, and that it only exists if we have a protagonist in head-to-head conflict with forces of antagonism through which only one can win out. If a sequence does not have a turning point, we can identify which element is missing, and then make an informed judgement on whether this sequence can get away without a turning point (given the context of what goes around it) or if it's absence fundamentally undermines the story.

If a sequence does have a turning point, it can still be a problematic sequence if the events it drives forwards are not relevant ('causally linked') to the top level story and the overarching aims of the protagonist.

13.1.6 Plot and character

You set up a key question and a quest for your protagonist and settled your audience down with an expectation that these things are now being addressed. If your characters then act out events that do not progress the spine of this plotline or which disconnect the character of your players from the things they should be doing, your story will become confusing.

Go and have another read of Chapter 5.2 – Plot-driven or character-driven? – to be sure that your plot is a direct result of your players' personalities (a result of the in-character actions that they take), and that your characters are defined by the actions that they take when in conflict (not by the things they say or the clothes they wear).

I am analysing a story at the moment in which the protagonist is a clearly intelligent, educated individual, holding down a responsible job and with assertive tendencies towards his staff and the things he finds irritating. He then goes into town and behaves like a buffoon, cannoning from one disaster to the next and treated with derision by his friends. This is clearly not the same character. The writer wants to deliver acerbic comedy one moment, via a strong and cynical character, and slap-stick, cartoony stuff from an incompetent the next. The same character cannot realistically deliver both types of comedy, so although both types are well written and sometimes hilarious, they cannot believably be the same character.

There are mechanisms for making this work. We could have him take illegal substances and undergo some form of Jekyll and Hyde character switch that will carry the audience with him. It is also possible, of course, for a character to have great competence at one thing – say, their day job – and utter incompetence at another – say, dealing with the opposite sex. Indeed, this can add greatly to a character's appeal and makes for the very best three-dimensional characters; but be very careful that any overlap between these two is handled consistently, or your character will fall apart instantly in the mind of the audience.

13.1.7 Fighting the flab

Even if your baseline is fine, and your inciting incident is in good shape, it is still the case that the next most common problem with a story is Act II flabbiness. The main plot inciting incident is good, it raises a key question that is clear. The climax and resolution bring this key question into sharp and unavoidable focus and resolve it to complete satisfaction. But there are all those acres of empty space between the inciting incident at the end of Act I and the climax and resolution at Act III. If you make Act II the length you would naturally want it to be, then the whole story is too short. If you pad it out, it loses vibrancy because the padding is unconvincing. This is a very common problem, particularly for novelists, where the wide open spaces that need filling are just enormous.

The answer lies in subplots. Your story currently looks like this:

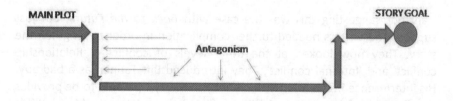

The inspiration behind your story includes an excellent problem and antagonistic forces for the protagonist to face. It's all brilliant, but it simply isn't enough to sustain a hundred minutes or 100,000 words. What you need to do is to search for subplots in the form of new forces of antagonism, in order to shape your story to look like this:

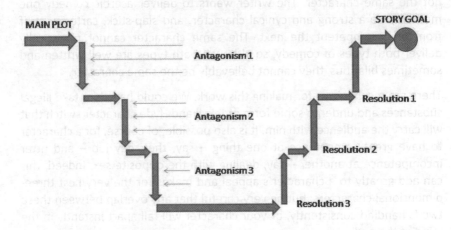

Where do you find these? Well, it's very hard to say without knowing your individual situation, but the first place to look is at the different levels of conflict discussed in our chapter on Conflict and Antagonism. If you think about *Back to the Future*, the main plot conflict Marty faces is with the science of time travel and the ability to do it a second time in 1955 without the technology available in 1985. This is an 'external' conflict with forces over which he has virtually no influence. He has to work with the laws he's given, and he has almost no control outside of these laws. In the context of the diagram above, this provides the diversion of Antagonism 1.

The first subplot is provided by conflict at the 'institutional' level – or, more sensibly in this context, the 'low control' level – whereby Marty disturbs the course of history and effectively wipes himself from existence. This provides the diversion of Antagonism 2 in the illustration, because he has to put historical events back in place before he can return to dealing with Antagonism 1.

I am not suggesting this was the case with *Back to the Future*, but just suppose the writers needed further complication in order to lengthen the story. They now looked at the other levels of conflict – 'Relationship conflict' and 'Internal conflict'. They introduced Biff Tannen as a bad guy. His interference in the relationship between Marty's parents-to-be provides the diversion of Antagonism 3 with conflict at the 'relationship' level. Biff is directly interfering in Marty's ability to get his parents to meet and fall in love. He has to resolve this before he can return to dealing with Antagonism 2.

The writers also went on to provide an overarching 'internal conflict' whereby both Marty and his father doubt they can ever achieve anything. Marty reveals this during Act I as he fails the music audition and considers giving up. Later, when he is trying to persuade his father to ask his mother to the dance, he realises how frustrating this same attitude is, and delivers the philosophy he himself was lacking in Act I: 'if you put your mind to it, you can accomplish anything.' By the end of the story, Marty's father has his first novel delivered to the house. George holds the book up to Marty and proudly teaches his son the same lesson his son had taught him back in 1955: 'if you put your mind to it, you can accomplish anything.' The writers use this internal conflict to deliver the philosophical premise – the theme – of the whole story as well as to deepen the conflict and antagonism on to all four levels and provide the basis for George's fundamental character growth that defines the story's overarching philosophy. We, the audience leave the theatre feeling we, too, could assert control over our lives and our future if we show the right spirit and don't just leave everything to fate.

Interestingly, if you think about it, because all the plotlines are both causally linked and dependent upon each other, the whole of *Back to the Future* eventually turns on one man's self doubt, and that single punch that turns that self doubt around. Here it is in diagrammatic format:

Back to the Future - Story events are causally linked and dependent

MAIN PLOT
Key Question: Can Marty get back home to 1985?

Antagonism 1
External conflict. The time machine cannot be powered in 1955. Can they harness a lightning bolt to make time travel happen? Plan to do so *is frustrated by:*

Story Resolution
Because of 2, Marty is able to hit the lightning bolt and makes it home to 1985.

Antagonism 2
Relationship conflict. Marty's parents don't meet. Subplot aim: Can he get them together?
Plan to do so *is frustrated by:*

Resolution 2
Because of 3, George's parents kiss on the dance floor.

Antagonism 3
Relationship Conflict. George is weak and unattractive to Lorraine. Can George appear strong to Lorraine? Plan to resolve conflict *is frustrated by:*

Resolution 3
Because of 4, George becomes strong, and is now attractive to Lorraine.

Antagonism 4
Internal Conflict: George's self doubt threatens to scupper everything.

Resolution 4
George overcomes self doubt and punches Biff's lights out.

A 'world' conflict is compounded by a relationship conflict, which is compounded by internal conflicts, which cause further relationship conflicts, until it was all reduced to that one single moment when George finally makes a fist... and everything unravelled back from there.

So Act II is flabby if there simply isn't enough 'Progressive Complication'. You need to search the other levels of conflict and find ways of layering in this kind of beautiful complexity to force the main plot to take mazy diversions before it can be resolved.

13.1.8 Conflict regression

It is also possible at the Act II level that a flawed story is suffering from conflict regression. This occurs when the protagonist has been put through a conflict of epic proportions too soon, leaving further turning points a little pale in comparison. Repeating a turning point of similar scale is still not satisfactory. If Rambo has already battled 200 soldiers and scraped through, lining up a further 200 against him will not grip as the first 200 did. When a third gang of 200 appear, we think about nipping out for a pint. We know what happens because we've seen it already. You need to design your story so that each plot-line builds turning points that scale upwards, increasing progressive difficulties, as the story advances.

This does not apply across plot-lines, of course. The set up and inciting incident of a subplot in Act II, for example, do not have to trump the recent main plot inciting incident that climaxed Act I. Hence, shortly after the extreme drama of the Act I climax of *Back to the Future* (Marty is trying to escape terrorists, and is dramatically sent back in time), we get the relatively modest sequence 4 climax to the Act II setup asking the question: will Marty find Doc Brown in 1985?

13.1.9 Character arcs

In great stories, at least one character takes a journey of learning and personal growth. Their problem at the outset – although presented through action – is really their flawed approach to a social issue. They deal with something inappropriately, and are faced with difficult consequences. By the end of the story, they have learned appropriate behaviour, and will never fail in the same way again. In *Back to the Future*, George McFly is struggling in life because he won't stand up for himself. We recognise that his lack of assertiveness and self-belief means that he is bullied by Biff and cannot be attractive to Lorraine. By the end of the story, he has learned – and we have learned with him – that a bit of spine can take you a long, long way. If we simply let life wash over us we won't get what we want, whereas if we are proactive and determined we can get life to give us what we want.

If none of your characters learns or grows, your story may still have positive aspects, but it will not be as good as it could be. Most writers, particularly scriptwriters, try to give as many characters as possible some form of personal growth across the story progression, and this is great if it can be done naturally.

The growth of a secondary character can also provide for a subplot. In *Back to the Future*, Doc Brown could have been a 'functional' character; simply there to give Marty the foil he needed for his main plotline to play out. But the writers looked at Doc Brown and developed his story. In Act I he is attacked and killed by terrorists. Marty attempts to warn The Doc in 1955, but he refuses to accept information about future events. To fix this, Marty returns to the future ten minutes early in order to prevent the original death. This whole subplot bears almost no relation to the main story, but serves to bring complexity to the conflict of Act I and Act III and to 'humanise' it. In other words, the main forces of antagonism come from the somewhat unemotional meta-physics of time travel. The Libyans, the Doc's 'death' and Biff are used to personalise the conflicts so that we can relate to them.

13.1.10 Sequences, scenes, subplots

Next in line is to take everything we have talked about above for the main story, and go through your composite events checking for all the same things. Here is the checklist we used in the step outline:

Ask yourself: does your story event have:

A Protagonist

    A protagonist aim

Forces of Antagonism

    Antagonist aim

Protagonist/Antagonist aims in opposition?

An event inciting incident?

Event key question raised?

Protagonist has a value under threat?

Value at start?

Value at end? (Should be significantly better or worse than at start)

Event has a turning point?

Event key question answered?

Delivery in subtext?

And of course, this check should validate any event, be it an act, sequence, scene or an entire story. We will undertake an in-depth scene analysis, with a detailed example in a moment, in **13.2 – Scene analysis.**

13.1.11 Falling in love with detail

Despite the flexibility allowed by structural drift, you need to be honest with yourself. Often, if your story is just not vibing nicely and you are conscious there is something wrong but cannot put your finger on it, it is a good bet that you have fallen in love with some detail and are refusing to allow it to be removed. During step outline and all points before writing the first full draft, it is so easy to be seduced into putting gorgeous detail and – worse still – dialogue into the piece, resulting in a reluctance to remove a scene that really has to go. Try to spot when you are keeping something because it has a hugely attractive aspect to it, rather than recognising that this material is in the wrong place or in the wrong story altogether. You might even have written it in originally simply because you didn't want to forget it, then you went into greater depth because you loved writing it, and now you have a single area of detail in the delivery, in which you have invested time, effort and brilliance. You have fallen in love with it and are bending the rest of the story out of shape to accommodate it.

You need to provide yourself a strategy for dealing with loved but misguided/misplaced material. As discussed earlier, the secret is to build up a repository of good ideas – not just for this story, but forever. Jokes, character traits, subplot ideas, iconic images and moments, genius dialogue – none of it needs to get lost, but just because something is brilliant does not give you any good reason to crowbar it into this story. I love custard. That doesn't justify putting it on my fish and chips.

The test for such material comes from the relationship between plot and character. If your plot is your character and character is your plot, then everything that happens in any given story event will be leading you towards your protagonist's goal. This should be unavoidable. If your players are acting in accordance with their characters, they should be driving the story forwards inexorably and defining the plot for you. If an event doesn't do this, there is a good chance it is a symptom of misplaced genius.

Do you have events that are not connected to the progression towards the (clearly stated) goal of the protagonist? Do you have characters who do amazing/hilarious/ frightening things, but which are not part of the spine of a plot or subplot? Be brave. Be honest. You know where it is. Operate now. Remove it from your story and put it in 'TheDump' ideas repository. You are creative and can come up with more material at the drop of a hat – it's what you love to do. Your beloved but discarded work will definitely find a home one day, and when it does find its rightful place, its wonder will shine through. In the wrong place, it won't work and it will kill everything else around it.

13.1.12 Forces of antagonism

Are your bad guys really bad? Do they keep progressing their own cause, or do they stand still, simply waiting to be done over by the good guy? Are you such a nice and sensitive person yourself that you are not making your forces of antagonism convincing enough?

Most of us writers are thoroughly nice people. Arty, pacifists who don't have a mean bone in our bodies. We've all heard how most writing is autobiographical – well guess what. Your protagonist is You, and you are going to great pains to ensure he gets all the weapons he needs to deliver the messages you want delivered by your story. And you hate your antagonist. You despise him. And you aren't giving him enough attention to make him real. None of us wants to be bad, so we don't deliver the negative forces in our story well enough. Focus on your forces of antagonism – it may make you feel guilty and uncomfortable to work closely with your bad side – but try to get into it. You won't go to hell. [7]

Map out the antagonist's own character and plot development and make sure they represent a genuine 'story' in their own right. Also ensure that it is through the positive and proactive initiative of the good guy that the forces of antagonism are overcome, not through the incompetence or lack of conviction of the bad guy. **Stories are born out of conflict**, so the conflicts you create must be impressive. For this to happen, your forces of antagonism must be impressive, too. Remember, your protagonist can only be as good as the challenges he must overcome, so make the antagonistic forces so harsh, uncompromising, intelligent and convincing that your own friends and family will be shocked that you had such evil inside you at all.

Incidentally, conflict is part of real life, too. If you are spending a great deal of time and effort pouring oil on troubled waters and trying desperately to calm things down and remove conflict from your real life and the lives of others, you are probably not living an appropriate life at all. People often become writers in the first place because they can express themselves in writing without fear of being slapped down. Start trying to get used to conflict in your real existence, and notice how you deal with it; let it roll sometimes – join in and escalate things occasionally – it can be quite an effort – or at least don't be the one to dive in and try to remove it. It will

---

[7] This might not apply to everyone, of course, but I meet writers like this all the time. Some of us are just too nice to get anywhere. It is often part of a more general lack of self-belief, which will seriously undermine your ability to get published. Believe in yourself and your story, and you will have a much better chance of getting somewhere.

make you a better writer. See who else responds in the real world if you sit on your hands. You will be amazed how much more life there is to lead if you accept that conflict is part of every day. You will also get a lot more story ideas and realistic, convincing characters if you allow conflict into your everyday life. It might make you a stronger person, too.

13.1.13 Analysis and subtext

Still got problems? OK. Next, look more deeply at the subtext. Pick a few key moments in your story – probably most usefully in the scenes running up to a major turning point – and measure off the subtext between each of the participants relative to the audience, like we did earlier for the Jeeves and Wooster story – **4.1.3. – Extract from The Inimitable Jeeves By P.G. Wodehouse.** If there is not much subtext across all plots there will be no interest. No intrigue. No story. It's like measuring for a current across the poles of a battery and finding no life. There's a battery in your hand, but there's no spark.

Your story probably ticks a lot of boxes, as I said at the beginning of this section, in terms of drama, head-on conflict, life truths and so on. But if there is no subtext, then there is no soul. Revisit the chapter on subtext. Additionally, ensure that your main plot and subplots have clear key questions. Raising these key questions is the trick in raising lively subtext of the more advanced forms discussed, because your audience will absorb real-time action in the context of the impact on other plot lines.

13.1.14 Still not found a fix?

Your story stinks. Get a proper job.

Seriously, if you still have problems, maybe it's in the detail. Go through the next section on scene analysis, then go back to the beginning of this chapter and start again from the top. Don't just plough on to the full draft regardless. You must find a remedy first if you possibly can. I promise that any problems that exist now will only be magnified by the full draft. They won't be hidden by great dialogue or made beautiful by fantastic scenery. They will get bigger and worse. Now is the time to act.

13.2 Scene analysis

A scene is the smallest meaningful component of a story. An event defined through conflict that palpably shifts the fortunes of a protagonist. Although this is very much a theatrical or filmic term, it applies equally to a novel or any other story form. And of course, although I am analysing a scene here, the same approach can be applied to any story event, or indeed, an entire story.

13.2.1 Scene analysis example – *Back to the Future*

Let's take a look at a 20 second scene from early in Act II of *Back to the Future* to see how it breaks down. You should be able to do this to any scene at all. This was selected at random by students, who decided to choose, at random, the first full scene after the exact middle of the film, i.e., 54 minutes. I could have chosen an easier one, myself, but I wanted to show them that these principles apply to any scene at all.

We are at the point where Doc Brown has realised that Marty's interaction with his parents-to-be (George and Lorraine) has interfered with the course of history. His parents didn't meet when they should have done, and his actions mean Marty is being wiped from existence. Marty must reunite his parents in love before he can return to 1985, so Doc and Marty are at the school his parents attend. The plan is for Marty simply to introduce George to Lorraine. They fell in love easily enough in the original course of life, so surely nature just needs the opportunity to take its course once more, as it did so successfully the first time around.

As the scene runs, Marty introduces George to Lorraine, but she ignores George completely. It becomes evident that she is much more interested in Marty.

Scene Objective: The scene objective is for Marty to introduce his parents to one another so his future father can ask his future mother out on a date. (This is what would be written on the index card.)

Protagonist: There are three main roles that are of equal importance to the scene: Marty, George and Lorraine, so it isn't obvious who wears the protagonist's armband. The way to choose your protagonist is to ask, 'for whom does a value come under threat in this scene? Who moves in value terms from negative to positive, or vice versa?' That is your protagonist. One could argue that George is the protagonist, and yes, the scene does turn on his value (hope?), but he moves from being 'without a girlfriend' to 'even more without a girlfriend', so although this works, I would keep looking. Marty moves from being potentially dead but feeling positive, because he has a plan to fix his problem, to 'much more likely to being dead', and negative, because the plan fails. This shift also takes place in subtext (the other characters do not know what is at stake for Marty) so I think Marty has the greater claim on a shift in values.

Protagonist Aim: Marty's aim is to get his parents to meet and fall in love.

Value under Threat: The value that is under threat for Marty is 'life'. His very existence depends upon his parents meeting and falling in love.

189

Conflict: The conflict comes in several forms at this point in the story, but for this specific scene, there are three key conflicts opposing Marty's aims:

The space time continuum. Marty has to change the course of history to get his future birth back on to track.

George's self doubt. We know that George is not at ease with himself or others, let alone girls. We also know that Lorraine has knocked him back once or twice already and that he 'can't take that kind of a rejection'. George has to overcome this self-doubt if Lorraine is even going to notice him.

Lorraine's love for Marty. Marty replaced George at the moment his parents were supposed to first meet. This has led to her becoming infatuated with him, Marty, instead of falling in love with George as history intended. This has put Marty in conflict with Lorraine.

The test of true conflict is to see if it is in opposition to the goal of the protagonist for the scene. The starting point has the course of history betting against Marty's future existence, so there is clear opposition to Marty's desire to get the space/time continuum on track and live. Marty's need is for his parents to meet and fall in love. George's self doubt and Lorraine's desire for a relationship with Marty are also directly opposed to Marty's aim, so the conflicts are good.

Turning Point: Marty begins the scene from a (relatively) positive value for 'life'. He has a simple plan to fix everything, so at the scene setup, things look promising. However, when he introduces George to Lorraine, things don't go as expected. She is so besotted with Marty, and so overcome by his presence, that she doesn't even acknowledge George. Marty's actions change unexpectedly from the matter of introducing George to Lorraine to the job of fighting Lorraine off himself, whilst George succumbs to his self doubt and sneaks off in the background.

Lorraine is then dragged away to class by her friends, and she is all the more in love with Marty. She didn't even notice George.

The test for a turning point is to see if the scene switches the value under threat from negative to positive, or vice versa. In this case, the (relatively) positive starting point for Marty's 'life' has been severely undermined. George doesn't have the belief to sweep Lorraine off her feet. Lorraine is too obsessed with Marty to notice George, and Lorraine has said to Marty that she likes a 'strong man'. Marty's future existence is even more unlikely than it was at the beginning of the scene. His fortunes have gone from positive to negative (or you could say, from negative to dramatically more negative. It amounts to the same thing). The scene therefore has turned.

Text and Subtext

Note that the value that turns (Marty's life) is not directly addressed by the content of the scene. This is a sure sign that the story is moving in subtext.

What we understand from the action of the scene is not directly presented in the action of the scene.

The surface level, textual content of the scene is an attempt by Marty to hook up his friend George with a girl he knows, Lorraine. The textual result is failure. However, there is a great deal going on under the surface. The subtext is oozing out, as prescribed, at every level. Let's measure some of *Back to the Future's* knowledge gaps.

Dialogue and action

At the basic subtext level – **Dialogue and Direct Action** – when Marty walks up to Lorraine and says (text): 'Lorraine? I'd like you to meet my good friend, George McFly.' What we hear him say, in subtext, is: 'you two need to get it together or I'm going to be wiped from existence.' In text it's just teenage banter and relationships. In subtext, life itself is under threat.

George then swaggers suavely towards Lorraine. We know that he doesn't really walk like that. We know that the way he leans against the lockers next to her with overt confidence is not the real George. And when he says: 'It's really a pleasure to meet you,' we cringe for him as Lorraine falls back heavily against the lockers, involuntarily blurting out Marty's name, because we know what is really going on. She is so besotted, she can't even bring herself to be polite to George. Indeed, she doesn't even notice he is there. In subtext, we recognise that Marty's plan and George's chances of a date with Lorraine or a boost to his confidence are both going horribly wrong.

Empathy

This beat also resonates with us in subtext. We empathise with both George and Lorraine – we remember George's position in our own lives (or at least, some of us do...) – approaching a girl with a vain hope that a relationship might develop and yet knowing – just knowing – that it is all going to lead to a desperately embarrassing rejection. We relate to George's position: knowing that we have to do something and having no belief that it will work out well. We relate to Lorraine's position: in terms of George, having to deal with someone we want out of our face, and in terms of Marty, having to face and talk with someone we are totally in love with – someone who doesn't know or respond to the way we feel.

Lorraine ignores George completely. She reaches out for Marty, asking him how his head is after the earlier accident. He shies away from her touch, saying he is fine. In subtext, she is saying, 'I want to take care of you,' and in subtext he is rejecting her. Because of our position of 'privilege' (we know more than Lorraine – he's trying to set up George, not himself) we get a strong subtext: 'this is all wrong! She doesn't realise he is her son! Something has to be done!'

But she tries again, telling Marty how concerned she's been for him since the accident, whilst George slinks off in the background. This is the turning point. In subtext, we realise that the plan cannot possibly work now George is gone, and Marty is floundering around as he fails to get Lorraine's attentions off him and on to George.

The school bell rings, Lorraine's friends drag her off to class. We see her face and realise that she is even more in love with Marty now that he has approached her at school than she was beforehand. As yet, Marty does not know this...

Subplot and implication

In privilege subtext, we know as much as Marty, but much more than Lorraine. We know that he is trying to get his parents together to ensure his future existence, so everything he does we interpret in this context which, of course, Lorraine doesn't.

Also in privilege subtext, we, the audience, know more than Marty in that earlier scenes told us that Lorraine is infatuated with him. We recognise that Marty doesn't realise this yet, so in subtext we are already thinking, 'this plan is horribly naive.' The subtext has us preparing for things to go wrong, whilst at the same time, Marty and the Doc are preparing for things to go right. (Remember the conscious and subconscious plot progressions moving in opposition to each other?)

George is going to make a great effort to overcome his own self-doubts and be brave enough to actually ask Lorraine out. We know more than him, in that Lorraine is infatuated with Marty, and his advances are more than likely to be rebuffed.

As the scene plays out its resolution, the camera pans across to rest on the face of Doc Brown, who has looked on as the scene unfolded, just as we have (we discussed earlier the possibility of a character 'representing' the audience. Usually, this would be Marty. In this scene, it is Doc Brown). This encourages us to 'zoom out' and think about the bigger picture; in other words, we read the subtext in terms of the sequence, act and story levels. At the sequence level, we realise Marty is now further away from achieving his sequence aim: to reunite his parents in love. At the Act level, we realise he is further distanced from his act aim: to be in the time machine, coinciding with a lightning bolt having reunited his parents. At the story level, we feel he is now further distanced from his main plot aim: to get back to 1985.

Subterfuge

In subterfuge subtext, Marty knows more than Lorraine and George. He is a time traveller from the future, and he is their future son, he's trying to get their romance back on track for his own survival, and he has to keep these things secret. A juicy set of knowledge gaps that persists through all the Act II scenes.

All this from one low-drama, 20 second scene containing one minor turning point and a couple of dozen words.

13.3 Planning a scene

With a cynic's hat on, an interesting method to plan out a scene goes as follows.

Look at the value under threat for the protagonist through the scene and check its value at climax. Say, we want the protagonist to succeed.

Set the start of the scene up with this value at the opposite pole. The protagonist is failing. The scene is an attempt to succeed.

Set the forces of antagonism in direct opposition to the possibility of the protagonist turning this value from the beginning to the end.

Define the events that will progress the scene: the action through conflict that will force a turning point. The protagonist looks like he might succeed! Then the forces of antagonism slap him down, and it looks overwhelmingly like he will fail – but no! He snatches success from the jaws of defeat! The protagonist succeeds, and the scene has turned.

Ensure the mechanisms you use are not clichéd or predictable – find more interesting ways to deliver the scene than the first ones that spring to mind.

Ensure the whole thing is awash with knowledge gaps; i.e., delivered in subtext.

Only resort to this kind of approach if you really have no inspiration to instinctively take you rollicking through a scene. It's all a bit contrived, really, isn't it?!

THE WRITER'S DAY, THE SALESMAN'S HAT

A good many young writers make the mistake of enclosing a stamped, self-addressed envelope, big enough for the manuscript to come back in.

This is too much of a temptation to the editor.

Ring Lardner (1885 – 1933)

14 The commercial world

Like all areas of creativity, there is a clear division between two different mindsets that must come together to make a work of art into a commercial success. On the one hand, we have the creative individual – the 'artist' – giving blood, sweat, tears and years to wonderful new creations for the world to enjoy. On the other hand, we have the commercial bread head – 'the businessman' – looking clinically at this same creation as a 'product' and trying to decide if there is any money in it or not.

Very rarely do these two people see life in the same way. They live in different worlds and work by different imperatives. More often than not, they can barely communicate. I would go as far as to say that the very best artists, by their very nature and instinct, are almost impossible to manage or categorise in the way that a businessman would like, and have less chance of 'making it' than a lesser artist who is more commercially amenable.

As I mentioned in the introduction, Hollywood film companies speculate, on average, $100,000,000 on a single film. I left all the zeros there so you can see them all and appreciate – it's a big number – one hundred million – and it's a big risk. And that's the average in 2009. For this reason, story departments (or more likely accountancy departments) need to be as sure as they can that this isn't money down the drain. If they could, they would take all of the guesswork and subjectivity out of it, but they can't. The nearest they can get is to work very hard to find 'High Concepts': stories that can be expressed in a sentence and which have a highly marketable hook. One of my Hollywood production company partners is looking *only* for concepts – short stories at most – to take to the studios. When the studios see a hooky title, intriguing logline and a concept that lends itself easily to attractive marketing then they begin to see dollar signs. They only need to add a famous name or two to be most of the way to a financial success. Sad but true. Whilst you and I bleed from our foreheads, desperately trying to make every word meaningful and perfect, the studios are looking for a poster.

Look at Harry Potter. What a fantastic high concept. Some people amongst us are secretly wizards. They exist in a secret world right in amongst us mere mortals and they can do magic. How perfect is that?! Oozing subtext and conflicts and sci-fi magic whilst feeding the dream of all young people. Perfect. Supreme. However, then look how the stories were delivered. The wizards go off together to their own wizarding school. The subtext is removed, because they all know that they can all do magic. The plots are reduced to one dimensional battles with a standard 'bad guy', and the potential of the high concept is not delivered. I know it is not done to say this, but I don't think the Harry Potter stories are delivered to their maximum potential. The world bought into Harry because of the fantastic power of the high concept, but although they take us to a wonderful world, the subtext potential was missed in the actual delivery. I'm not suggesting that the stories are bad – of course not, and as I say, the high concept and the world created by J.K. Rowling are simply perfect. What I will say is that the Harry Potter stories (particularly in their film form) leave us a little dissatisfied, because the subtext is not fully exploited. The stories are weaker than they should be and the films will not stand the test of time as they should. Check the ratings. You heard it here first.

But do note how much can be achieved with a great high concept. It is really, really beneficial to you as a writer and to the potential success of a story.

Once they have their 'high concept' they throw a team of in-house screenwriters at it, whose job it is to crowbar in all the concepts, techniques and principles espoused in this book, a couple of mega-star actors and the rest is down to the accountants.

So when they see something that *might* be brilliant, but is hard to measure, they baulk. Just as you would baulk if someone asked you to double your own mortgage to show confidence in a work of art. Would you remortgage your house for your own story?! Suddenly, we aren't so sure about just how highly we value our own work. It may genuinely be great, but even then there's no guarantee of a return. We want other people to take these risks. And yet if you can come up with something brilliant, but which *can* be measured in ways that might give them some confidence that it is not only brilliant, but to some extent provably so, they smile broadly and ask if you would like to sign here, here and here.

What they can measure is the presence or absence of the principles in books like this. So the first commercial advice I have is: work to these principles. Don't try to be clever until you are fully professional, financially secure and can call the tune. The musician, Sting (Gordon Sumner), started with hot little pop songs and moved on to more indulgent Jazz after he'd cracked the big time. Spielberg made *E.T.* before he could gain commercial support to make *Schindler's List*. Woody Allen started with the spoof: *Casino Royale* before he made the work of art that is *Manhattan*. You are well advised to walk before you can run, learn your trade and play a long game.

Have a go at being a businessman for your story. To begin with, write the poster. What will be your one-liner that will get the mood and vibe of your story across? This is known as the 'log line' or sometimes the 'strap line' – the catchy sound bite that hooks you in one go, that they strap across the poster and the guy says in a deep voice on the trailer. For example: 'In space, no-one can hear you scream' was the perfect scene-setter for *Alien*. *Back to the Future* went with: 'Meet the only kid who ever got into trouble before he was born.'

Many agents, publishers and producers will ask to see a title, logline and story summary. The summary is the equivalent of the 'blurb' that would be written on the back of the book, or in a newspaper summary of a movie plot. People always read the back of the book, and often base their buying decision on what it says. I don't think there is any more difficult challenge in writing than getting the back cover blurb right, and you will grow to hate doing it. It is definitely proof that you have a high concept story if you can do it easily. Ironically, the better your story, the more subtext it will have, and therefore the more difficult it is to get across in a small number of words. (This is why the industries pass on great stories and don't understand why they missed them.)

But it has to be done, so my advice is to look at the inciting incident and the implications of the main opposition conflict that the protagonist must overcome to answer the key question, and use these as the basis for the summary. If you feel yourself trying to force the subplot overview in as well, are you really sure your main plot is that strong?

More valuable would be to try to get the initial submission to include the treatment rather than just the summary. The treatment is the whole story in something between three and ten thousand words. For a novel, this is likely to be the short version you wrote earlier, or it may be that they will request the first three chapters or fifty pages, or five thousand words. For a film script, it should be relatively easy to write a short but comprehensive version of the entire story in a synopsis word count, because film stories are much shorter than novels.

In my experience, if you tell your industry target that you have a 'presentation pack' that is ready and waiting to make their lives nice and easy, they will accept it gladly, irrespective of their own specific criteria, so I would advise that you make a presentation pack out of those items listed that seem to work best for your story. Let's take a look at that now.

14.1 Packaging your material

OK. So you have taken quite a journey. From a first few paragraphs showing a rough idea of your inciting incident, key question and resolution, you have now got an impressive full (manu)script, a 5000 word treatment, summary and/or pitch, slugline and a monster of a step outline that was the tool to pull it all together. Now we have to make it attractive to the businessmen. The process looks like this:

> Create a presentation pack containing a covering letter, a brief CV of your writing achievements and relevant experience, and the 'taster' for your work. The taster will vary according to the request of the agent, production company or publisher. (The best target is an agent, so we will use this term from now on.) Most literary agents will ask for the first three chapters or fifty pages. Most film agents will initially want to see a title, logline, one-page summary or perhaps the treatment. Your presentation pack has a space ready for whatever they request. I use a gloss white folder from the stationers to pack everything inside. For a book, I also include an illustration – a 'cover design' – as this can give a terrific feel for how you see the look and vibe of your story. (This said, cover designs are a terrifying discipline all on their own, with years and years lost to discussion and opinion to get the design right. It is important because people do judge a book by its cover, and it is very, very difficult, but I still feel my own image does a lot to help create good first impressions.)

> Do not fret too much about precise formats. I have heard long and heated arguments about how film companies reject anything that doesn't have the title in capitals in the right position on the front matter, or the right number of staples (or 'brads') holding it together, and publishers rejecting a masterpiece because it had spelling mistakes.

Rubbish. Yes, of course, you must take a pride and do the best you can, but as long as it is clear and concise and well presented, and the story comes across, then there really aren't hard rules. Don't be too gaudy. Don't try to be 'different'. Do make sure you use a grammar and spell checker.

I generally try to set myself apart by being right down the middle. No cleverness, no gaudiness, no gimmicks. I keep all the peripheral material (CV, mugshot, biography and so on) brief and to the point, then let the writing speak for itself, and I think the industry professionals are pleasantly surprised to see this approach. In particular, the professionals dislike extraordinary hype – they see straight through it – and absolutely detest anything that encourages them to give you a deal on the basis of your personal desperation. Avoid trying to pull emotional levers – it has them avoiding you like the plague.

Establish a list of 'targets' to whom an approach will be appropriate. (See 'Resources and Support', below for how to find them.) Do not just spray your work out all over the world. Agents list the kinds of material that they are looking for, and a small amount of effort on your part can focus your efforts appropriately, thereby removing a large proportion of the dreaded rejections you will receive and saving time, effort and money for everyone.

Initial contact with the agent probably involves a telephone conversation or an email to solicit interest.

The aim of this initial contact is simple: to get permission to submit your presentation pack. Focus only on this aim. Don't go into too much detail. Above all, don't go all emotional about how this is your last chance and your life will be wrecked forever if you don't make it soon.

You have two messages that they want to hear. They want to know about:

1. The genre and nature of your material to tick the box that says your work is appropriate to their list.

2. The existence and nature of the presentation pack.

That's it. Unless your approach is fundamentally misguided (sending a slasher horror film to a children's book publisher or some such) the agent's notice will be drawn to the simple professionalism behind your approach. A presentation pack is exactly what they like to see – remember what we said at the beginning? If you can stand there holding up a gold necklace, they will drop the buckets they are wading through and come running towards you to examine it more carefully.

To prepare for this first contact, get very slick at presenting the 'high concept' of your work. You need a snappy rehearsed paragraph that will instantly have them wanting to know more. If they ask what the story is about, and you say, 'Well, it's pretty difficult to explain...' then you are instantly dropping out of the picture. If a story is difficult to explain in a few words, it will be difficult to sell, so they are already thinking it's not for them. Worse still, is if you start rambling:

'Well, you see, there's this weird church right? And the bloke who's running it is, like, this dictatorial weirdo that nobody realises what he's like, but he's convinced this woman to collude with him and – oh, this is in Idaho, by the way, and, oh, it's 1970, and, well the reason he's like this is because when he was growing up, right, his mum had a problem with a local pheasant plucker, who used to come round and – he was an immigrant from Italy, and his dad, who thought the American government had it in for him, so it made him go a bit paranoid, so...'

Can you imagine being on the other end of this phone? You must stay high level, and you must have a snappy paragraph ready. The job at this stage is not to tell them the story. The job is to get them to request more. Don't go any deeper; if the agent seems to be enticing you to go into depth, just talk about how the presentation pack nicely nutshells it all. If they ask for more detail, I make a little joke about how they are already interested... If they want to know more, they will request the presentation pack, and that is your job done at this junction. [8]

Get the contact's name and agree a timescale after which you will expect to hear from them. Most agents and publishers are extremely good about fulfilling their promises. Honestly. If they agree to read your material, they will do it. It will take two months longer than they said it would take, but they will do it and they will respond. They are also mindful of the emotional connection between a writer and his material, and are diplomatic and, if they agree to read your material, they are generally pretty sensitive in giving feedback and reasons for rejection. They are unlikely to enter into feedback or communication with you if they reject it immediately, only if they take a step or two forwards with you.

---

[8] Just to be clear, the logline is different from the 'high concept'. The logline is the snappy one liner on the poster – part of the marketing. The high concept is the one or two sentence version of your story. For example, in *Back to the Future*, the logline is 'Meet the only kid to get into trouble before he was born.' The high concept is: 'a kid goes back in time, meets his parents, and his mother falls in love with him'.
The logline sells to the public. The high concept sells to the industry.

Once rejected, do not revisit the same person, hassling them for more information unless invited to do so on the basis of a requested rewrite. You are, of course, in love with your material, you are hungry for feedback that will help you improve and you cannot understand why they don't get it. It is always tempting to try to connect with this industry contact to ask what you should change so that they will accept it. You are wasting your time and theirs.

14.2 Handling rejection

Remember, for the most part, material is rejected – even if it is quality material, well above the bottom line of creative merit – because:

It is not appropriate to their areas of interest/specialisation and/or the established relationships they have with partner publishers, producers, marketers and so on.

They have no resources to commit to new clients at the moment (financial or human).

Above both of these items, of course, would be that your work is simply not good enough, but if we assume that it is, there is still every chance that you will gather many rejections before you get the fabled deal (and, indeed, continue to collect rejections *after* you've got your first deal!). Most of the larger agents live almost entirely off projects that are internal to the industry; projects that are pretty much guaranteed to make them money, so why speculate on unknown quantities?

For the most part, books in particular are a by-product of celebrity. Bookshops generally don't sell books, they sell 'names', so agents spend most of their week involved in brokering deals between celebrated authors (or celebrities from any other field) and the publishers who want to use these celebrity profiles to sell books. Celebrity is used to sell books in just the same ways as it sells sunglasses, diets, cars and anything else with a price tag.

Note carefully that this has nothing to do with literary merit.

It has everything to do with marketability. For the most part, the works that I have seen that are of the highest literary merit are also the least likely to get a deal, because they are unlikely to generate a financial return. How much Tolstoy have you read? Could Dostoevsky get a deal today? Precisely. If someone turned up with great literature along these lines, would you invest in it? Precisely. Nor me. David Beckham is bringing out an autobiography – would you invest in that if you were a publisher? Of course you would – and he isn't even a writer – but he's a Not-Writer who sells more books than 99.9% of authors. Yes, you say, but he's not writing stories. True. But Jordan (Katie Price) sells stories. If you were a publisher, would you invest in those stories? Yes. Would you even bother to read them first? No. The content doesn't matter. They will sell because of who she is. They have a marketing handle. If they happen to be great stories too, that's a bonus, but there will be no problem – you will give her a deal first on who she is and the fact that she will sell. The content of the book is an irritation that can be dealt with later. Literary merit comes a distant third.

The point is, you must not beat yourself up as you receive rejections. You WILL receive rejections, and you have to be objective about it. You are emotionally involved with your own work, and you will naturally feel somewhat attacked by any form of criticism, but you must develop a thick skin. You are approaching people effectively for their money, and money is not sentimental. You have to accept that there are many reasons why companies reject material, and whether your writing is actually any good or not is rarely going to be the main reason.

I am a sensitive soul, and I can't pretend that rejections from important potential opportunities do not hurt, but for the most part I see rejection in a philosophical light. I only write for me. I don't write for anyone else or specifically to achieve some publishing goal. I write for me, I write forever, and I write because I love doing it, whatever the world thinks. If I happen to click with a large enough percentage of people then lucky me, but lack of commercial success would never stop me from writing. I listen to critics, because they might have something of value to say, but ultimately, I am my own harshest critic, and rarely take action on the basis of another's opinion unless it confirms a doubt I already harbour.

You must write your own material from the heart, and disregard all opinions about it. There is no other way to write. When you put yourself on the line by presenting your work to a public, however wide, there will be brick-bats as well as bouquets, and you need to "meet those two impostors just the same" (Kipling, *If*) – in other words, accept both extremes gracefully without believing too much in either. From within my sensitive self, I have grown to finding a great deal of value in honest criticism. I actually get a little embarrassed when people shower praise on my work, and find myself trying to get people to tell me what they didn't like as well as what they did. I like praise, of course, but I value criticism. On a practical level, it's more useful!

So accept rejection. You won't ever *like* rejection, but it goes with the job, and learning to handle it helps you to get on and do the right things. How you manage rejection might be the difference between success and failure.

14.2.1 Take responsibility for your work

Many authors somehow feel that if they get attention on the basis of their brilliant ideas, this magical entity called an 'Editor' will descend unto them from the skies and will write their stories for them in the perfect form to make lots of money. No, they won't. Editors (agents, producers...) want something that is basically finished. They may request changes and help to polish and finalise your work, but they won't write it for you.

My experience is that editors do a fine job of selecting appropriate authors and material for their lists, shaping a book to 'house style', and preparing your book for the printer, and have an invaluable role in so doing, but if they are allowed or encouraged to change the content they spoil the book; not because they don't know what they are doing but because it is not their story! How could they possibly write your story for you?! Take responsibility and ensure that every single sentence is how you want it. Then stick by what you have done unless, as I say, someone's criticism rings a bell with your own feelings about the work (or, of course, if someone pays you hard cash to change it in specific ways).

Rewrites are very common in the movie business, and it is difficult to resist wholesale changes suggested with a wave of the hand by some industry bod whom you see as a valuable contact. You rush off and spend weeks crow-barring in his recommendations, then come back and he waves his hand again and suggests a couple more things. After several circuits, the story has lost its spine and the industry bod looks at the mess he's made... sees it's rubbish, can't understand why he ever got involved and moves on. I generally agree to make simple changes – particularly if I feel they are right – but generally, I will ask for a deal before agreeing and implementing changes. A substantial advance on a book would do it, or an option on a screenplay. Otherwise, don't do it. Find someone who likes the story as it is.

I have a thin clear plastic folder containing the half-dozen contracts I've had with agents, production companies and publishers. I also have a bulging lever-arch folder full of rejections. (I know, unbelievable, isn't it?) And I don't believe it would be possible to have the one without the other. I keep the rejection letters with pride because, eventually, getting published is all the sweeter for them.

14.3 Resources and support

The writer's lot is, by nature, a solitary one. It becomes very hard to keep an objective view of the beast you are creating, and it becomes very difficult to prevent madness from setting in when removed from normal society for long periods while you write it. This said, most writers only begin doing what they do because they don't know any other way to live, and most like the solitude. Many – perhaps sadly – greatly prefer the world in their head to the one they are forced to live in the rest of the time, so are relieved when they are able to shut the door on the rotten old real world and immerse themselves in the other one they have made for themselves.

I recognise in myself a combined need. I love being on my own and writing. Ideally, I write as a 'day job' and, once sated by the writing hours, I become a joyously sociable person. On those days when I am denied my personal time alone with my writing world, I am a distracted misery until I am again able to satisfy my need.

The key point is that you must make time for writing but not take that to an unhealthy extreme. When I was working in an office and had young children at home, I used to write from 5.00am to 7.00am. Every day. If I could get the odd 45 minutes here and there on top of that – lunchtime, train journey, whatever – it was a bonus, but those early morning hours were my time for me which, most importantly, did not detract from my commitment to my family. It is not helpful to allow your obsession for writing to cause you to let your nearest and dearest down. You will know that most successful people in any field commit the fabled 110% to their chosen course and follow it without compromise. Some writers interpret this as a call to chuck in the job, abandon the world, get a bed-sitter somewhere and lead a hermit's life. Maybe this works for the odd individual, but I do not think it is wise. Writers need to lead a 'normal' life if they are to understand normal people. Separating yourself implicitly separates your experiences, and when you write from the heart, it will be in a different place from your audience's heart, so the chances that your writing will resonate with a section of society are reduced, particularly if you get lonely and bitter. All that happens is that you start to write stories... for the lonely and bitter. You cannot genuinely study human nature by looking at the internet from the solitude of a converted attic. Well, you can, but it won't inform your writing particularly well. You need to be in groups and parties and families – integrated into society; remember the 'sense of belonging' in Maslow's hierarchy? – that has to be achieved before you can get near 'fulfilment'. The two are dependent.

This also overlaps with the 'creative constraints' we talked about earlier. Removing all other responsibilities from your life creates a situation where you have acres of time to write your story. You can think deeply and make detailed plans. This might seem like a good thing, but guess what. Nothing gets done. Days drift into months and years, and no finished product emerges into the open air because there is always tomorrow, whilst those who envy you the time you have as they are forced away from their writing by life's responsibilities still manage, somehow, to generate meaningful output. When they can snatch time with their story it is precious and valued, and the output is intense because the writer wants to make the most of that time. Time forced away from writing allows a build-up of creative energy – we think and we plan when we are driving or bathing, taking a break, sitting on a train – so when time is found to deliver, it is productive time. Time is limited, and the more it is limited, the more creative you become with it. So embrace family. Embrace friends and social events. Do right by your work and your other commitments. But...

...write every day. Force it into your schedule and make it a priority. Be determined to value that time and to make it productive.

14.3.1 Getting contacts

If your situation allows, the best advice for those who want to write is to train as a writer. Go to college and study writing: Journalism, Creative Writing, Film School, Publishing. In my thirties, I attended a short course at the National Film and Television School in Buckinghamshire and was stunned at how useful it would have been to have gone there full-time. Not only because I would have mastered my craft a lot earlier, but – perhaps most importantly – my peer group of film student friends and colleagues would have been precisely the network I would have needed to find vehicles for my work. The students studying to be directors and cameramen and composers and actors need material to work on, so the writers at film school are in huge demand, and their work is converted into film there and then, week after week. The graduates go on to take key roles in film and television; you are one of them, and they are your mates. When they need a writer, they give you a call. When you need a director of photography, you have a list of them in your little black book. Sadly, getting published or produced is much, much more about who you know than what you write. There is almost nothing more important to a writer than his contacts, and becoming involved with the right people as part of education or career puts you at a great advantage.

It is absolutely no coincidence that the most successful contemporary authors in the same field as me – Clive James and Bill Bryson, for example – both worked on newspapers. Not only did this sharpen up their writing skills, it gave them the contacts they needed to get published and, once they had a book out there, the newspaper gave them the exposure they needed to a buying public. Perfect. Other humorous writers worked as stand-up comedians or in radio and television – Ben Elton, Tony Hawkes and Dave Gorman, for example. Danny Wallace started out as a producer at BBC radio. Try to make your day job a place where you can advance your writing career.

If you are too late to go back into education towards a writing career, try to cross-train so that you are involved and ideally, so that you are writing every day. My training in IT wasn't useful – so I became a technical author. Suddenly I was writing every day. If you work in a corporate job of some sort, in IT or accountancy or whatever, apply for the same kind of job, but within the publishing, newspaper, theatre, film, radio or television industries where you will meet and interact with people who can help you get some exposure. Find a way to write every day, and find a way to work in the area where you heart desires to be.

The Writers' and Artists' Yearbook

Assuming you were not at school with Spielberg, and cannot go back to school now or get a job at Universal, what next for you? The main source of contacts is a book entitled: *The Writers' and Artists' Yearbook*. An annual publication, it lists all agents, production and publishing companies (as well as newspapers, magazines, competitions and much else besides) along with a brief synopsis of the company's specialisation and what they are looking for. Work through this book and highlight the companies that are appropriate for your genre of work.

I would advise that agents should be your first port of call. They are more open to new writers and are geared to handling initial approaches from unknowns. If nothing else, they are more likely to accompany a rejection with some indication of what you need to do to improve your chances, and if they do take you on, they will have a specific avenue in mind that is most likely to prove successful. They are unlikely to take on anything that they aren't very confident will generate a return. Indeed, received wisdom has it that it is harder to get an agent than it is to get a publisher. This said, my first breakthrough was with a direct approach to a publisher, even though I had an agent at the time who was unable to place the same material. Go figure. In *The Writers' and Artists' Yearbook*, you can see which publishers are open to direct approaches, and most have a means of making an initial approach via telephone or email.

Remember at this point which role you are playing. You are wearing the salesman's hat, and you are dealing with the business and commercial side of your project. Media businesses are terribly wary of dealing at the business level with the 'artist'. All too often, the artist is a sensitive and emotional person, particularly when discussing his or her own creations, and very, very difficult to negotiate with on a business footing. However loveable artists might be as people, businesses avoid them. Agents are the interface. Agents talk creative to the artist and then talk business to the businessmen.

Some of the very best artists are, almost by definition, so purely into their creativity that they even actively dislike the vulgarity of businessmen and the prostitution involved in selling their art. We can all sympathise with this attitude, but if we ever want to sell anything, it is better to embrace the way the world works and spend a proportion of our time wearing the mask. Most media company staff are creative themselves, and they are a lot easier to deal with than other industries, but the fact remains, if you can show an understanding of the commercial world and the business imperatives, you will be a great deal more attractive to the people trying to package and sell your work, and therefore you will be much more likely to be signed up.

Web resources

Film production companies get most of their work through internally managed projects, agents and what they call 'first look' production houses who give them first refusal on the interesting nuggets they find. The bigger production companies and studios will never deal with an unknown or unrepresented writer directly. Film agents are also listed in *The Writers' and Artists' Yearbook*. I also found some success once through a web-site called **inktip.com** which provides a link between scriptwriters and the industry, and seems to have decent links into genuine film makers. It is also an interesting place to punt your scripts, because, over time, you gain an awareness of the point at which people are dropping your work. Statistics are available to you concerning the numbers of people who viewed your title, slugline and premise. If they are interested by these top level elements, the individual will go on to read a summary, then perhaps the treatment, and ultimately the whole script. Over time, you can see, for example, large numbers attracted by the top lines, then reading the summary, but dropping out before the treatment. You can look at the summary and see if you can sharpen it up and get more people moving to the next stage. There are many other web resources; have a trawl around and see the **Useful Links** in the next section for more web sites that might work for you.

Competitions

In books or film, competitions are a wonderful way to get a profile and make contacts. My first movie business success was a competition win. It was called the Euroscript Film Story Competition and was advertised in *The Writers' and Artists' Yearbook*. First prize was to work up my story with a professional scriptwriter, and between us we produced my first screenplay. The screenplay didn't then sell, but the competition win greatly enhanced my ability to get people to talk to me and look at my work. If you join inktip, for example, you will often see a stipulation that submissions are only accepted from 'published or produced writers, or competition winners.' It also shows that you are beginning to hit home with your material and should continue along the same lines. Perhaps above all it gives you contacts and feedback from people who can tell you something useful.

Web site

Get yourself a web site. It is cheap and easy to put up all the basic information you need on a well designed web site. It gives you something authoritative at which you can point prospective agents and buyers, and allows people to find out all they need to know about you and your work from one easy access point. Many authors these days decide to cut out the publisher altogether, and sell their own work from their own website. There are positives, because the profit you make on a book is all yours, whereas through an orthodox publisher you must pay off a retailer, distributor, publisher and agent before you get your cut, which leaves you with something like five percent of the cover price (before tax). This said, do take a look at **Self Publishing**, below, before you run off down this route. There are down-sides.

A well designed web-site can help give you some credibility with a prospective contact, and make life a whole lot simpler than preparing personalised presentation packs, licking stamps and sending out hard copy material. Most of us really struggle to find the time to sell ourselves when what we would really like to do is crack on with the next creative masterpiece. A web site can greatly help save time and can make an excellent impression for you.

Live work

As we said earlier, books in particular are largely a bi-product of celebrity. A great way to set yourself apart from the pack is to get on stage and put on a live show. There are many opportunities to enter the live arena, from local clubs and interest groups to hundreds of literary and arts festivals (at which the audience is far more benign than for traditional stand up comedy. You really don't need to be as nervous as you might otherwise be!). You can also film yourself and put the film out on YouTube or your own website – you just never know how effective it might be. Indeed, nobody really knows how effective such activities can be. What we can say is that it cannot do any harm and adds enormously to your appeal to a publisher, because you come with marketing potential, not just another book to punt.

Collaboration

There are two types of collaboration. The first is with a friend. I have written collaboratively, and found it to be much more fun than working alone, because there is a social aspect to it. But is 'fun' a good thing? A matey collaboration can swiftly turn a working session into a weekly opportunity for nine beers and a curry. I guess the answer to this depends on the relationship you have with your collaborator.

The main advantage is being able to inspire and bounce ideas off one another and to develop the script more quickly as you share the workload. Comedy, in particular seems to benefit from a team approach (and from the beers), so it is mostly a matter of organising who is doing what and agreeing the overarching story. There are innumerable examples of collaboration on story (including, of course, Robert Zemeckis and Bob Gale on *Back to the*

Future) and, if you can find the right partner, I suppose it is a great way to write. It really depends on your personality and the working relationship you can set up with the partner.

The second type of collaboration is with a 'professional' consultant. There are many people advertising, particularly on the internet, to help fix your story. They will, for a fee, become your collaborative partner. I do this myself, so I suppose I must admit a certain bias, but I have very clear boundaries in that I believe I only have a role in guiding the writer, not the story. That might sound odd, given my knowledge of story, but no amount of knowledge will ever qualify a story consultant to write someone else's story for them. A consultant could help cynically make a story more commercial, or help wrap it up for presentation, but should avoid getting his hands dirty in the story events himself; as I say, I try to help writers to find their own voice and deliver their own story, and help with the kinds of practical lessons that this book has attempted to impart. (If this sounds appealing to you, take a massive positive step for your career by contacting me via www.baboulene.com immediately for a story evaluation that will let us know in what ways I might be able to help, whilst ensuring you remain completely in control of your story. And I'm so cheap it's almost embarrassing...)

Seriously, a consultant is unlikely to be a good 'collaborator' at the story level and I would be wary of them making changes to your story. As soon as they do, it is no longer your story and is more likely to lead to frustration for you. The same goes for books called things like: 'How to Write A Massive Bestseller' or such like. Don't go near. They mostly approach the task with a structure-led approach that will fail and frustrate you. They may be able to point out the kinds of story problems that, again, we have discussed in this book – inciting incident not raising a key question; key question not answered at resolution; and so on. You can accept help with the structural and interface issues, but I think it is important that you provide the whole story from your own head.

Similar (and free) assistance is available from creative writing clubs and collaborative ventures with friends. For me, if a story is frustrating me, rather than getting another writer in to see what they would do, I put it to one side and work on other things for a month or two. When I pick it back up again with fresh eyes, I tend to find it looks a whole lot different from the view I had before I walked away for a while, and I find new inspiration. Other stories find themselves in a bottom drawer for decades, and I never get around to picking them up again, which I guess tells its own story about the value and quality of that piece of work.

It is worth noting that the studios generally work on the basis of a story taking on a life of its own. If they are interested in your script, they sign you up for what is often called a 'packaging deal'. This buys them the time to send it out to 'the talent' whom they think might like a piece of the action. If the actors and directors and others they trust come back with an enthusiastic thumbs up and demand to be counted in on the project, then the story begins to get a team around it, and is said to 'have legs'. If the film company receive positives from a complete set of professionals it would take to make the film, then it has the implicit green light from people they trust and they 'option' it from you (pay you for control of the story for an agreed length of time, usually around 18 months). In this time, they continue to follow the progress of the story as it builds itself up a buzz and a reputation. If people want to be part of it then it naturally develops into a hot project, all by itself. If it doesn't get the buy-in then it goes cold, you get it back 18 months later and can go and try to sell it again elsewhere (Yes, you get to keep the money from the option deal!)

Publishers work in a similar way, with submitted manuscripts getting 'sponsors' from within the editorial team who fight for it to have a place in the catalogue. Eventually, colleagues buy in, reaching a critical mass that takes it to an offer of a deal.

You will find you adopt something like this approach with your own stories. The ones that continue to inspire tend to get completed. The ones that sit in a drawer whilst you work on things you find more attractive at that moment may or may not ever get finished. So don't be concerned if you have to shelve one for a while. It is part of a fairly standard development process that can tell you a lot about your story and how you feel about it.

Self-publishing

Strange game, this. Quite often when I do an author event, I find myself working next to another author who is selling books he has printed up himself, and he's making five or ten times more money than me per book sold. It can be a little irksome, to be honest, and I want to make a small fire in a critical area.

I have done a little publishing in my own right as well (my children's books are self-published), and these days it is perfectly feasible to do it oneself. We can all work up a book using, e.g., Microsoft Word or OpenOffice Write. We can create a cover in Photoshop and we can pay a friendly neighbourhood printer to build it for us. I know someone who had ten books printed – just for his own satisfaction – for £300. A run of 2000 to 3000 books, of a standard style and type like my humorous books, work out at around 60p a book (2009 prices). You can even get an ISBN number from

Nielsen for yourself (the UK ISBN agency – www.isbn.nielsenbookdata.co.uk)[9] and this act alone puts your book on all the shops' systems, including magically appearing on internet book shops like Amazon, who automatically give a page to everything that has an ISBN number. So, self-publishing is amazingly accessible, cheap and simple.

But that doesn't mean you can make any sales.

I would warn away from self-publishing for the simple reason that, without any marketing, you will struggle to sell 100 books, let alone thousands. Unless you have a clear route to market with a target audience who are going to want your product, forget it. You will end up trying to store 1,900 books around your house for the rest of time.

If you have a little marketing planned beyond your family and friends, the rule of thumb for calculations is this: of the number of people exposed to the marketing 10% will notice it. Of that number, 10% of them will make a purchase. In other words, do your revenue calculations on the basis of 1% of the people you reach with your marketing actually putting their hands in their pockets. This is dependent upon the type of advertising under discussion, and the power of the chosen media – a live show, for example, will reach a smaller audience than a poster, but will result in a higher percentage of those making a purchase.

Marketing is the key to success, and the key to marketing is a 'marketing handle'. If you have a good marketing handle, then marketing works. Without marketing, self-publishing is unjustifiable and driven by vanity. Which brings me to...

Paying to be published

Simple one this: don't do it (except for unashamed vanity). If you don't get a positive response from the agents and publishers, the temptation is there to take a deal with one of the 'vanity publishers' who offer you a publishing deal on the basis that you share the risk by paying them a little up-front cash. In return, you get to tell your friends you got a publishing deal. The fact is that the great majority of these companies make their money from the cash you give them up front. They make their money from your vanity. That's why they are prepared to give you a deal where no orthodox publisher will. They aren't really giving you a publishing deal. You are paying them to organise the printer for you.

---

[9] Actually, you have to buy a minimum of ten ISBN numbers, but it still is not going to break the bank. They also have a free listing service, which puts the basic details of your work in the public domain.

They use your money to print a short run of books, they give you a dozen or so for free, put your book on Amazon in just the way you could do for yourself, and that is it. You're done. They do very little more, and there will be little or no marketing effort.

The only way that any sales will be made is if **you** put in the marketing effort by yourself. If you are successful and your book becomes a bit of a seller, it will be on the back of your own personal efforts and, guess what, you have to share the returns with the 'publisher' you paid to take your rights from you in the first place! If you get a movie deal from your book, the publisher you paid will get 50% of the returns from that movie deal on a standard contract!

I can see no benefit to vanity publishing whatsoever. If you are tempted to vanity publish then don't; self-publish instead. You get the same result, but get to keep ownership of the rights to your own work.

14.3.2 Writers' software packages

There are many software packages available for the writer, but you don't really need any beyond a word processor. Use Microsoft Word, or if you want an excellent freebie, OpenOffice Write.

Just so you know, when you have a publishing deal and you deliver your book to your publisher in, for example, Microsoft Word, they will convert it into a 'built' book using design software, such as Adobe InDesign. For this reason, it is unnecessary to go too mad with the pretty pretty stuff, as it will have to be stripped out and redone in the book building software, so only do that which is necessary to make a good impression with your delivery. The design and build software will be used to generate a final version in PDF (portable document format); this is appropriate for the printer to take to press.

If you are one of these severely anxious people when it comes to film script format and you wish to be absolutely sure of yourself, the scriptwriting industry favours (for no better reason than because everybody else uses it) a software package called 'Final Draft'. Rest assured, oh, severely anxious one, that although the industry does estimate that a page of correctly formatted script equates to a minute of screen time, they will not reject your script purely on the basis that you've used a five centimetre margin for 'Dialogue' rather than two inches. They are looking for a decent story, not an anally retentive format policeman, and if they do take your material, they will rewrite it many, many times, and will end up with a wholly different format, known as a Director's Script, so excessive concern on your format is not worth the nervous energy.

For excellent free scriptwriting software for stage, screen, radio, film, comics – use Celtx; not only excellent but absolutely free.

Also remember what Willy Russell says: your script is an *ambition* to be a film. It's not a film. Before that ambition can be fulfilled, it must first be <u>read</u> by people absorbing the story. So write it clearly as a story. Don't put in scene numbers and camera direction and all that cobblers. It just distracts from the story, particularly if you don't do it properly. And it peeves the director if you start doing his job for him. Present the story as a story, and worry about conversion to other media when the time comes.

This said, pride alone should dictate that you format your script to the traditional style, and it just feels nice to produce something that looks official. I hereby admit that I do find Final Draft excellent, and because it is purpose built for the job, it tends to be quicker to use than Word and has a good deal of shortcuts that move all the housework out of the way and allow you to get on with the writing. It also has additional resources for scriptwriters, such as a scene-level view that just lists all the scene headers. And, sadly, no-one has paid me to say that. So use Final Draft or Celtx so it has the 'feel' of a script, but do not do the job of the director – just deliver the story.

Nothing else is required, beyond the trusty old dictionary, thesaurus and a kettle with stamina. I would certainly avoid all software packages that tell you they will write the story for you, claiming all you have to do is put in the odd noun here and verb there. I admit I have never tried using one of these packages, but my feeling is that if this is where you find yourself, you should probably think about a different career.

14.4 Useful links

www.inktip.com

www.writersandartists.co.uk

www.writermag.com

www.thenewwriter.com

www.writersnews.co.uk

www.isbn.nielsenbookdata.co.uk

www.openoffice.org – I created an entire book right through to print-ready PDF using OpenOffice Write. And it's completely free.

www.finaldraft.com for the preferred screen writing software that costs money, or

www.celtx.com for one that is excellent and free.

And whether you are a producer, an experienced or aspiring writer, for the very, very best in story evaluation and development consultancy, you want:

www.baboulene.com

IN CONVERSATION

Anybody can sympathise with the sufferings of a friend, but it requires a
very fine nature to sympathise with a friend's success.

Oscar Wilde (1854 – 1900)

15 Introduction to the conversations

In putting this book together, I was absolutely determined firstly, as you
know, to avoid writing a rule book; secondly, to avoid a purely theoretical
and academic work, of low practical value to aspiring writers; and thirdly, to
try and garner the views of individuals from all the main media who have
found success through stories: a scriptwriter, a publisher, an actor, a
novelist, a comedy writer, television writer, a playwright – and as you can
see, I was so fortunate with the responses I got, it is almost beyond belief.

I do not apologise for repetition of some of the text from these
conversations in the body of the book. It is important that the relevant
information coming from these professionals gets nailed home, and that it
is acknowledged as coming from them, so when you see something you also
saw in the body of this book, just take it as read that it must be important!
There are also subtle differences in the point they may be making within
their personal context and that which I make in mine, so it is still worth
paying attention through what seems to be a repeat.

So first and foremost, I must give my warmest thanks to Bob Gale, Mark
Williams, Willy Russell, Lee Child, John Sullivan and Stewart Ferris for their
time, patience and expertise. What follows are summaries of the

conversations I had with these lovely gentlemen, who have in common that they all make their living from Story.

First up, then, from the screenwriting angle, its Hollywood legend, Bob Gale.

15.1 In conversation with Bob Gale

Bob Gale attended film school at the University of Southern California, and went on to become a scriptwriter, producer or director of an impressive portfolio of Hollywood productions, including, of course, co-writer (with Robert Zemeckis) and executive producer of the *Back to the Future* trilogy.

Back to the Future exhibits most of the principles that lie beneath a good story, and, perhaps even more of an accolade than being my favourite story, it is one of the top 100 movies of all time (according to the internet movie database and every other serious poll ever taken).

More recently Bob has become a respected expert on story theory, employed by major film studios as an expert witness, undertaking story analysis in court cases involving accusations of plagiarism and spending his time proving beyond reasonable doubt and that sort of thing.

I talked to him about his thoughts on what makes a story tick.

What do you think about theories on how to write?

First and foremost – don't let anyone tell you they have a 'method' for making a story into a success. Nobody does, and if anyone says they do, they are lying. There is no magic formula, and mercifully, there never will be. If there was such a method, there would be no bad stories, and I don't think that's the case now, is it?! All you can ever do as a writer is write your own story your way. Master your craft, of course, by reading stories, and learn from what other writers say about what worked for them, and from teachers about story theory. The information you can get this way is all interesting, and adds to your personal ability, but you must accept all these opinions only for what they can do in helping you to establish for yourself a working method that works for you.

Remember, even with a formula or rule book that seems incredibly convincing or appears to be globally accepted, all that's happening is that someone is giving their opinion; and often that someone hasn't actually had any success themselves. Don't forget, for hundreds of years, everyone accepted that the universe revolved around the Earth. The moon, the stars – it all revolved around us; there was even scientific proof that this was the case! Then along came Copernicus, and suddenly all that theory was rubbished and all those experts were proved wrong. Formal learning in a creative field is only useful if it helps you to find your own voice and establish your own personal method.

Do you consider story structure in your own development process?

Sometimes. Of all the magic 'how to write' methods, I specifically don't agree with any that are based around so-called 'act structure'. Stories develop around characters and their behaviours, learning and growth. Of course, structure does exist, and as you write your scenes, your story will gain a structure under the surface, but it's not a starting point for development.

For example, people talk about acts and how they must deliver the story in three acts or five acts, but "an act" is really a practical construct of plays created for the theatre, to provide a way to change costumes and switch scenery around – but "acts" should not be a benchmark in defining how you create your book or film story. You can certainly try to define where acts start and finish once a screenplay is complete (I'm not sure why you'd want to, but you can) but there's no sense whatever in trying to write a story driven by acts – or even consider acts – unless it is genuinely going to have a curtain going up and down, or the modern equivalent – advertisement breaks in a TV story. For a novel or film script – forget about acts. I don't know where the act boundaries of *Back to the Future* are, and I don't care, because it doesn't matter.

How do you develop your own stories?

All writers face the same starting point. We start with a story idea and the challenge is to get from this idea to a beautifully developed story that remains faithful to that original idea. We have to deliver that idea using characters and plot – and the way I do this and simultaneously keep that faith is to ask and answer questions that the idea naturally evokes.

Let me tell you how *Back to the Future* came together. Like any other writers, Robert Zemeckis and I started with an idea, and ours looked like this:

"A kid goes back in time. He meets his parents when they were young and his mother falls in love with him."

That was it. The idea. The starting point. From this, we can reasonably deduce that the story will have three characters – a son and his parents. What do we reasonably know about these characters? Well, if his mother is going to fall in love with the son instead of his father, he must have different qualities from his father. So we said, what if, instead of his father being paternal to him and telling him how to behave, it was the other way around? After all, in 1955, his father is just a kid himself, so why should he be paternal? Marty from 1985 could be the streetwise, strong one, and his father can be unassertive and learn from his son. It is this difference between them that attracts his mother to Marty instead of his future father. Excellent. So the character of George McFly takes on some shape, as does the character of Marty and Lorraine, and the story is developing through this knowledge of character.

If he goes back in time, how did he time travel? We decided it should be via a time machine, so we had to ask more questions: Where did it come from? Who built it? What does it look like? Maybe a corporation is making it. Maybe it is government property and gets stolen. Maybe it's a product of a crazy inventor. Bingo! We knew that was right, and Doc Brown was born – our fourth character.

How, what, where, why…? We asked questions relating to our premise , and for each answer we came up with, there was a set of logical implications that began to build the story. So, for example, we asked ourselves, if Marty goes back in time, what will he do when he gets there? When we put ourselves in Marty's position, we all assume we would invent something we know about from the future that would make us famous, don't we? So we said, wouldn't it be great if he invents rock and roll? What would this mean to the story? Well, it would set the timeframe – it meant that he had to go back to around 1955. It also meant that, somewhere in the setup, Marty had to show he can play music, so his band in 1985 and his ability to play guitar and his musical ambition got its place in the story setup, and therefore in his character.

Similarly, we thought, wouldn't it be great if Marty invented the skateboard? Same thing – we decided if Marty was to invent the skateboard in 1955, then we needed to establish him as a skateboarder in the setup. You can see straight away from these two small examples that Marty's character is emerging all by itself – *the character actions deliver behaviours* – he's going to be a guitarist in a band and he's going to be a skateboarder – and this in turn affects the plot – he enters a Battle of the Bands competition and he gets about town on a skateboard. Plot driven by characters reacting in accordance with their natural character.

Just from these few questions and answers leading to more questions and more answers we have characters and behaviours that drive our story, in service of that original idea. We know that Doc Brown is a crazy scientist who invents a time machine. We know Marty is a streetwise cool kid, who rides a skateboard, plays in a band and goes back in time. We know that Marty's mother, Lorraine, in 1955 is a romantic. She's looking for a boyfriend and is constantly thinking about love. We know that Marty's dad, George, in 1955 lacks confidence and is unassertive, and that is why Lorraine will fall for Marty instead of George when they meet. Look at that! All directly deduced from the original idea, which means the characters and behaviours make sense and the story has cohesion and integrity as a result.

Sounds good. What next?

When we liked what we got from the questioning process, we wrote the resulting story event on an index card, and put it out there as a scene or sequence that would need to be there. The index card would say something like: 'Marty invents rock and roll'. This, in turn, would require another index card, which we knew must come before this one. If Marty is going to get on stage and play rock and roll in 1955, we'd better establish he can play, so we wrote on another index card: 'establish Marty can play rock and roll', and we placed it chronologically to the left of the one saying 'Marty invents rock and roll'.

Over time the process of asking questions and finding answers puts out more and more index cards, and the story develops in front of you. I would recommend that you get off your computer and do the same. Get a pile of blank index cards, write the scene aim on each and further index cards that establish what needs to be in place to facilitate the scene taking place. When you lay the cards out on the floor you can see your story in front of you much better than you can see it on a computer screen. You can move things around and work with your instincts to see what goes where.

Is there any organisation of these questions and answers?

It is initially pretty random – we just let our imagination go and the questions and answers take us where they do, but there is a natural logic to the index cards that is quite intuitive. Most events find their natural place in the order of things, and the whole story takes on its own shape.

This said, we thought strongly about the ending early on. If you don't know where the story is heading, you can't aim towards it, so we did focus on the ending. Initially, we knew two things about the ending: firstly, that we wanted Marty to make it back to 1985, and secondly, we wanted him to come back to a better life than the one he left in the first place. Most time travel stories end up as salutary tales of how bad everything will be for you if you screw with time. We wanted ours to be positive and different, so we made Marty unhappy to find himself in 1955 – he never wanted to travel through time in the first place – and his basic aim was to get back to his girlfriend and his life in 1985. We also made him screw with time accidentally [by interfering with his parents' meeting], and find himself obliged to fix things up before he could go home. This gave us excellent dependency – the main plot couldn't resolve until the subplots did, and the clock was ticking down. We also needed something more than simply his return to 1985 as the endgame. He had to come back for a dramatic purpose, which is why we came up with the idea of Doc Brown being shot and apparently killed in 1985. Marty had to get back earlier than he left in order to save the Doc, and suddenly the story worked beyond the matter of getting back to his old life.

As it develops, how do you write the individual scenes?

In writing scenes, the primary question is to ask whether the action does its job in delivering the big picture. Not all scenes need to carry conflict and antagonism and 'turn' and so on. If all scenes carried that much power throughout your story, I think it would be hard to watch. The scene where 'Marty invents rock and roll' carries none of the things that the rule book guys would tell you a scene has to have. There's no antagonist, for example. The scene doesn't even deliver towards the main plot or any sub plot, but does it work? Judging by what people I meet tell me, it's the single most memorable scene in *Back to the Future*. You have to just be creative and natural sometimes, so if you write a scene in the way it 'feels' it should be, and it does the job you asked of it on the index card, it's probably right.

I like to work hard on the dialogue. A lot of writers struggle to deliver realistic dialogue. It's just one of those things some people have an ear for and others don't. Sometimes I put an actor or person I know in my mind when I write the dialogue for a particular character in order to give the character a distinctive way of speaking. I check my dialogue by looking at the words on the page and saying to myself: 'if the character wasn't identified for this line of dialogue, could I tell who it was from what they say?'

Dialogue is critical and needs a lot of thought. Sometimes the problem is that characters talk unnecessarily. In particular, you cannot have two characters tell each other things the audience already knows, or worse still, things that the two characters already know. It's a common difficulty and it totally ruins the realism of your story if you get it wrong. You will find yourself in this situation, and you must find clever ways to get around it. Don't just let it happen.

In *Back to the Future* we had loads of setup exposition that the audience needed to know before we could get into the meat of the story and we had to find ways of getting it out there without just stating it or letting the story drag. For example, we needed the audience to know in advance how George and Lorraine first got romantically involved, so we had Lorraine in 1985 feeling wistful about her past. She tells her children the story of how she met their father. Now, the kids already know this, so we had her daughter, Linda, interrupt her and say:

'Yeah, yeah, Mom we know – you told us the story a million times! Grandpa hit him with the car. You felt sorry for him, so you decided to go with him to the Fish Under the Sea Dance'.

And this is natural conversation. Parents always repeat themselves and kids always roll their eyes because they've heard it all a million times, so we got the exposition out there that way. Don't just settle for your first ideas and say, 'that will do.' Question everything and find innovative ways to deliver your story.

What advice would you give to new writers?

There are a couple of wise sayings out there that are the truth for all writers. David Mamet said: 'Ask who wants what from whom; ask what happens if they don't get it – and why now?' For me, this is more interesting than talking about acts and inciting incidents and rising action and so on, because it makes you focus on characters, behaviours and drama rather than technical stuff.

Once *Back to the Future* was well underway with Universal, they priced it all up and told us we had to lose a million dollars off the budget. The movie could be made, but it had to be made at a price, and we were a million over. Our story was finished. We didn't want to make such a significant change, but it was not negotiable. Bob [Zemeckis] and I wandered around the back-lot at Universal and we realised our climax was the key. At the time, we had an ending that revolved around Marty and Doc Brown harnessing power from a nuclear facility out in the desert. It was a million dollar location shoot all by itself. We could take out the million by changing the ending to one that didn't require a location shoot – one that could be filmed on the studio premises. But... changing the ending? That was a tough challenge. If the change wasn't going to ripple through the entire story, we had to deliver the same ending, but in a different way. [*The sequence objective remains the same, the method of delivery changes.*]

We worked hard and came up with the idea for the bolt of lightning, and it turned out that this new ending was much stronger than the one we had previously. The constraints that had been put upon us by the studio forced us to think more deeply, and we ended up with a better story because of it. This happens a lot, and the point is this: Placing constraints on a writer results in ingenuity. The monster in *Alien* was brilliantly kept from view for three quarters of the story. This excellent use of implication was not a conscious decision. The reason it didn't appear was because they couldn't get a convincing, scary enough monster out there cheaply enough, so they had to imply it instead. This constraint made it the best monster ever, because we in the audience made it up in our own minds. Similarly the shark in *Jaws*. It's a truly great movie, but the shark is only scary before you actually see it. These days, seeing that plastic shark is pretty much a joke, but *not* seeing it was really powerful. So embrace constraints. Try to force yourself to do better than your first idea.

This said you must not consider budget when developing your story. Apart from anything else, the first thing that happens to your story is that somebody reads it. They need to enjoy the story as a good read. Later on, there may well be changes made for budgetary or other practical reasons, but you must not let these factors influence you and your creativity.

My main advice if you are writing a screenplay is that it is very difficult to sell original material to producers or studios, because the financial risk they take is so enormous. These guys are much more likely to take on something that someone else has already shown some belief in, so if you can get a book published or a community play staged or a short story or a radio play out there or any other exposure through any other medium to give it some credibility, the movie business is far more likely to pick up on it from that point than it is from cold.

Other than that, like I said at the beginning, nobody knows the secret of how to write a hit – because there isn't one. The best advice is to be true to yourself and to write your story your way.

15.2 In Conversation with Lee Child

Lee Child is one of the most successful novelists on earth, ever, selling tens of millions of Jack Reacher novels the world over, and yet he had no formal training in creative writing or story theory.

He learned his trade on the job whilst working in television on the ITV network in the UK. There he was involved with shows including *Brideshead Revisited*, *The Jewel in the Crown* (TV series), *Prime Suspect*, and *Cracker*. He was involved in the transmission of more than 40,000 hours of programming, writing thousands of commercials, news stories, and trailers. He began to write novels seriously when he was fired from ITV during a restructuring.

You had no formal training. What are your views on formal training?

I suppose formal training does different things for different people, and all of us get interested in the process once we're involved, but one absolute truth I am certain of is that the only essential training for writing is reading. If you are starting to write and you haven't read a thousand books first, you're not ready. To be a writer you must be a reader. After that writing is simply about personal confidence.

Did television teach you about story?

I learned a lot from working in television productions, but television changed out of all proportion for a very specific reason between 1980 and 1990 – a reason that intrigued me – and it was all down to a little device nestling in the viewer's hand. In 1980, people sat in the chair and committed to one channel for the evening because they couldn't be bothered to get up. By 1990, they didn't have to get off their backsides to change the channel. They could do it from the chair. Channel hopping was invented and suddenly the world changed. We had to give people a reason not to change channel. One of the ways we did this fascinated me. Before the ad break in a football match we would ask a trivia question, and found something basic in the make-up of a viewer meant they simply had to know the answer. It didn't matter if it was the most banal question – who won the FA Cup Final in 1895? Nobody knows, nobody cares, and yet there is something fundamental in our makeup that wants to endlessly raise and – most importantly – find answers to questions. I believe this is something writers need to understand. We raise and answer questions. Big questions that arch the full span of the story, small questions that arch a sentence or paragraph. Medium questions that span a chapter.

So stories are about questions?

It's interesting to look back to the very reason we developed language in the first place, around 100,000 years ago. If you imagine how life was at that time, people would have been occupied the whole time with the business of survival. Nothing more. Getting through the day, and trying to be as sure as they could that they live through tomorrow. Language developed because it helped us to ensure survival. Why? Because it helped the human animal to co-operate. With language, a dozen or two people, working together, could be more powerful than any other creature on earth. So the roots of language are elemental, and the roots of stories equally important – they came into being as an extension of the need to survive.

It wasn't fiction at that time. Story telling allowed hominids to project a life state to one another that educated and gave an advantage to the receiver of that education. We don't know when fiction became a part of the picture, but clearly you can see how that would be a natural progression. From educating one another with the story of how three men fought off a sabre-toothed tiger, it could become more engaging and encouraging to the receivers of story if the tiger was captured, killed and brought back for dinner. Heroes were born. Stories still resonate with those elemental parts of our being. We are hard-wired to project ourselves into stories and to seek out and receive an emotional benefit from that story.

A good story will make us feel anxious and uncomfortable, but will end in understanding and hope or consolation. When my daughter was young I would hold her in my arms then pretend to drop her, only to catch her again a foot lower. It's only a game, but it's elemental in the same way. She learned a small, repeated lesson about trust and security and her relationship with me from that game. And that game does to a child what an author should do to its audience.

So what comes first in your story development process?

First and foremost in making a story work is character. In the plot v character discussion, I have no doubts – it's a nonsense argument, because character is, always and forever, the essential primary driver. Look at the Lone Ranger. Everyone knows the Lone Ranger, but not a soul on earth can tell you a single event from a Lone Ranger story. We buy into characters, not authors or plots. It's as simple as that. Nobody goes into a shop looking for a Lee Child book. They go into a shop looking for a Jack Reacher book. We don't say, 'Have you read the latest JK Rowling?' we say, 'have you read the latest Harry Potter?' This is why I created Jack Reacher as the vehicle for my stories, and have not varied him from day one. I know people talk about character growth and development, but as soon as your character grows and develops, he hits the ceiling and cannot grow or develop any more, and you have to start again with another character. I prefer other characters around Jack to change and learn and grow. The crooks can learn severely harsh lessons. I'll leave Jack as he is.

So I wanted Jack to be reliable and consistent in reader terms, because once someone knows what they get from a Jack Reacher story, they are more confident about investing in another one. I don't mean financially – we all stand there in front of the bookstand and wonder why we're thinking so long and hard about investing a few quid – but what we're really agreeing to invest is far more valuable: our time. A book takes a lot of our time, so if we know what to expect from a book, we can invest with knowledge of what we are likely to get from the investment, and the consistency of Jack Reacher as a character gives a reader the confidence to pick up my book rather than someone else's unknown quantity.

Why do you think Jack Reacher is so successful?

Jack Reacher is a strong character for many reasons to do with our fundamental being. In our real lives there are many basic things we want and believe in that we don't get. At work, we suffer injustice from the megalomaniac who runs the department. We wish we could punch him in the face and we can't. We just have to suffer in silence. When someone is burgled we want revenge, but we don't get it. We want to see that burglar punished, but of course even if we get our hands on the crook, we don't punch him. It's not how civilised society works, so even if we do in some sense 'get justice', we don't service our animal need for a knee-jerk, vengeful, violent response. So Jack Reacher represents us in these terms. He can do all those things we can't do. He works outside the law. He's highly moral, and caring – like us – but he's brutal with the bad guys and capable of meting out that form of justice. We all wish we were him or could call him to sort out our own life needs. I believe that's why my books sell – I am fulfilling an elemental need in my readers.

The second key factor in a story after character is suspense. As I said earlier, raising questions is the means by which a story can tantalise its audience, and choosing how and when you answer the questions, and therefore pay off the suspense, is your story. This is also the key to developing your story. I begin with an idea and the suspense drops out of the natural, logical questioning of that premise. So, for example, my next book has a premise that Jack Reacher wanders into a town and finds an elderly lady who is in need of protection. That's the story in a sentence. So, logically, the first question we have to ask is obvious, isn't it? What does she need protecting from? OK, so I introduce this mysterious establishment just outside of town, and that is at the root of the problem. So, the question is, what is the establishment? OK, so I made it an ex-military establishment, and it turns out it is nine-tenths underground. It's enormous in comparison to the proportion on the surface. So what's it for? What's the problem it is causing? Who is inside and what are they doing? Why is the old lady in their sights? Clearly, from interrogating the premise, we can see that at a key point in the story, Jack Reacher is going to have to go inside this secretive establishment and pit himself against the unwelcoming, overwhelming and intimidating odds that will be stacked against him when he does.

I don't really plan too much beyond this process. I start writing by instinct and, although I generally have an idea for the main events, the detailed story and possibilities just kind of open up for me as I go along.

The third key element of a good story for me is 'education'. I think a good book should leave the reader knowing more about life than when he began.

What advice would you give to aspiring writers?

I don't understand it when writers talk about having to be disciplined and asking about how to 'find the time' to write, and wanting a method for getting going. I can't help with advice there because if you need help in these areas you are probably not motivated correctly to ever be a writer. Writers must be desperate to write – driven – hungry – forcing themselves to leave their writing to go and do other things, not the other way around. I work in my office in New York. I do around four hours a day from about noon. I feel that's about as much as I can do and remain productive. I'm not one for working in coffee shops or any public place, and I'm a little suspicious of those that do, because again it points, in my opinion, towards incorrect motivation. Many people I meet adore the *idea* of being a writer – the romantic image – but see the day-to-day job of writing as impossibly lonely and difficult.

I don't have any great secret for success – I don't think anybody does – but I can tell you a sure fire route for failure: sitting at a desk surrounded by 'How To Write A Blockbuster' rule books as your starting point means you are dead in the water from the kick off. Forget it. You must write because you are driven to do so, and writing should really be instinctive during the creative process. It's mostly about confidence. Those who go looking to rule books and gurus are doing so because they lack confidence, not because they need rules, and when they sign up for a course of some sort, they may or may not get confidence, but there's a good chance they will get hooked into following a formula. Just use courses and seminars to get reassurance that you are on the right lines and get yourself the fundamental knowledge that all storytellers should have, then just forget all that, tuck yourself away and write your story your way. There is no other way. After that, it's a numbers game. If you write a story so you love it, there will be a proportion of people out there who will love it too. If that is a significant percentage, you will make a living. If it's not, you'll have 100 copies printed around the corner and have something to be equally proud of, because it's your story. The commercial side is a different world – different issues – nothing to do with the story. Just write it, and worry about all that afterwards.

On the commercial side, it is really important to be professional. Treat every interaction with a publisher or agent as if it was a job interview – not a discussion of your art. Make a plan – you are selling units in shops now, not writing a story or being creative, so design your career around a solid, visible representation of what you plan to do as a commercially attractive professional writer. Publishers feel good about these things. I write a book every year – that's 14 books out there now – and they like it that next year's is finished and I'm working on the one for the year after that. If I wrote a book every five years, I'd have two out by now, and I wouldn't be such an attractive commercial proposition. Remember, publishers are money men, not book men. They are looking at you as a potential business partner – not as a brilliant artist. If they feel it will be difficult to work with you, it won't really matter how good your creations are, they will probably find someone else.

Ultimately, we end up where we started: I believe the only training for writing is reading. Read 1000 books and then have the confidence to write your book your way. If you are correctly motivated and then go on to write lots and lots of words, if they click with a proportion of the populace, you have a chance of success.

15.3 In conversation with John Sullivan

John Sullivan grew up in a working class environment in Balham, South London. He had no formal story theory training, but he did have an innate drive and ability to tell stories. He drew his material from real-life – the people and the world around him – and he learned and perfected his trade simply by doing it. Indeed, he started out by selling lies at school. Boys in need of a convincing alibi came to John in a collar-tugging sweat and gladly parted with a few bob for John to come up with a story that went down well with the authorities. And he's never stopped – he's carried on making up convincing stories ever since with a roll-call of classic television comedies, including *Only Fools and Horses, Just Good Friends, Dear John and Citizen Smith*.

This is what he had to say to me on his approach to writing:

When you sit down to work, what is the starting point for you?

As a writer, you must always start with the story, and for me you have to look at real life to find story ideas. When you think you have an idea, you ask questions of it to see if it develops. That's the starting point. If it does develop, then I get what I call a core to the story; the overarching event that drives the characters into conflict and is behind all the other events in the story. For example, in *Only Fools and Horses*, I might have an idea that's something like: "Rodney asserts his independence" or "Delboy falls in love" or "Rodney brings home a policewoman". All of these provide a basis – a foundation to build on by asking the question, 'What events will come out of this premise that will drive these characters? How will the characters respond to this premise?'

If I'm going to start from, say, 'Rodney asserts his independence,' then it seems obvious that the story will need a reason why Rodney would want to assert his independence, so to me it must begin with him being walked over by Delboy. Logically, this will make Rodders angry with Del, and angry with himself for letting it happen and immediately we have conflict, and we have the starting event from which Rodney can try to stand up for himself.

I know I'm on to something worthwhile if I can clearly see – even in these early stages – the nature of the relationship between the characters. There must be a bond between them, and the conflict driven in by this core idea will test that bond and drive the story. Already you can see, in the logical progression of 'Rodney asserts his independence,' that it is going to work, because there is conflict: the characters' bond and loyalty is being put under pressure, and we all want to know what will happen in the end.

Then it's all about the ending. The ending is all the world to a story, and I have to get the ending in my mind before the rest can really know where it's going. So I have my basic signposts. Rodney gets walked over. He wants to do something about it and they go into conflict. Rodney asserts his independence. The ending is the result of him asserting himself. I could see the possibility that Rodney could finally assert himself at just the wrong moment and scupper a potential million pound opportunity that Del had been carefully building in subplot. Del walked all over Rodney at the beginning and paid the price for that at climax when Rodney asserts himself. Now I have more story events generated by the 'make a million' subplot that must happen to create that ending and the story has another new line of development.

So we have the core of a story. What next?

What I've been saying makes my approach sound very scientific, but it's not really. I don't think about it as much as it seems – I just do it – and what I would do next is just write. I have my basic signposts, so it doesn't matter what I write, I just write. Too many people pussyfoot for weeks and months thinking about it, when there's no better way than to get stuck in. It doesn't matter if you end up throwing away nine-tenths of it, just go for it and write. Loads of stuff, and more ideas just come as I do it. I'm well known for over-writing. I used to write 30 minute stuff, but the over-writing was so extreme that in the end *Only Fools and Horses* became 50 minutes. It was a more natural length for me to work to. But I'd much rather have too much material and cut it back than start trying to pad it out. I can't stand padding. You know you're onto a loser once you've got the padding out. Just write and let the ideas come and write some more.

What difference does it make to the story that it is comedy?

The fact that I'm writing comedy doesn't make much difference to the story. If you have a good story, then the chances are that the same story can be delivered as a comedy or a serious drama – it doesn't make any difference. The story still has to be there and carry power. When you turn up to see Shakespeare, the bloke on the door has to tell you whether you're supposed to laugh or cry when someone dies, because it's not about the story half as much as it's about the way you set the audience up. Comedy isn't necessarily cheerful, the same as drama isn't always serious. In fact, the humour in a drama is often massively funny, because it's so natural and unexpected, and the tragedy that lies behind some of the best comedy – and in the lives of some of our best-loved comedians – is well known.

For example, in the ninety minute special we're doing on Delboy's childhood, one of the core themes is that the kid Del is clever and street-wise and becomes the provider; and his dad becomes jealous of the way his son is so resourceful and is making him look bad. Del's trying to help, but he's unwittingly putting a wedge into his parent's relationship. At the same time, Del wants his mother's love – he's desperate to impress her, even though he is simultaneously undermining his father. He's a kid, so why wouldn't he be like that? Just like the episode we talked about earlier: real world, human bonds and loyalties tested – it could be a serious life drama just as easily as it could be comedy. Look at Harry Enfield's Wayne and Waynetta. Hilarious characters, but if you work in social services you'll be looking at them and thinking it's a documentary – real people dress like that and do things that are terrible, sad and wrong, not funny at all. It's funny because we recognise the reality in those characters.

Many writers struggle to get going with a story. How do you organise yourself?

I find I get far more productive the more I put myself under pressure. Writing is seriously hard work and I've put my pen down so many times at the end of a project and thought 'never again...' But it really takes that kind of pressure to bring out the best in a writer. If I had all day and all year without a deadline, I wouldn't produce half so much as I do under pressure, and what I would produce would lack that urgency and edge that comes from writing in a cold sweat.

There's a special kind of urgency that comes from writing for an audience too. You have to go less time without a laugh when there's an audience. There's nothing worse than a silent, squirming audience in a comedy production. When it's filmed, you get more time to play with between laughs, but I'm not sure if that luxury is such a good thing.

If there's no audience I often have a character who represents the audience. So if the plot is moving forwards through the interaction in the pub between, say, Delboy and Rodney, Boycey might be there to ask the questions the audience would ask and looks puzzled and gets enlightened and so on in tune with the point of view of the audience. You talked about the film 'Back to the Future' – no clearer example of a lead character who represents you and me and leads us through a story which really happens to other people.

Any tips and tricks?

In my stories I like to play on audience preconceptions a lot. The audience overlays an expectation on just about everything, so you can use this. For example, if you make your character really proud of his white suit, then show a puddle outside on the road, the audience adds two and two... then of course you make him successfully step round the puddle and not get his suit all muddy. He's very pleased with himself... only to walk into someone and get a coffee spilled all down his front. It keeps the audience guessing. People relentlessly try to put themselves one step ahead, and you can use that.

Again, this doesn't apply only to comedy. Audience preconception works in any genre. Alfred Hitchcock said, 'the monster isn't half as scary as the build up to the monster'. A girl walking alone in a dark old house. The camera goes into close-up as she looks to the left and Hitchcock would deliberately put her a little off-centre, leaving the camera angle wide on the right so we immediately, subconsciously, assume a hand is about to come in and grab her from behind her head on the right. Just in time, she'd swing round to the right and scream... and we'd scream... and there'd be nothing there. The girl breathes a sigh of relief. And we all breathe a sigh of relief with her... and the hand would rush in and grab her from the left. Brilliant use of audience preconception to keep leading them the wrong way and then frighten six bells out of 'em.

Another tip I use – writers naturally fall towards two characters for an interaction, but I generally like to have three characters. It tends to offer more opportunities when you have a third point of view in the mix. Also, I can have two of them gang up on the other one, and then one can switch allegiance as a nice plot turning point.

As you write, question what your mind gives you. Ronnie Barker said to me, 'try to think of the odd angles'. Too many writers go for the obvious and regurgitate standard stuff we've seen a thousand times before. Try to rethink it and look at it another way and do something different.

What factors do you think ensure a good story?

Well, conflict is constantly at the forefront – you can't get far without conflict – and yes, I think about character development. Of course, a character is unlikely to grow much across the course of a single sitcom episode, but even in that genre I'd look for them to develop across the series. It's difficult, of course, because if they grow too much then they change and you lose your basic starting position for the next series, so it tends to be the forms of growth that don't fundamentally change a character. For example, by the end of the story in which 'Rodney Asserts Himself', Rodney would go from being walked all over to asserting himself. A story built fundamentally on character growth, but because the assertiveness results in him spoiling things for Del, they can all end up back where they started. Del didn't make a million. Rodney *did* assert himself – but it didn't work out properly, so it doesn't stop me from writing another episode from the same character starting positions the next week.

What advice would you give to aspiring writers?

If I was starting out from scratch today, I would write the best stuff I can and send it off. Then I'd write more of my best stuff and send it off again. It's not complicated! All you have to do is keep going and improving and sending it off. If your writing is good enough, you will get success in the end.

15.4 In conversation with Mark Williams

Actor Mark Williams is best known as one of the stars of the popular BBC comedy sketch show *The Fast Show*, as well as for his role as Arthur Weasley in the *Harry Potter* films. He has also starred in *Shakespeare in Love, The Borrowers, 101 Dalmatians* and many other film and television roles. I should mention that, despite the image portrayed by the characters he plays and the catchphrases he has turned into household expressions ('I'll get me coat...'; 'This week, I have mostly been eating...'; and 'Suits you, sir,' among the favourites) Mark is an English graduate of Brasenose, Oxford, and has an unparalleled knowledge of the acting profession. He also provided some fascinating insights, so my first question was...

Do actors generally learn any story theory?

Actors have massive variance in theoretical knowledge and formal learning. Some get right into that stuff, acting with a formal knowledge to their performance; others are just naturals, picking up their own ideas for what works for them and learning from experience and from working with others as they go along. The minimum that all actors need to know is that it is all about the character, of course, and we are employed to make the character serve its purpose to the story.

If you think about it, the story can't happen without an actor. The actor is the interlocutor between the audience and the story, and the character is the medium that connects the two. This means, as actors, it is our duty to the story to be true to the character. If we are not true to the character, we will not communicate the story as intended by the writer. We must be generous and understanding to the character. We mustn't mock the character or step outside it, because as soon as you do that, you are damaging the story.

So what is your approach to a story? What do you look for?

When I assess a story, what I'm really doing is interpreting my character. To do this I ask questions of my part on three levels:

Who do I speak for? By this I mean you have to appreciate the cultural position of the story. What politics are under scrutiny? I'm looking for the provenance of the story and the target part of an audience where you are trying to resonate. The story will be giving over a message – maybe a moral or a lesson – and I have to understand my part in delivering that all-important message.

Secondly, what am I trying to say for the character? Not the words that come from the character's mouth, but the piece of the story puzzle that the character delivers. This can mean several things at different levels. For example, the journey of the character could have a strong influence on the message from the cultural perspective, given above, but more likely this is about the character's position in the story, and the specific functions the character plays in delivering the story. It's really important you don't try to make the character something it isn't, so if you're a servant serving a king, you can't go thinking 'that's not good enough. I want to be king!' and starting to change the part that must be delivered for some ego reason. I have to speak with the characters voice, and from the place he fits into this story. It's about his story position.

Thirdly, I get right into the character. What can I add as an actor? What can I bring to this of myself? When a part gets an actor it is inevitable – totally unavoidable, in fact – that the actor will bring something to the part that was unexpected by the writers. If an actor is any good, and has done 1) and 2) properly, this is generally a good thing, whereby the actor is able to give life to the character in the correct spirit – the one intended by the author and required by the story. I feel that if I've done my homework in terms of 1) and 2) the chances are that I can add something from my own imagination that will help make the character as good as it can be.

To give you an example, when we first worked on *Harry Potter*, I was coming to grips with Arthur Weasley, Ron Weasley's dad, and Julie Walters was playing my wife, Molly Weasley. Julie and I spent time discussing how our characters might have met; where we met; how come we have seven children; how long we'd been together and what shared loves and values our relationship might be based on. We decided that we met at college and had been together since then, so we gave them a kind of studentish attitude and a 'Jolly Hockey Sticks' characteristic that they share because they've been together so long. Obviously, JK Rowling didn't write that into the books, but having that provenance and understanding helps me to 'be' the character and helped Julie and I to deliver something that makes the Weasley family, as an entity in itself, feel real.

And, from an actor's viewpoint, what will put you off a story?

When I read a script the worst things for me – the things that will have me turn the role down – are firstly clichés. Writers need to work hard to be original and avoid cliché. The other thing is tautology. Repetition loses the audience in a finger snap, and if two characters have to tell each other something that the audience already knows, it's all over. Forget it. The writers have to be smarter than that and find other ways of delivering that information without taking up time. I also hate writing that gives great long pauses. Writers love to ask their actors to 'look thoughtful' or 'pensive' before delivering lines, and it's so unnatural. You end up standing around wondering what to do with your hands and it's just not real life. People don't do that – the opposite is more true, where one person decides they know what the other is going to say before they finish speaking and they crash across the ends of each other's sentences, but the message still gets across fine, because that's more real – it's how people speak and interact and understand one another in the real world.

How should a writer consider the actor in his writing?

Writers must have huge flexibility. A film is a result of a collaboration; there's a long chain of people involved in a final product, and they are mostly dynamic, smart people with ideas, experience and imagination, and the best stories arise when there is flexibility to embrace the suggestions these people can bring to the party. Most writers will tell you that the final story ends up on the screen looking and feeling different from the original idea; somewhere between a fair bit different and unrecognisable, but my guess is that most writers are ultimately pleased with the outcome. If they are not pleased it's because it was done on the cheap and that could have been avoided when they signed the deal if they had the experience to know what they were signing up to. On the other hand, you get people who just dig their heels in and defend the one idea and you end up thinking: that's because it's the only idea they've got. Their defensiveness will suffocate the possibilities of their story.

That sounds terrible! Surely the writer must decide on the story?

For writers this sounds negative, but it's rare that the process removes the beating heart of the story. Of course, at its centre, the basic story is set before the time we begin filming. You can't start changing the story line once the camera is rolling, so – assuming the story is strong – then the flexibility I'm talking about is all about delivering scenes. The scene aim doesn't change, so the story doesn't change, but the flexibility is still vital within the scene context to giving the story life. From the writers' side, we do get lots of rewrites, and in rehearsals and even on set there is usually a lot of suggestions and changes and imagination going into how the scene can best be delivered, but it's more pure acting stuff – you know – I'll say, 'look I'm supposed to freak out and smash the room up and whack Billy here with a soup ladle when I hear this line, but that's not what my character would do. He'd be catatonic – paralysed in horror – remember how he was earlier? – not smashing the place up.' And that changes the response of the other characters and the reactions around him. It's the same story, delivered in different ways.

Or it will be practical thing: make-up might say, 'look, if you're going to bash him up with a soup ladle, will we see it in live action on camera? Will there be blood?' Because that's much, much harder – and more expensive – to organise. Suddenly we need special make-up and maybe special slow-motion cameras or whatever to show the detail of the soup ladle mayhem. So the director will check his pockets for cash and if the money and the time are there, and if the genre of the movie or the demands of the atmosphere demand it, he'll either say, 'sod that – can the soup ladle – we'll go with catatonic horror.' So the storyline gets delivered with integrity – but at a tenth of the price. Or he'll say, 'oooh, yes. Love it, darling. Dark lighting please Mr DP (Director of Photography), and we'll have an iconic world first five minute brutal murder with a soup ladle thing.'

When a story begins to build towards becoming a completed film, it's an incredibly powerful collaboration and the most exciting and remarkable thing to be a part of. There are a lot of links in the chain, and endless opportunities for it to go all wrong, but it is also pure magic to be in there seeing it come to life. Decisions have to be made there and then. Not everything can be decided in advance, so it's edgy and nerve-racking and wonderful. When the pressure is on, that is when greatness happens.

What advice would you give to writers?

If you don't want your story to get the 'benefit' of lots of other input, and you don't want it changed for better or for worse on the way through, you have to make sure it is so totally complete before you show it to anyone that you can defend every line because of its relevance to everything else. A truly great story won't change because to change it simply doesn't make sense. Also if you write a book, it's more likely to keep its integrity in book form, because publishers don't make changes like movie people do. There are fewer people in the chain and a much smaller investment risk. If you think about *Harry Potter*, the movie people can't change anything at the fundamental story level, because whatever they do in, say, movie number four must line up with what's already set in stone in books five, six and seven, so the story can't change very much. So make sure you know your work, that you finish it to the point where absolutely everything has earned its place on the page, take responsibility for its shape and form. Then you can strongly argue the case for keeping things as they are.

Think about characters. Stories are all about the characters and what they do. That's it in total. You must make your characters real and differentiate them and then be sure that they have a reason to be there. Like I said, the main thing an actor wants to lock on to is a character's purpose – the duty to the story – the duty that is our job to deliver on the story's behalf. At the scene level, we deliver the character's character. At the story level we deliver the character's 'message'.

Mostly though, my advice is not to lose the magic. Stories are magic, and actors are the key to the magic happening. When someone says 'sit down and listen to me. Once upon a time...' there's a magic that happens and it is the job of everyone involved, starting with the writer, to get a hold on that magic and keep it alive in the mind of the audience.

15.5 In conversation with Willy Russell

It's no exaggeration to say that Willy Russell is one of the most influential people in the world of theatre of the last century. He is also a published author and a hugely successful musician, but is best known as a playwright, and the theatre runs and the films that have been made from his plays, including the massive hits, *Educating Rita; Shirley Valentine; Blood Brothers;* and *John, Paul, George, Ringo and Bert.*

Willy's background is working class and he originally had no formal story theory education. My first question to him was about how he thinks stories work, and he lost me in the first sentence, so before you read on, in order to save you, dear reader, from the visit I just had to make to the dictionary, I looked up the word 'atavistic' – it means 'relating to deep instinct; behaviour originating from our distant genetic past'.

Why do you think stories exist? How do they work?

EM Forster in *Aspects of the Novel* talks about the 'atavistic worm' – our innate human need to know what happens next. Our brains are wired up to instinctively drive for answers and to understand everything that might affect us. We writers have to use that innate drive to engage the audience, and we have to learn how it works.

When someone comes up all excited, grabs you by the arm, and says, "Hey! Listen to this...!" it presses that innate button inside us, something primal switches on and we are somehow pre-programmed to accept a story. At that point, the storyteller and his audience enter an unwritten agreement at a primal level. The audience will trust that the storyteller will deliver a context, the necessary back-story, and then the events that will change or enhance our understanding of the world.

"Heeey! Listen to this! You remember Sandra's fifteenth birthday two months ago? You remember she got off with that old bloke? Get this – it turns out he is her teacher at college and – guess what – she's only pregnant. Yeah! Up the duff. Anyway, they've ran away together, and you'll never guess what her mum's gone and done..."

Well? You want to know, don't you? The atavistic worm. The innate need to know what happens next and to learn about life from how people reacted. If you can learn to work with that you cannot go far wrong. But the audience will only trust you for a while. If you fail to set up a context quickly enough or if your back-story fails to give the story sensible, promising direction, you have broken that trust, the magic dissipates and you have failed as a storyteller.

The basis to our primal response is the need of the character, and that need must be one we can relate to – again at a primal level – in order to engage and understand. I don't ever like abstracting too far away from the lives of real people and real characters. As soon as your story goes so highbrow and clever, and goes on about 'issues', you've lost me – and everyone else as well. Keep it real – real characters, real behaviour.

How do you develop a story?

Well, my stories start from an idea, of course. With *Blood Brothers*, initially, I just had the one idea, which I mulled over for literally years. It went like this:

"A woman with many children gives away one of her newborn twins. They grow up in different circumstances and one causes the death of the other."

I spent years pushing this around in my head. Then reading Ibsen's *The Doll's House*, gave me the key that I was looking for to really make *Blood Brothers* work. Two women make a pact – a secret pact. The mother gives one of the twins away to the other woman, and they agree to never tell anyone. From that moment you, the audience, are a party to that pact where none of the other characters know the truth – not even the twins themselves. From that moment to the end, you have a driving, innate need to know what happens when others find out, especially when the twins find out about each other.

That's fascinating – and supports my theory of subtext

But hold on. I also deliberately tell the audience at the very beginning basically what will happen in the end. I know it sounds odd, but knowing where the beacon is that we are heading towards is not only vital to the writer in knowing where the plot is going to go, but it heightens the tension in every single scene, because the audience understand the implications far more than they would have done if I had kept it all secret and we'd had a revelation at the end. As it is, the emotion builds towards the inevitable with far more power than it otherwise would. The audience shouldn't be asking: 'where is this story taking me?' it should be, 'I know where the story is taking me – how on earth are we going to get there?'

Back to the Future is an example of a story built on this same mechanism. Marty makes stated plans at the setup of each plotline, so every scene carries an extra dimension, because we all know exactly where he's trying to get to.

So you know the story idea and the ending. What next?

Apart from building basic knowledge of where my story was going, I also knew up front some things that I *didn't* want to do with it. For example, I knew I didn't want a sort of 'tennis match' situation, where we go from one twin and his development in a poor world followed by the obligatory scene where we go see the other kid addressing similar issues in his high class world, then back to the poor kid and so on. So I knew they had to meet and interact without knowing who each other were, and that made me think immediately – they are going to fall in love with the same girl. Of course they are. So in comes Linda, and we have our key five players. The twins, two mums, and Linda. I also knew I had to strictly avoid all the cliché stuff surrounding identical twins. I knew immediately I wasn't going to go near any of that identity confusion between them or some mystical biological connection driving behaviour and so on. If they grew up in different circumstances, they would have such different clothes and hair and voices and attitudes that you wouldn't necessarily know they were twins, so I thought I would try to be original and work more on the opposites of the obvious. Here they are, identical twins in the same places, and no one even knows it.

The basis of the story kept giving me ideas, and I took the good ones. The corny or bad ones still helped with direction; knowing where you won't go is almost as helpful as knowing where you do want to go.

Once I knew the main beats of the story, to the point where it was broken down into a series of manageable chunks it wasn't half so scary to deliver. I had effectively reduced the hugeness of *Blood Brothers* to a series of sketches. From there, I just tried to make it gripping on a minute by minute basis – the atavistic worm. If you can keep the audience engaged minute by minute, you will ultimately succeed overall, right? It can't be any other way, so I just got into it and tried to be creative in finding original ways to deliver the story.

Is it different to write for the stage than for other media?
I knew the whole thing was going to be a musical, but I realised quickly that the power of the story had to be delivered by periods of acting and dialogue. This was because the story had to be delivered with comedy, and comedy in song is a difficult and awkward rhythm for an audience. Comedy needs the rhythm and timing of the humour, and music enforces its own rhythm and timing that would spoil the comedy. Because the story is ultimately so bleak and tragic, I knew the comedy had to be strong enough to provide a catharsis to this, so I knew it wasn't an opera style where everything is delivered in lyric, and that the songs would be interspersed with largely light and humorous acted scenes.

The stage as the medium also brought me two things that I've always found painful but which turned out to be positives. I had a limit of seven players at the time, and this restriction made it impossible to deliver *Blood Brothers*. Literally impossible.

So I got round it by getting the narrator to keep switching hats and playing different roles. He would rock up in the first scene as the milkman, nip back to his position and deliver as narrator, then return centre stage as the mother's doctor. I felt it was really important not to lie to the audience about this – trying to dress him up and pretend – they can always see through that, so I made a feature of it. Everyone can see him changing hats. When he appears in front of her as the doctor she says: " Hey! I thought you were a milky!" and he replies, as he applies his stethoscope, "Finished with all that and went into medicine." It gets a big laugh, and we're delivering three characters for the price of one in interesting and engaging ways.

The point is that this restriction forced out great humour and ideas that really improved the play; things that never would have come out if I hadn't had those restrictions. This happens a lot. Restriction feels like pain, and can cause big headaches, but it nearly always turns out to be a positive.

Creative limitations seem to be generally accepted as positive

That's right. Painful but positive. To be honest, I've never ever been able to write well without personally being under pressure to deliver. I know it sounds weird, but even now I have to take a commission, take some money, then sit squirming in a cold sweat until finally, at the last minute, when I'm all ready to hand the money back and start apologising for letting everyone down, it comes. The story pours out of me with urgency and edge that comes from desperation. I know this doesn't sound like fun and it's not. It's horrible, and I always promise myself I won't ever put myself through it again, but it's the only way to get the good stuff out. My very first play was for Christmas. I agreed to write it and the December deadline was absolutely unmoveable. Ever since then, it's always been the same: the pressure and the deadline seem to drive me to deliver worthwhile writing.

What advice would you give to aspiring writers?

Firstly, remember that a script is nothing more than an ambition. It's on paper and it's going to need a lot of people and their individual disciplines to bring it to life, so write it as a story that can be read. Don't do all the structural stuff or camera angles or all that guff. Just give us a great story, and let the other stuff come from the appropriate person at the appropriate time. You are delivering a story, so don't distract the reader by trying to do the job of the director or the cameraman.

Secondly, there's only one real learning you need to be a storyteller, and that's to read. Read absolutely everything on earth that has ever been written in your chosen sphere. It's simple – an apprentice learns from a master, so what kind of playwright could ever consider himself learned without reading Shakespeare? Read, read, read. It's all been done before, so when you get to a junction in your story you will know where to take it next if you've read everything that's been done and recognise what the situation demands. Almost as importantly, observe life. Stories are about characters and behaviours, so watch people and think about what they do and what drives them.

Thirdly, I would say never be grateful! And never do it for free! The world will accept you at your own valuation, so even if it's a modest amount, always value your work and insist on payment.

Fourthly, I would say, "Just Do It". Lots of people do courses, and think deeply, and mooch about for years. The truth is that a real writer needs to write. He often doesn't even particularly want to write, but he needs to write. It's a strangely masochistic, love-hate thing, but he can't stop himself. If this isn't you, forget it. There are people out there who are driven like maniacs to write, and you have no chance of keeping up if you are doing it for the pose or the romance of saying you're a writer. It's hard work, and the successful ones just refuse to accept that what pains them so much is not worth continuing with.

Finally, I'd say do it yourself! If you want to be a playwright, don't sit in a room writing scripts and hoping some top producer is going to descend upon you with a million quid and a team of people to make your play for you. Start more modestly, and get something made. A school play, a radio play, a community play. You will get a track record, you will make some contacts, you will develop your storylines, and above all you will get invaluable experience from working with actors and directors and an audience that will see your ability grow exponentially. *My Big Fat Greek Wedding* started off as a one-woman stage play by Nia Vardalos... with Tom Hanks' wife sitting in the audience. The film *Memento* started off as a short story by Jonathan Nolan in Esquire magazine. Even *Slumdog Millionaire* started off as an Indian novel called *Q & A* by the author Vikas Swarup. None of these works would have found success if their authors hadn't put themselves out there in a more modest way first.

15.6 In conversation with Stewart Ferris

Stewart Ferris is the former managing director of Summersdale Publishers – a leading independent UK publishing company, and author of more than 40 books himself, including two books to which you really should treat yourself, entitled *How to get Published* and *How to be a Writer*. He also distinguished himself in 2001 by giving a first break to the much loved humorous author, David Baboulene...

Over the last 15 years, Stewart has commissioned around 700 books... and rejected 10,000!

So, what is Rule 1 for authors in approaching a publisher?

Rule one for authors on submissions to agents and publishers is probably: 'don't'. The most common first error aspiring writers make is submission way too soon. They reach the end of their first full-length manuscript and the elation surrounding their achievement – and it is a considerable achievement – is to spray it out all over the civilised world. In the background, over the years of writing it, they've built up a list of all the agents and publishers, and with the most immense enthusiasm they begin mailing out ten copies a day for a month.

Sadly, the subject of redrafting hasn't entered the vocabulary. The manuscript they are sending out is half-baked at best. There is a saying out there somewhere which says: 'there are no such things as writers; only re-writers', and there are no exceptions. Your writer hero – whoever he or she may be – is an obsessive, sweating re-writer, and would happily admit it. When I write, I do so in the full expectation that I will redraft TEN times, and I will never – ever – allow myself to show anybody drafts one to five. Seriously.

Draft 1 – Type out a rough version of the whole book

Draft 2 – Tighten the structure, fill in holes

Draft 3 – Develop the characters

Draft 4 – Improve the dialogue

Draft 5 – Work on the language and imagery

Draft 6 – Restructure parts of the work

Draft 7 – Add layers of conflict

Draft 8 – Improve the crucial opening pages

Draft 9 – More work on the character development

Draft 10 – Proofread for mistakes

We all over-estimate the quality of our latest draft. Reading it with a cooler head a few weeks or months later will be a sobering experience. If you ever choose to send off anything earlier than draft 6, you are simply requesting a rejection – enjoy it when it arrives.

I can relate to that – what's rule 2?

Rule two of submission is to remove the writer and artist in you and replace yourself with a deeply professional salesman's head on the body of an acutely commercial businessman. A totally different animal from the creative type who wrote the book; one who is aware that a publisher takes a substantial investment risk in a book, and the likelihood of recouping that investment is the principal driving force behind his decisions. It may not be what we would want to focus on in an ideal world, but it has to be, or we go out of business. So publishers appreciate writers who are cognisant of commercial imperatives.

And the first commercial reality is whether the publisher will want to work with you or not. If your presentation is slapdash and you are unprofessional as an individual, a publisher simply won't want to work with you. Your book will be rejected before it's even got to square one, so the brilliance or otherwise of the story will not be a factor. Of course, we all know the stories of the A&R man who rejected the Beatles and the publisher who rejected JK Rowling and the studios who rejected *Back to the Future*, and so on, but I have absolute sympathy for these people, because the reason for 98% of rejections is almost never anything to do with the quality of the creative product. We have limited resources to sift through the slush pile. The fact is that the quality of the initial presentation is a pretty reliable indicator to the quality of the story, so going through all those hundreds of bad presentations so as not to miss the one in a million that might hold a worthwhile story is simply not viable. So it is essential that you get your first big hits in professionally and beautifully. Nice, neat presentation in line with the submission requirements. Get a great title, a great subtitle, any supporting information right up there. You can be out of the running in seconds if your title is turgid, the genre unclear, the 'message' of the work impenetrable on first impressions. If I can't see these things on first pass, I think: 'I don't care how good the story is, because I can't sell it with these toplines.' It really doesn't matter if the story is a cracker if the top level marketing acumen in missing.

Look at it like this. When a potential reader chooses to buy a book, he is making his decision on the basis of the range of books that have made it into his consciousness. To get in to that position, the author (and hence the agent and publisher) first had to sell it in its basic form to the organisations that can get it into the heads of your potential audience. Your first book, Mr Baboulene, [*Ocean Boulevard*] didn't catch the imagination of the buyers at

WH Smith, so it didn't find its way into the airports and railway stations and high streets, so it never got to the point where your potential audience *could* make it part of its purchasing decisions. It had no choice. Yes, your book is terrific, but of course, the WH Smith buyer never reads any of the books he buys. He makes a decision on the basis of the sales tools the book arms him with – the topline messages he will use to sell the book – and what he's looking for isn't a 'great read' – he's looking for a great marketing punch; a book that a punter will like the look of enough to part with £9 or whatever. Your second book, Mr Baboulene [*Jumping Ships*] had that title and design and immediacy that *did* catch the buyers' eyes and bingo – it sold out its first print run in ten days. Don't forget, it didn't sell out because of the persuasiveness of your prose – nobody important outside of the publishing house had read it at this point. It sold out because the shops bought it – not because the punters bought it. Selling to the shops is what put it on to the radar of the public. Suddenly you are selling in bigger numbers, snowballing with reader reviews and being interviewed by the BBC.

So you must be as professional and commercial in your presentation as you can possibly be, and stress the genre and marketability of your work. Of course, there will be small things wrong in your presentation – the odd typo and grammatical error is inevitable – but overall we know instantly – within seconds – if a writer is proud of his work himself, will take responsibility for the final product and its quality, and is likely to be conscientious, helpful and professional on the long road we must take together to deliver a package that will sell. If an author hasn't even bothered to spell-check his manuscript that tells us enough to be pretty sure it's not going to work for us.

So, our first hoops to jump through:

> Did the author contact us first and get their work solicited?
>
> If not, has the author obeyed our submission guidelines?
>
> Is the material appropriate for our brand and list?
>
> Does it have a strong title?
>
> Does it have a clear genre?

If the answer is 'no' to any of these, instant rejection is almost inevitable.

The sixteen elements that influence a publishing/agent's decision:

The book	The market
Quality of writing	Competition
Fresh ideas/ new angle	Trends
Format of the book	Related events
Title and subtitle	Niche

The author	The publisher
Reputation	Size of company
Personality	Direction of company
Previous books	State of company
Self-publicity	Internal politics

What else leads to rejections?

I would advise against trying to set your submission apart with gimmicks or gaudiness. I know it is tempting to try to set yours apart, but mostly it makes us worry. I had a submission once that had dried flowers attached to the front. When I was putting a pile of submissions together to take home, this one caused a pile of others to slide off on to the floor. You can guess what I thought. Suffice to say, I didn't take it with me – it was too awkward. If you make your submissions clean, clear and professional, you will have instantly cleared the first hurdle. Set yourself apart by going straight down the middle, doing what we ask and making our lives easy.

And what leads to green lights?

It's always good to see a CV of relevant experience or biography surrounding the subject matter. This can give clues to commercial advantage, so show the publisher or agent all the pluses that might reduce our risk or contribute to the likelihood of achieving sales. With your book the fact that you had been on stage before and were happy to be outgoing in marketing terms was a tremendous advantage.

When we meet an author who is a shy or reclusive mouse we know that commercial activity is likely to be limited because of the way he or she will perform on the radio or TV or at a literary festival or signing event. A lack of commercial awareness or go-gettem attitude is not a showstopper for publication, of course, but all these factors go into the mix.

What happens inside the publishing house? What's the process?

Well, every submission initially gets assigned to a reader. I suppose it is true that you might simply be lucky or unlucky at this point, but they are empowered to make an instant and autonomous decision to reject if there are clear problems with the submission – along the line of those mentioned above – a reader quickly becomes capable of recognising those that, for one reason or other, are non-starters, and this is the fate of the vast majority of submissions.

They will look at the high level criteria I mentioned, but more attuned to the material:

- Does the book have a good title?

- Is it well written?

- Is the author appropriate to our list and aims?

- Does it have a clear genre?

- Are there high costs involved in publishing this? For example if it has a million words, many colour pictures, or requires the securing of rights, it might make the work less attractive because of the cost of production.

What happens to those that the initial reader likes?

The initial readers will bring to the weekly editorial meeting any that they feel are worthy of consideration. At this point, I would say we are talking about between 5 and 10 books out of every 100 submitted. Most of these will still be rejected – we probably publish roughly one book in every 100 submitted.

At the editorial meeting, submissions are circulated and discussed in summary form. Anyone at the meeting can volunteer to give a second reading to new material on the basis of that summary, so the imperative here is to have a really strong title and compelling top-line messages. The story in concept form is critical to passing this test. The titles that are picked up by volunteers finding them attractive are put on the agenda for the next meeting, and they are through to the next round. On this basis, you can see how it works. A good book begins to get 'fans' inside the company. Your books have real, genuine fans within Summersdale; people who think your books are hilarious. They will talk about it and it will get a buzz around it and it becomes compelling. From that moment it will generally live or die on its own genuine merits. Commercial considerations are a part of this, don't forget. All the readers work within a commercial publishing environment and are sticking their necks out for a commercial success, not necessarily for a work of art they love.

Are you sensitive in your rejections?

We try to be, but the primary thing to remember is that a rejection is very rarely any sort of reflection on you or your capabilities. There is no need for your ego to be bruised. Remember, 98% of submissions are rejected without any consideration of the literary merit of the material. This sounds depressing, but it is an advantage for the wary. You can avoid rejection by avoiding the most common reasons for rejection listed earlier – wrong publisher for the material; the list is full (a call in advance to solicit the material avoids this one); lack of resources to commit to the work; market statistics on the given genre; a similar book already in the pipeline within the publisher; technical reasons to do with costs; none of these things are within the author's control and none are a reflection on the quality of the work, so firstly, go through ten drafts before sending it out; secondly, contact the target agent or publisher in advance to ensure they are on the lookout for work like yours and will accept your submission; thirdly, ensure your presentation is professional, and your chances of acceptance are hugely increased.

Should a writer contact a publisher who rejects them?

Generally, no. Certainly not if a rejection letter is from your initial submission. It is unlikely to contain useful information towards your personal improvement, and nobody got so involved with your work as to be useful in conversation with you. These rejections are generally 'stock' template style letters that are not personalised, so there's no point in contact.

On the other hand, if your work got past first base, and you have had any dealings with the publisher – you have a name and have had some communications with an individual moving things forwards – then you have a right to know why you were rejected. However, the conversation should still be unnecessary as the rejection letter should give the reasons. You should be able to rely on the contents of a rejection letter at this stage to be a genuine critical appraisal with the real reason why your material has been rejected.

Should a writer get an agent?

The simple answer is 'yes'. If you can. However, received wisdom suggests it's even harder to get an agent than it is to get a publisher. A good agent is probably very busy already with deals within the industry – selling a spin-off book by a celebrity or a tie-in with a TV show or something. They don't generally like to take on unknown authors, because it involves a lot of work and a slim chance of success. If you do get an agent you can be pretty certain you are on to something, and that they are confident they can sell it.

If you think that an unknown author is likely to get 10%-15% of the publisher's net income from a book – say, 30p to 50p per book – and the agent is only going to get 10% – 20% of that, you can see that it has to sell big to have any chance of being a worthwhile investment of time and effort. Let's say you have a best-seller – 100,000 book sales might make you, say, £40,000 before tax, and the agent will take, say, 15% of that. You make £34k. He makes £6k. Not a great deal of money for truly exceptional sales. Most don't get anywhere near this kind of performance.

It's not all doom and gloom, of course, because sales build over time. A writer in this position will sell at least another hundred-thousand with the follow-up, and the agent will be out there selling overseas rights and film rights and all the rest of it. My point is, when talking about a new writer, an agent can end up doing a lot of spadework for potentially very little return.

* * *

As I mentioned at the top, Stewart Ferris has written or commissioned a range of books on how to write, including *How to get Published – Secrets from the Inside* and *How to be a Writer*. For a much more complete understanding of this area, I recommend you visit Stewart's website, which is **www.stewartferris.com**.

FADE TO BLACK

[This] is not an end, but a beginning.

Martin Luther King (1929 – 1968)

And you have a dream...

16 Postscript

In summary, what are the main points arising from the conversations with story professionals and the book as a whole? What are the principles that lie beneath all good stories?

Here are the main points that I believe you should understand and apply in your own work having read this far. If you don't fully understand any of the bullet points below, I suggest you recap on the relevant chapter, or look to other material presented in the **References** section after this one:

Stories are implicit to our psychology. Our instinctive drive to understand what is going on – to remove doubt, to ask and answer questions, and to bring life back into balance when emotional stability is rocked – is key to the civilisation we have built and to our personal sense of safety and security. 'Intelligent' people follow a story structure in the way their brains work. Stories that put the character's world out of balance, that raise questions and introduce doubt and jeopardy, will resonate with the human mind.

Stories work when they are delivered in subtext. The more subtext there is in a story the higher the story quality and popularity will be. Subtext is delivered through the mechanism of 'knowledge gaps'; gaps in the knowledge held by different participants in a story. Knowledge gaps are delivered via dialogue, action, questions, promise, sub-plot, suggestion, implication, misinterpretation, subconscious aims, subterfuge and metaphor.

Stories exist through 'character actions'. The actions and reactions taken by a character define both the plot (action) and define the true personality of the players (character). In a great story, this leads to both plot and character being essentially the same thing.

True character only emerges through putting the protagonist under pressure and forcing him to make decisions and take action under pressure and through conflict.

At least one character should learn life lessons, change and grow across the telling of the story. This doesn't mean they have to win, succeed or even survive, as long as the lesson is clearly delivered to the audience.

The story development process begins with an idea, which leads to a short premise. Questioning of this premise drives out 'obligatory events' which form the basis to your story and are, implicitly, cohesive in terms of that original premise.

The ending is best defined in the mind of the writer as soon as possible, in order that all component events know where they are heading.

An understanding of structure is valuable, particularly in problem resolution and story analysis. Turning points can be identified in any story event, at the points where the forces of protagonism go into conflict with the forces of antagonism, and only one can win out. Turning points are the link between created character events and the underlying structural components.

Structure is NOT a starting point for – or even a part of – story development. Create from the heart and say balls to structure; optimise and refine your story with the head, using knowledge of structure.

If you want to be a writer, read a thousand books.

If you want to be a writer, write every day.

Writers produce their best material when under pressure from personal, practical and creative limitations.

Achieving success on a modest basis first – community play, radio work, short story – is the first step towards success. Working, training or otherwise harvesting contacts in a relevant writing industry is a great benefit.

Have confidence in your story and your ability. NO-ONE else could possibly write your story for you. Write your story, your way, and let the world make of it what it will.

Write from the heart. There is absolutely no other way to come up with good stories. Rewrite with your head; structuring your story, then analysing and improving it using solid principles.

And finally, be professional and unemotional in your efforts to sell your writing. And never work for free. This is really important. If you value your work at zero, the world will accept you at your own valuation and give you nothing. Businessmen will devote their time to the products in which money is invested, because that is where the risk lies. If you can't get any money for your work, move on to the next target. When you finally write something hot, you will be amazed at how your lifetime of pushing on the industry becomes a rush as the industry pulls on you, and at that point, money is never an object.

So we are back at the beginning: the quality of your product is king. Create a story of unrivalled excellence and tell it brilliantly. Then the rest is the easy bit: take it to market as the market dictates, and you will get published and/or produced.

I wish you all the very best of luck with your projects.

David Baboulene
November 2010

If I can help you with your story, do please contact me via:

www.baboulene.com

17 References

Aristotle. ~B.C.350. *Poetics*. Trans. GF Else 1967. University of Michigan.

Booker, C. 2004. The seven basic plots: why we tell stories. London, Continuum.

Forster, EM. 1927. *Aspects of the Novel*. Edward Arnold, London.

Freud, S. 1932. *The Interpretation of Dreams*. (Translated from the German)

Goldman, W. 1983. *Adventures in the screen trade.* Grand Central Publishing, New York.

King, S. 2000. *On writing: A memoir of the Craft.* Hodder and Stoughton, London.

Levi-Strauss, C. 1978. *Myth and Meaning.* Routledge & Kegan Paul, London.

Levi-Strauss, C. 1984, *Anthropology and Myth*: Lectures, 1951–1982, trans. Roy Willis, 1987.

McKee, R. 1999. Story: substance, structure, style, and the principles of screenwriting. Methuen

Maslow, A. 1954. *Motivation and Personality*. New York: Harper and Row.

Pinker, S. 1999. *How the Mind Works.* WW Norton & Company.

Pinker, S. 2007. The Stuff of Thought: Language as a window into human nature. Viking Press.

Propp, V. 1968. *Morphology of the Folktale*, trans. L. Scott.

Stanislavski, C. 1937, *An Actor Prepares*. Translated by Elizabeth Reynolds. Hapgood, London.

Vogler, C. 1998. The Writer's Journey: Mythic Structure for Writers. Michael Wiese, USA.

Whipps, H. 2008. *How the Hyoid Bone Changed History*. LiveScience Magazine

Motion Picture Association of America. 2008/9. Film statistics and research. (www.mpaa.com)

INDEX

FURTHER READING...

"Interesting, raucous and very, very funny to the point that some bits will make your eyes water.

The story on Barbados is one of the funniest I've ever read."

TALKSPORT

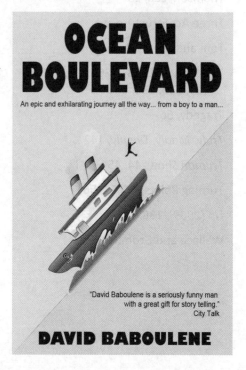

"This truly absorbing and at times astonishing tale will have you laughing out loud... Baboulene has an engaging, informative and gripping style... a real page-turner."

In Touch Magazine

About the Author

David Baboulene is a published author of two humorous books, two children's illustrated books and an academic work on story theory. He has had production deals in Hollywood and the UK for his film stories. He works as a story consultant for producers, writers, writer training and film development organisations.

David gives seminars on story theory and writes regularly on the subject, including a monthly column in *The Writing Magazine and Writers' News.*

He is currently writing his Ph.D. thesis at Brighton University, proving his theory on the defining and measurable importance of subtext to story quality.

David lives in Brighton with his wife and four children.

Delegate Comments on the Story Seminars

Every session provided a 'eureka moment' for me; another sudden insight into ways to improve my stories and find direction for me as a writer."

"A wonderful combination of technical knowledge balanced with the recognition that story must come from the heart of the individual. Your seminars have helped me enormously."

"Made something very complex beautifully clear."

"Hugely entertaining and motivating."

"It would be hard to improve these seminars. I would recommend them to everyone."